plurall

Esta obra está no **Plurall**.
Baixe o app no seu celular
ou acesse **http://plurall.net**
e descubra uma nova
forma de estudar!

AASGJ3BKG

Atenção! Somente serão liberados conteúdos
e serviços relacionados a esta obra.

Ajuda: @plurallnet

SOMOS
EDUCAÇÃO

Organizadora:
Editora Saraiva
Obra coletiva organizada e produzida pela Editora Saraiva

Editor responsável:
Vicente Martínez
Licenciado em Tradução/Interpretação pela
Universidad Pontificia de Comillas (Madrid)
Editor de conteúdos didáticos

Coordenadora:
Gisele Aga
Licenciada em Letras pela FMU - Faculdades Metropolitanas Unidas
Professora de Inglês na rede particular de ensino e em cursos de idiomas
Coordenadora pedagógica em cursos de idiomas
Editora de conteúdos didáticos

TIME TO SHARE

Jornadas 7

Editora Saraiva

DESENVOLVIMENTO DOS CONTEÚDOS:

Adriana Beatriz Saporito
Licenciada em Letras e graduada em Tradução/Interpretação (Inglês-Português) pela Faculdade Ibero-Americana de Letras e Ciências Humanas.
Professora de Português e de Inglês da rede particular de ensino.
Editora de conteúdos didáticos.
Autora de Inglês para os anos iniciais do Ensino Fundamental.

Amini Rassoul
Bacharel e licenciada em Letras (Inglês-Português) pela USP.
Professora em cursos de idiomas e faculdades.

Ana Lúcia Militello
Licenciada em Letras pela Faculdade Ibero-Americana de Letras e Ciências Humanas com habilitação em Tradução/Interpretação.
Editora de conteúdos didáticos.

Carla Maurício Coelho da Silva Vianna
Licenciada em Letras pela UFRJ.
Professora de Inglês da rede particular de ensino.
Editora de conteúdos didáticos.
Autora de Inglês para os anos finais do Ensino Fundamental.

Cristina Gaglianone Pinto Cesar
Bacharel e licenciada em Letras (Língua e Literatura Inglesas) pela PUC-SP.
Mestre em Linguística Aplicada e Estudos de Linguagem pela PUC-SP.
Professora de Inglês em cursos de idiomas e faculdades.
Editora de conteúdos didáticos.

Daniella Bergamo
Graduada em Tradução/Interpretação e licenciada em Inglês e Português pela Faculdade Ibero-Americana de Letras e Ciências Humanas.
Pós-graduada em Educação — Currículo e Prática Educativa — pela PUC-RJ.
Professora de Inglês da rede particular de ensino e em cursos de idiomas.

Lisiane Ott Schulz
Doutoranda em Letras pela Universidade de Caxias do Sul (UCS) em associação com a UniRitter.
Mestre em Educação pela Universidade de Caxias do Sul (UCS).
Bacharel em Letras – Tradução/Interpretação (Português-Inglês) — e licenciada em Letras — Inglês e Literatura — pela UFRGS.
Professora do curso de Letras — Português e Literatura Brasileira — pela UCS.
Professora de Inglês das redes pública e particular de ensino e em cursos de idiomas.

Luciana Santos Pinheiro
Especialista em Estudos Avançados da Língua Inglesa pela PUC-RS.
Mestre em Letras pela Universidade de Caxias do Sul (UCS).
Doutora em Linguística Aplicada pela UFRGS.
Autora e editora de conteúdos didáticos.
Professora universitária e da rede particular de ensino.

Sueli Valente da Silva Caparroz
Graduada e licenciada em Letras pela Universidade Nove de Julho.
Professora de Inglês da rede particular de ensino.
Autora de Inglês para os anos iniciais do Ensino Fundamental.

Time to Share – Jornadas – 7º ano (Ensino Fundamental)
© Editora Saraiva, 2016
Direitos desta edição:
Saraiva Educação Ltda. São Paulo, 2016

Dados Internacionais de Catalogação na Publicação (CIP)
(Câmara Brasileira do Livro, SP, Brasil)

Jornadas Time to Share, 7º ano / organizadora Editora Saraiva; obra coletiva organizada e produzida pela Editora Saraiva; editor responsável Vicente Martínez; coordenadora Gisele Aga. – 1. ed. – São Paulo : Saraiva, 2016.

Suplementado pelo manual do professor.
Bibliografia.
ISBN 978-85-472-0838-7 (aluno)
ISBN 978-85-472-0839-4 (professor)

1. Inglês (Ensino fundamental) I. Martínez, Vicente. II. Aga, Gisele.

16-04731 CDD-372.652

Índice para catálogo sistemático :

1. Inglês : Ensino fundamental 372.652

CAE 603687 (AL)
CAE 603985 (PR)
2ª impressão

Gerente editorial	M. Esther Nejm
Editor responsável	Vicente Martínez
Editores	Alice Silvestre, Caroline Zanelli, Myrian Yamamoto, Renata Chimim, Renato Malkov, Vinicius Oliveira, Vivian Viccino
Coordenador de revisão	Camila Christi Gazzani
Revisores	Larissa Vazquez, Lilian Miyoko Kumai, Patrícia Cordeiro
Revisor linguístico	Robert Caudle Garner
Coordenador de iconografia	Cristina Akisino
Pesquisa Iconográfica	Beatriz Fonseca Micsik, Fernando de Almeida da Cunha Cambetas Junior
Licenciamento de textos	Erica F. Brambila
Gerente de artes	Ricardo Borges
Coordenador de artes	Narjara Lara
Design e Capa	Sergio Cândido com imagem de Christian Mueller / Shutterstock.com
Diagramação	C2 Artes
Assistente	Camilla Felix Cianelli
Ilustrações	Leo Teixeira, Vicente Mendonça, Zubartez
Tratamento de imagens	Emerson de Lima
Produtor gráfico	Thais Mendes Petruci Galvão
Impressão e acabamento	Corprint

Editora Saraiva
SAC 0800-0117875
De 2ª a 6ª, das 8hs às 18hs
www.editorasaraiva.com.br/contato

Avenida das Nações Unidas, 7221 – 1º andar – Setor C – Pinheiros – CEP 05425-902

INTRODUCTION

Let Us Not Be Bitter

Life is change, life is progress
Life is learning things, life is onward.

Oodgeroo Noonuccal

Extracted from: <www.poetrylibrary.edu.au/poets/noonuccal-oodgeroo/let-us-not-be-bitter-0719002>. Accessed on: May 23, 2016.

Viver é experimentar mudanças. É superar-se e aprender cada vez mais. Progresso é construirmos a nós mesmos de forma consciente e cuidando do mundo que nos rodeia. É respeitar nosso planeta, as diferentes culturas e formas de vida que nele habitam. Aprender um novo idioma é ampliar nosso contato com o mundo, mudar, progredir, avançar. É ver que o novo e o diferente têm muito a nos ensinar. Nesta coleção, você encontrará textos e áudios autênticos, expressões artísticas com diferentes linguagens (música, tirinhas, fotografia, pintura, grafite etc.). Você terá a possibilidade de refletir sobre temas polêmicos e atuais, de pensar sobre sua escola, sua comunidade e sobre seu próprio aprendizado, além de, é claro, atividades linguísticas. Esteja aberto ao conteúdo apresentado, veja, reveja, leia quantas vezes for necessário, pergunte aos amigos e professores quando tiver dúvidas, ouça as interpretações que cada um tem, use livros, revistas, internet, compartilhe suas impressões, seja ativo no processo de aprendizagem à sua maneira!

ALBERT NAMATJIRA, *MOUNT SONDER, MACDONNELL RANGES* C.1957-59 WATERCOLOUR AND PENCIL ON PAPER NATIONAL GALLERY OF AUSTRALIA

GET TO KNOW YOUR BOOK

The units are organized by sections. Get to know a little bit more about them.

OPENING PAGES

This section presents several artistic manifestations and questions to activate your previous knowledge about the theme you are going to explore throughout the unit.

UNIT 3

Houses around the world

EXCHANGING IDEAS

1. Look at the opening image of this unit. This is a photo of an installation created by the artist. What is it?
2. This installation is part of a collection from a museum. People can walk into the room. What effect does the use of colors have on the visitor?
3. If you could choose a new place to live in, where would it be? What kind of housing would you like to have?

Cildo Meireles is one of the most important Brazilian contemporary artists. His work was displayed in important exhibits such as the retrospectives at the New Museum of Contemporary Art, in New York, and at the Tate Modern, in London. His work was also shown at the Museum of Modern Art in Rio de Janeiro and in São Paulo.

Your learning objectives for this unit are...

- to identify and describe types of housing;
- to name the parts of a house, some furniture and appliances;
- to read and write an ad for a house for rent.

MEIRELES, Cildo. *Desvio para o vermelho*. 1967-1984. Several materials. Inhotim, Brumadinho, Brazil.

- enciclopedia.itaucultural.org.br/pessoa10593/cildo-meireles
  Information about the artist Cildo Meireles and his artworks.
- www.tate.org.uk/node/237205/about.shtm
  Information, images and videos about Cildo Meireles' exhibit at the Tate Modern in London, England.

48 forty-eight

forty-nine 49

READING COMPREHENSION

It brings authentic texts about relevant topics in a variety of genres. The texts will help you get prepared for the real use of the language.

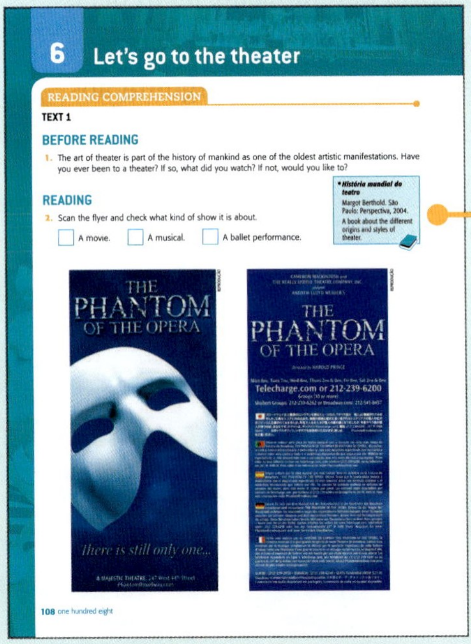

6 Let's go to the theater

READING COMPREHENSION

TEXT 1

BEFORE READING

1. The art of theater is part of the history of mankind as one of the oldest artistic manifestations. Have you ever been to a theater? If so, what did you watch? If not, would you like to?

READING

2. Scan the flyer and check what kind of show it is about.

☐ A movie. ☐ A musical. ☐ A ballet performance.

- *História mundial do teatro*
  Margot Berthold. São Paulo: Perspectiva, 2004.
  A book about the different origins and styles of theater.

108 one hundred eight

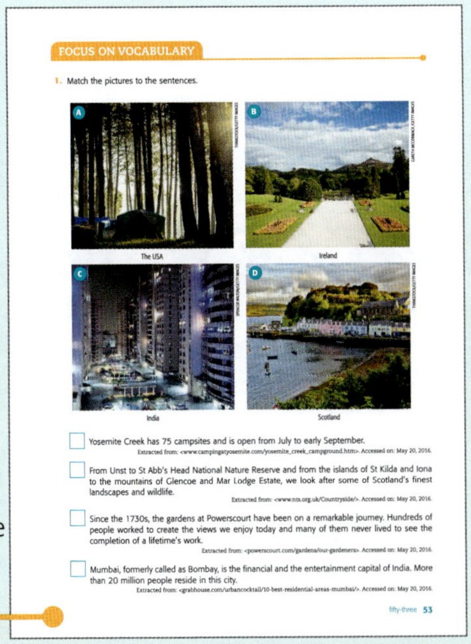

FOCUS ON VOCABULARY

1. Match the pictures to the sentences.

A The USA

B Ireland

C India

D Scotland

☐ Yosemite Creek has 75 campsites and is open from July to early September.
Extracted from: <www.campingatyosemite.com/yosemite_creek_campground.htm>. Accessed on: May 20, 2016.

☐ From Unst to St Abb's Head National Nature Reserve and from the islands of St Kilda and Iona to the mountains of Glencoe and Mar Lodge Estate, we look after some of Scotland's finest landscapes and wildlife.
Extracted from: <www.nts.org.uk/Countryside/>. Accessed on: May 20, 2016.

☐ Since the 1730s, the gardens at Powerscourt have been on a remarkable journey. Hundreds of people worked to create the views we enjoy today and many of them never lived to see the completion of a lifetime's work.
Extracted from: <powerscourt.com/gardens/our-gardeners>. Accessed on: May 20, 2016.

☐ Mumbai, formerly called as Bombay, is the financial and the entertainment capital of India. More than 20 million people reside in this city.
Extracted from: <grabhouse.com/urbancocktail/10-best-residential-areas-mumbai/>. Accessed on: May 20, 2016.

fifty-three 53

FOCUS ON VOCABULARY

Vocabulary practice is contextualized, so it will be easier for you to understand it. You will also have the opportunity to expand the vocabulary related to the topic of the unit.

LANGUAGE IN USE

This section will help you reflect about language in context and practice it with different kinds of activities.

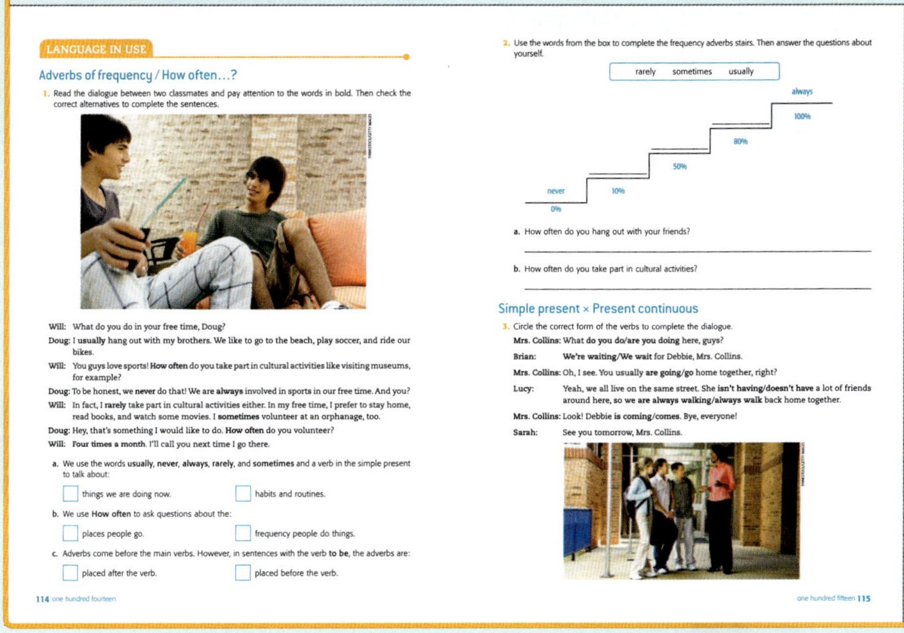
LANGUAGE IN USE

Adverbs of frequency / How often...?

1. Read the dialogue between two classmates and pay attention to the words in bold. Then check the correct alternatives to complete the sentences.

Will: What do you do in your free time, Doug?
Doug: I **usually** hang out with my brothers. We like to go to the beach, play soccer, and ride our bikes.
Will: You guys love sports! **How often** do you take part in cultural activities like visiting museums, for example?
Doug: To be honest, we **never** do that! We are **always** involved in sports in our free time. And you?
Will: In fact, I **rarely** take part in cultural activities either. In my free time, I prefer to stay home, read books, and watch some movies. I **sometimes** volunteer at an orphanage, too.
Doug: Hey, that's something I would like to do. **How often** do you volunteer?
Will: **Four times a month.** I'll call you next time I go there.

a. We use the words **usually**, **never**, **always**, **rarely**, and **sometimes** and a verb in the simple present to talk about:
☐ things we are doing now. ☐ habits and routines.

b. We use **How often** to ask questions about the:
☐ places people go. ☐ frequency people do things.

c. Adverbs come before the main verbs. However, in sentences with the verb **to be**, the adverbs are:
☐ placed after the verb. ☐ placed before the verb.

114 one hundred fourteen

2. Use the words from the box to complete the frequency adverbs stairs. Then answer the questions about yourself.

rarely sometimes usually

never 0% 10% 50% 80% always 100%

a. How often do you hang out with your friends?

b. How often do you take part in cultural activities?

Simple present × Present continuous

3. Circle the correct form of the verbs to complete the dialogue.

Mrs. Collins: What do you do/are you doing here, guys?
Brian: We're waiting/We wait for Debbie, Mrs. Collins.
Mrs. Collins: Oh, I see. You usually are going/go home together, right?
Lucy: Yeah, we all live on the same street. She isn't having/doesn't have a lot of friends around here, so we are always walking/always walk back home together.
Mrs. Collins: Look! Debbie is coming/comes. Bye, everyone!
Sarah: See you tomorrow, Mrs. Collins.

one hundred fifteen 115

LISTENING COMPREHENSION

Presenting different kinds of oral texts with a diversity of language variation, this section aims at helping you fully understand the messages of the texts.

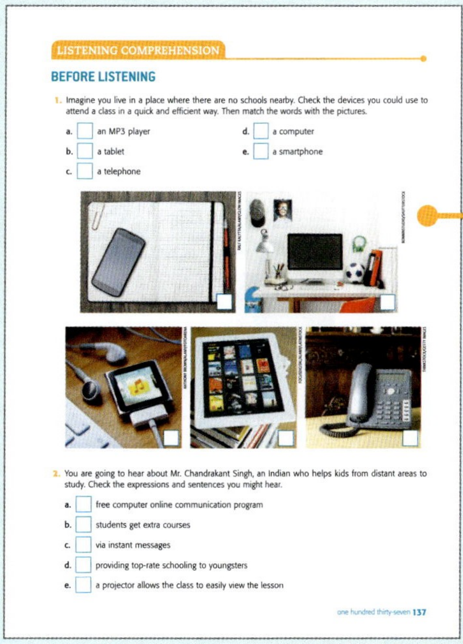
LISTENING COMPREHENSION

BEFORE LISTENING

1. Imagine you live in a place where there are no schools nearby. Check the devices you could use to attend a class in a quick and efficient way. Then match the words with the pictures.

a. ☐ an MP3 player
b. ☐ a tablet
c. ☐ a telephone
d. ☐ a computer
e. ☐ a smartphone

2. You are going to hear about Mr. Chandrakant Singh, an Indian who helps kids from distant areas to study. Check the expressions and sentences you might hear.

a. ☐ free computer online communication program
b. ☐ students get extra courses
c. ☐ via instant messages
d. ☐ providing top-rate schooling to youngsters
e. ☐ a projector allows the class to easily view the lesson

one hundred thirty-seven 137

SPEAKING

Suggestions of contextualized situations for the use of theme-based, communicative and linguistic aspects presented in each unit. The objective of this section is to provide you with an opportunity to use what you learned in other contexts and/or communicative situations.

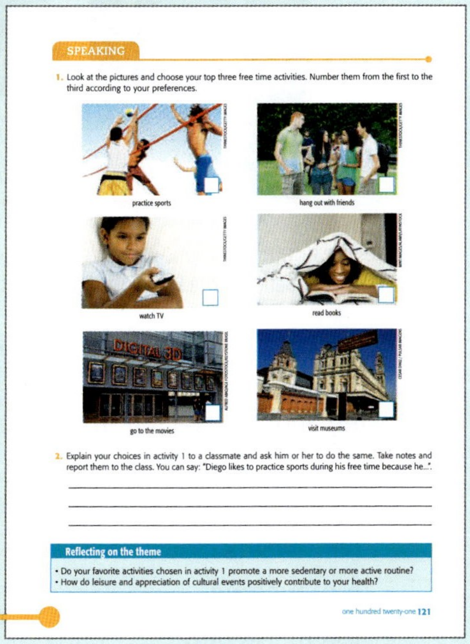
SPEAKING

1. Look at the pictures and choose your top three free time activities. Number them from the first to the third according to your preferences.

practice sports · hang out with friends · watch TV · read books · go to the movies · visit museums

2. Explain your choices in activity 1 to a classmate and ask him or her to do the same. Take notes and report them to the class. You can say: "Diego likes to practice sports during his free time because he...".

Reflecting on the theme

- Do your favorite activities chosen in activity 1 promote a more sedentary or more active routine?
- How do leisure and appreciation of cultural events positively contribute to your health?

one hundred twenty-one 121

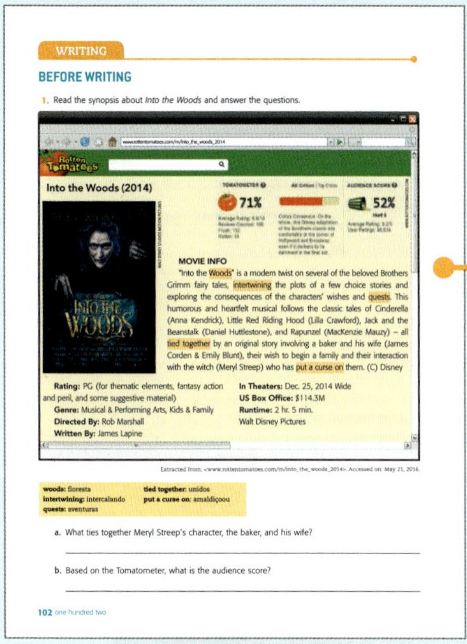
WRITING

BEFORE WRITING

1. Read the synopsis about *Into the Woods* and answer the questions.

Into the Woods (2014)

MOVIE INFO

"Into the Woods" is a modern twist on several of the beloved Brothers Grimm fairy tales, intertwining the plots of a few choice stories and exploring the consequences of the characters' wishes and quests. This humorous and heartfelt musical follows the classic tales of Cinderella (Anna Kendrick), Little Red Riding Hood (Lilla Crawford), Jack and the Beanstalk (Daniel Huttlestone), and Rapunzel (MacKenzie Mauzy) – all tied together by an original story involving a baker and his wife (James Corden & Emily Blunt), their wish to begin a family and their interaction with the witch (Meryl Streep) who has put a curse on them. (C) Disney

Rating: PG (for thematic elements, fantasy action and peril, and some suggestive material)
Genre: Musical & Performing Arts, Kids & Family
Directed By: Rob Marshall
Written By: James Lapine
In Theaters: Dec. 25, 2014 Wide
US Box Office: $114.3M
Runtime: 2 hr. 5 min.
Walt Disney Pictures

woods: floresta
intertwining: intercalando
quests: aventuras
tied together: unidos
put a curse on: amaldiçoou

a. What ties together Meryl Streep's character, the baker, and his wife?

b. Based on the Tomatometer, what is the audience score?

102 one hundred two

WRITING

This section proposes a writing task based on the theme and genre study of the unit as a closing activity. The task is divided in planning, production, evaluation and review of the work.

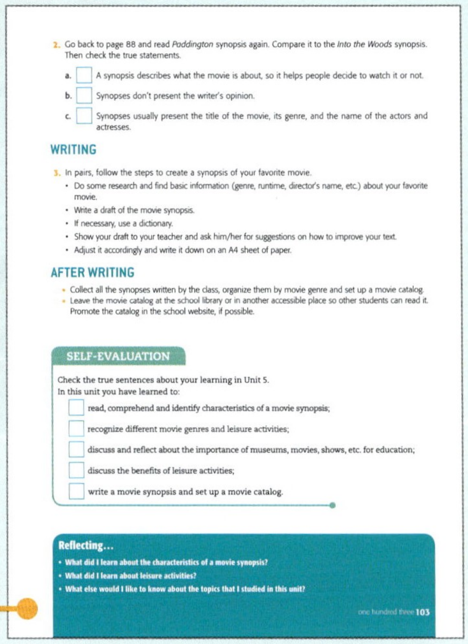
2. Go back to page 88 and read *Paddington* synopsis again. Compare it to the *Into the Woods* synopsis. Then check the true statements.

a. A synopsis describes what the movie is about, so it helps people decide to watch it or not.
b. Synopses don't present the writer's opinion.
c. Synopses usually present the title of the movie, its genre, and the name of the actors and actresses.

WRITING

3. In pairs, follow the steps to create a synopsis of your favorite movie.
- Do some research and find basic information (genre, runtime, director's name, etc.) about your favorite movie.
- Write a draft of the movie synopsis.
- If necessary, use a dictionary.
- Show your draft to your teacher and ask him/her for suggestions on how to improve your text.
- Adjust it accordingly and write it down on an A4 sheet of paper.

AFTER WRITING

- Collect all the synopses written by the class, organize them by movie genre and set up a movie catalog.
- Leave the movie catalog at the school library or in another accessible place so other students can read it. Promote the catalog in the school website, if possible.

SELF-EVALUATION

Check the true sentences about your learning in Unit 5.
In this unit you have learned to:
- read, comprehend and identify characteristics of a movie synopsis;
- recognize different movie genres and leisure activities;
- discuss and reflect about the importance of museums, movies, shows, etc. for education;
- discuss the benefits of leisure activities;
- write a movie synopsis and set up a movie catalog.

Reflecting...
- What did I learn about the characteristics of a movie synopsis?
- What did I learn about leisure activities?
- What else would I like to know about the topics that I studied in this unit?

one hundred three 103

SELF-EVALUATION

This last section gives you the opportunity to evaluate your learning by checking your progress and difficulties with the objectives listed in the beginning of the unit.

CONNECTIONS

This section presents texts, images and activities related to contents that you have learned in other subjects.

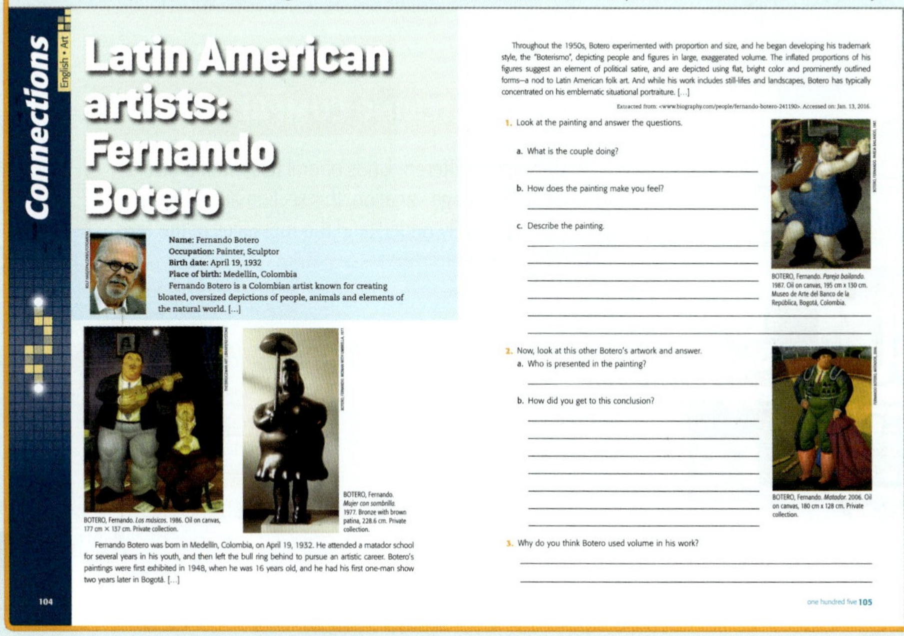
Connections — English • Art

Latin American artists: Fernando Botero

Name: Fernando Botero
Occupation: Painter, Sculptor
Birth date: April 19, 1932
Place of birth: Medellin, Colombia
Fernando Botero is a Colombian artist known for creating bloated, oversized depictions of people, animals and elements of the natural world. [...]

BOTERO, Fernando. *Los músicos*. 1986. Oil on canvas, 177 cm × 137 cm. Private collection.

BOTERO, Fernando. *Mujer con sombrilla*. 1977. Bronze with brown patina, 228.6 cm. Private collection.

Fernando Botero was born in Medellín, Colombia, on April 19, 1932. He attended a matador school for several years in his youth, and then left the bull ring behind to pursue an artistic career. Botero's paintings were first exhibited in 1948, when he was 16 years old, and he had his first one-man show two years later in Bogotá. [...]

104

Throughout the 1950s, Botero experimented with proportion and size, and he began developing his trademark style, the "Boterismo", depicting people and figures in large, exaggerated volume. The inflated proportions of his figures suggest an element of political satire, and are depicted using flat, bright color and prominently outlined forms—a nod to Latin American folk art. And while his work includes still-lifes and landscapes, Botero has typically concentrated on his emblematic situational portraiture. [...]

1. Look at the painting and answer the questions.
a. What is the couple doing?
b. How does the painting make you feel?
c. Describe the painting.

BOTERO, Fernando. *Pareja bailando*. 1987. Oil on canvas, 195 cm x 130 cm. Museo de Arte del Banco de la República, Bogotá, Colombia.

2. Now, look at this other Botero's artwork and answer.
a. Who is presented in the painting?
b. How did you get to this conclusion?

BOTERO, Fernando. *Matador*. 2006. Oil on canvas, 180 cm x 128 cm. Private collection.

3. Why do you think Botero used volume in his work?

one hundred five 105

Besides the recurrent sections in each unit, the series offer other sections with activities for pronunciation practice, boxes with cultural or linguistic information, extra vocabulary, and reading and/or learning strategies.

PRONUNCIATION PRACTICE

6 Listen and practice the -**ing** endings in the following verbs. Then choose the correct option to complete the pronunciation rule.

smile: smil**ing**
talk: talk**ing**
run: runn**ing**
listen: listen**ing**

We pronounce the -**ing** ending as
- [ ] /ing/.
- [ ] /in/.

This book also contains several appendices which contribute to your learning experience. Read more about them below.

FURTHER PRACTICE

Extra activities covering the unit themes with texts and listening activities that review the most relevant linguistic aspects.

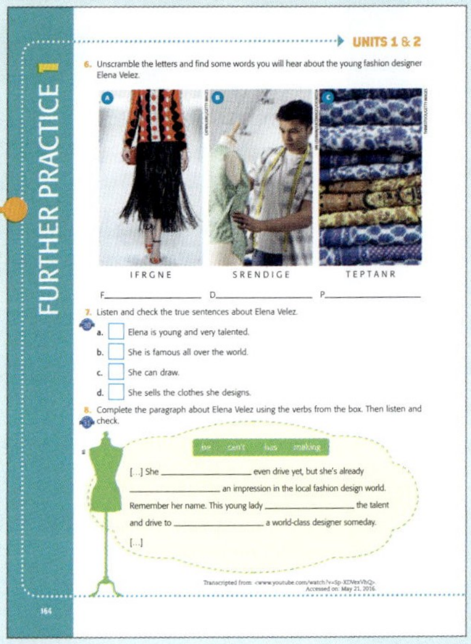

PROJECTS

Each book proposes two interdisciplinary projects with a wider scope. Based on a central theme and aimed at providing a deeper discussion about it, these projects culminate in a group closing activity.

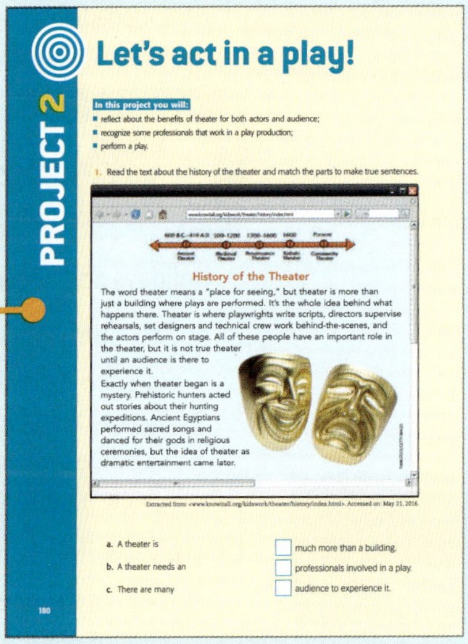

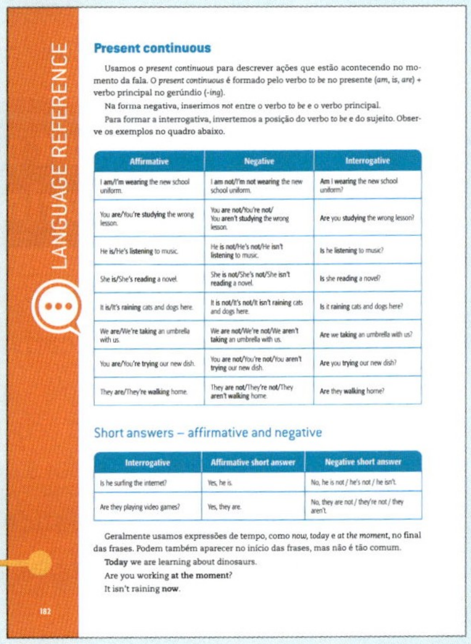

LANGUAGE REFERENCE

A summary of the linguistic aspects presented in the book. It can be used as reference material for studies.

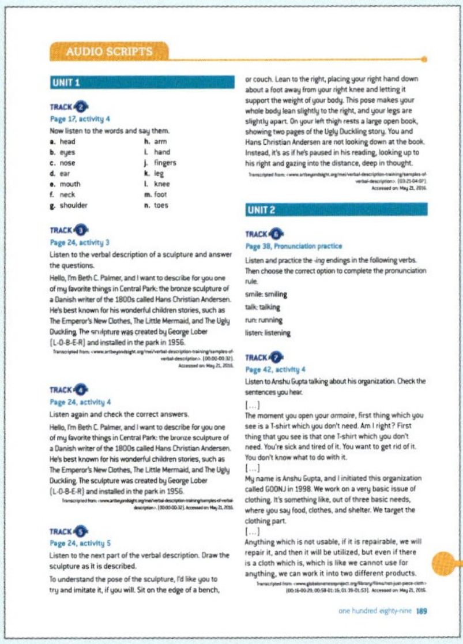

AUDIO SCRIPTS

The transcriptions of the audios used in the "Listening Comprehension" section. They can be helpful while doing some activities or for future reference.

GLOSSARY

A list of the most important words from each volume translated according to the context in which they appear.

CONTENTS

VICENTE MENDONÇA

UNIT

1

Changes

The image on the right is from the show *Dança das marés*, produced by a group of 62 young people born in Complexo da Maré, in Rio de Janeiro. It was directed by choreographer Ivaldo Bertazzo and written by doctor and writer Drauzio Varella.

Scene from *Dança das marés* by Corpo de Dança da Maré. Rio de Janeiro.

Your learning objectives for this unit are...

- to identify body parts;
- to use the present continuous tense to indicate actions that are in progress at or around the time of speaking;
- to read and write art catalogs.

EXCHANGING IDEAS

1. Look at the image. Describe the colors, lights and dancers.
2. The show is about the passage from childhood to adulthood. Which topics might probably be present in the story in your opinion?

KITA PEDROZA

- ***A alma da gente***

  Direction: Helena Solberg and David Meyer. Brazil: EH! Filmes, 2013. 80 min.

  Brazilian documentary which shows different people who were affected by art. The characters are 60 teenagers from Corpo de Dança da Maré, a group supervised by choreographer and educator Ivaldo Bertazzo at Complexo da Maré.

- ***O livro da dança***

  Inês Bogéa. São Paulo: Companhia das Letras, 2002.

  The book brings short biographies of important gymnasts and discusses the different kinds of *capoeira*. It also tells the history of classic ballets and informs about ballet steps, choreographers, dance companies and the most important ballet dancers of Brazil and of the world, including many photographs and drawings.

1 Changes

READING COMPREHENSION

TEXT 1

BEFORE READING

1. Adolescence is the period in which the most visible transformations in the body occur due to hormonal alterations.

Translated from: <www.brasilescola.com/educacao/periodo-de-transformacoes.htm>. Accessed on: May 19, 2016.

What are the main physical changes that happen during adolescence?

READING

2. Read the text quickly and circle the transparent words. Then tell a classmate what the text is about.

www.sexualityandu.ca/sexual-health/all-about-puberty/my-body-and-puberty

What's Happening to my Body?

As teenagers become adults, their bodies go through a lot of physical changes. The categories below describe some of these changes. Remember, everyone goes through these changes differently. [...]

CAIA IMAGE/AGB PHOTO

Physical Changes

Puberty is your body physically changing from a child to an adult. [...]

Are you feeling too skinny? Weighing in at more than before? Is your face looking a bit oily? Are your breasts feeling tender? Where are those breasts already? Are you shorter than the other boys on the court? Are all of your pants getting too short to reach your ankles? Relax, these are all normal questions, and if you're still waiting around for puberty, don't worry. Puberty will show up soon enough. [...]

Remember, puberty is different for everyone. Your changes are going to be different from the changes in your best friends, but don't let it worry you – each of our bodies takes its own natural course. [...]

Extracted from: <www.sexualityandu.ca/sexual-health/all-about-puberty/my-body-and-puberty>. Accessed on: May 19, 2016.

go through: passam por **breasts:** seios **tender:** sensíveis **court:** quadra

3. Read the text again and check the appropriate answers to the questions.

a. What happens to teenagers as they become adults?

- [ ] They go through a lot of physical changes.
- [ ] They go through some physical changes.

b. Do teenagers go through the changes the same way?

- [ ] Yes, teenagers go through the changes exactly the same way.
- [ ] No, teenagers are different, so they change in different ways too.

c. There are seven questions in the third paragraph. What are they related to?

- [ ] All of them are related to physical appearance.
- [ ] Some are related to physical appearance, and others are related to fashion.

4. Read the sentences and write **T** (true) or **F** (false). Correct the false sentences according to the text.

a. [ ] In the second paragraph, we can find frequent questions that teenagers will probably ask.

____

b. [ ] Puberty is a natural course, but not everyone goes through it.

____

c. [ ] Puberty can arrive soon for some teenagers, but others have to wait a little longer.

____

5. Read the text once again and answer the questions below.

a. Why is the title a question?

____

____

b. Does the text present a positive or a negative point of view about puberty? Justify.

____

____

c. Who can be interested in reading about puberty?

____

AFTER READING

- Who do you usually talk to about the changes that occur in the adolescence: parents, teachers or friends?
- What questions do you have about the physical and emotional changes that occur in this period?

TEXT 2

BEFORE READING

1. You will read part of an art catalog published by the Philadelphia Art Museum, in the United States. What kind of information do you expect to find in the text?

READING

2. Skim the text and check the best answer to the following question: What is it about?

a. ☐ It presents the story of the people represented in a painting.

b. ☐ It describes a work of art.

c. ☐ It presents the artist who made the painting.

> **Skimming** is a reading strategy that aims at quickly identifying the general idea of a text. To identify the central idea, it is necessary to search for elements such as key words, titles and text organization.

Blind Singer

William Henry Johnson

American, 1901–1970

About the Print

This lively image shows two musicians entertaining us with their voices, a guitar, and a tambourine. Facing us directly and standing close together, the man and woman catch our attention with their dynamic poses and their colorful clothing: a yellow hat with a blue band, a red tie, orange and blue jackets, and green shoes. Their bodies suggest movement: fingers strumming the strings of the guitar, hands shaking a tambourine, feet tapping, and hips swaying to the music.

William Henry Johnson would have seen musicians like these performing on busy street corners in New York City, where he worked and lived. [...]

His artistic style was influenced by the geometric shapes of West African sculpture, which he could see in the city's museums. He was also inspired by colors and patterns used by other great modern artists like Pablo Picasso.

WILLIAM H. JOHNSON, BLIND SINGER, CA. 1939-1940

JOHNSON, William H. *Blind Singer.* 1939-1940. Serigraph, 44,5 cm × 29,5 cm. Smithsonian American Art Museum, Washington DC, USA.

Extracted from: *Represent: 200 Years of African American Art.* Philadelphia Museum of Art, p.16. Available at: <www.philamuseum.org/doc_downloads/education/ex_resources/Represent.pdf>. Accessed on: May 19, 2016.

3. What is probably the occupation of the people in the painting? Choose parts of the text to justify your answer.

____

4. In pairs, read the catalog and check the sentences that are true according to it.

a. ☐ The people in the image play the guitar and the tambourine.

b. ☐ The bodies suggest movement.

c. ☐ William Henry Johnson used New Yorkers as inspiration for the painting.

d. ☐ William Henry Johnson did not live in New York.

5. Match the colors to the people's clothes and objects in the picture.

a. yellow

____

b. red

____

c. orange

____

d. blue

____

e. green

____

f. black

____

6. What parts of the musicians' bodies are mentioned in the description of the painting?

____

____

7. What are the artist's influences and inspirations to make this painting?

____

____

AFTER READING

- If you had to do a painting about people in the city, who would you choose to depict? Why?

FOCUS ON VOCABULARY

1. Read text 1 again. Write the questions that correspond to each picture below.

ILUSTRAÇÕES: ZUBARTES

____

____

____

____

> • ***Dork Diaries: Tales from a Not-So-Fabulous Life***
> Rachel Renée Russell. New York: Simon and Schuster, 2009.
> The book is about the typical routine of an American girl.

____

____

____

____

____

____

____

____

____

2. The words in the box are part of the text on page 14. Write them next to their corresponding synonyms or meanings.

colorful	dynamic	lively	standing

a. with many and vivid colors ____________________

b. full of life ____________________

c. energetic, active ____________________

d. not sitting down ____________________

Body parts

3. Look at the picture below and read the parts of the body. Circle the words you know. Then write the words in the corresponding spaces.

arm
ear
eye
finger
foot
hand
head
knee
leg
mouth
neck
nose
shoulder
toe

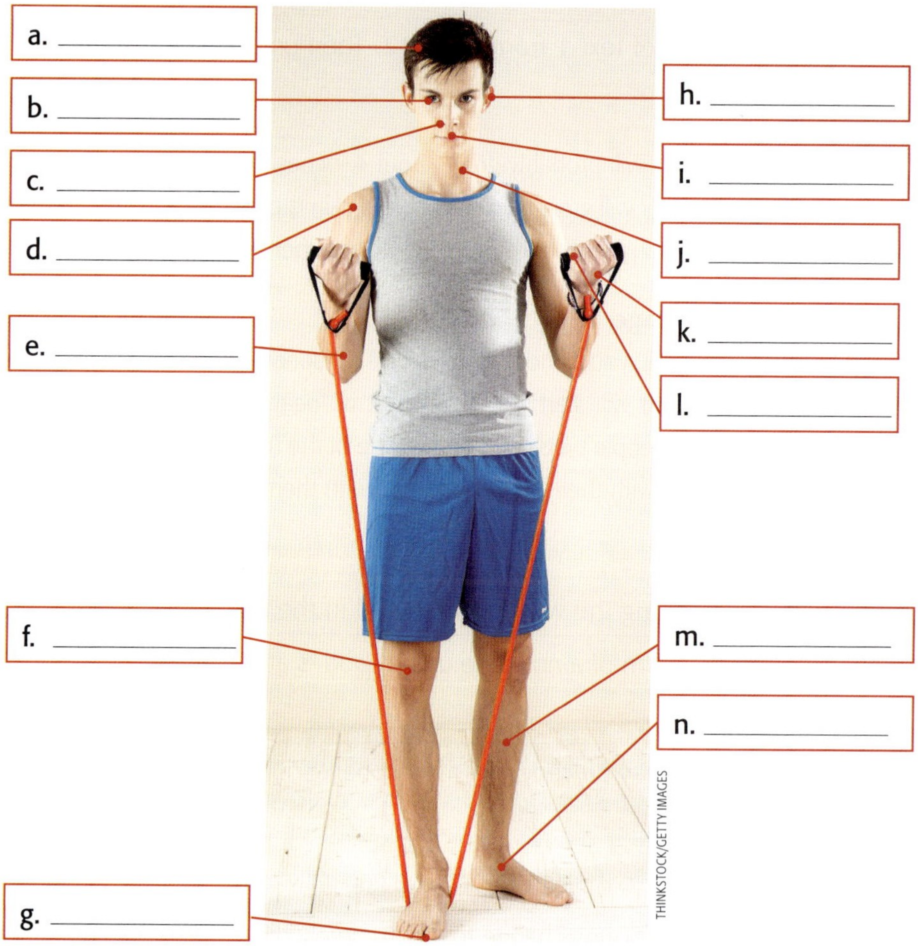

THINKSTOCK/GETTY IMAGES

4. Now listen to the words and say them.

5. Match the pictures to the descriptions below.

a. I have one big eye, a big mouth, two legs, and two arms.

b. I have two arms, two legs, a mouth, one head, five eyes, and one ear.

c. We have two heads, four arms, fours hands, and two big eyes.

IMAGENS: DISNEY/PIXAR

IT'S YOUR TURN!

Use your imagination and think of a new monster. Give him/her a name. Describe the monster to a classmate and ask him/her to draw your monster in his/her notebook. Use: *His/Her name is... He/She has seven arms, three eyes...* Then check if your classmate drew the monster described.

Regular and irregular plurals

1. Read the continuation of text 1 from page 12. Then underline the nouns that are in the plural form.

Hormonal Changes

During puberty you will probably grow about 4 inches per year. Your voice will change and might become deeper, pubic hair will grow thicker, and your skin is changing and you may get some pimples. These changes are all caused by your hormones, which are chemicals in your body that cause it to change.

Body Image/Self Image

[...] As you get older, you'll find that things like personality, confidence, intelligence, a sense of humour or having a good heart will start to define what is "beautiful", not just the way a person looks on the outside. In fact, most people would agree that one of the most attractive qualities you can find in a person is that they are happy with their lives and happy with themselves.

Extracted from: <www.sexualityandu.ca/sexual-health/all-about-puberty/my-body-and-puberty>. Accessed on: May 19, 2016.

2. Complete the chart using the words underlined in the text above.

To make the plural form of a noun we usually add **-s** at the end of the word. For example: ______, ______, ______, ______, ______.
When a noun ends in **-y** preceded by a consonant sound, change **-y** to **-i** and add **-es**. For example: ______.
When a noun ends in **-ch**, **-s**, **-sh**, **-x** or **-z** we generally add **-es** to the end of the word. For example: ______. Some nouns change to a completely different word in plural form. For example: ______, ______.

Imperative

3. Read these sentences from text 1 again. Then complete items **a** to **c** using the words from the box.

Relax, these are all normal questions, and if you're still waiting around for puberty, don't worry. Puberty will show up soon enough. [...]
Remember, puberty is different for everyone.

affirmative	don't	imperative	main	relax	verbs

a. The underlined words are ______ and they are in the ______ form.

b. The verbs "______" and "remember" are in the ______ form.

c. The negative form of the imperative is formed by ______ + the ______ verb of the sentence, like in "don't worry".

Present continuous (affirmative form)

4. Read the description of a painting, then choose the painting that matches the description.

Philip's body is turned so that it faces the right edge of the painting. His right arm, right side, and right leg are turned toward us. They are, therefore, closest to us. To understand his pose, I'd like you to try to imitate it now.

First of all, stand up straight. Now bring your left foot back so your left heel is a few inches directly behind your right heel and pointed to the left. Your feet should be at almost a right angle, with your right foot pointing straight forward and your left foot pointing to the left. This stance puts the right side of your body forward.

Now place your left hand on your left hip. Philip **is wearing** a sword, so imagine that you have a sword attached to your belt and your left hand **is resting** on the sword's handle. Your right arm should fall straight down to your side. Your right hand holds a baton, which is a stick about 2 and 1/2 feet long. The baton is a symbol of the king's power. Imagine you **are holding** the baton so that it is horizontal. If you were the stand-in for Philip in this painting, your chest would face toward your left, or the painting's right edge. And your face would be turned right, looking straight toward the viewer outside the painting.

BIS

Extracted from: <www.artbeyondsight.org/mei/verbal-description-training/samples-of-verbal-description/>. Accessed on: May 19, 2016.

JOHN MICHAEL WRIGHT, KING CHARLES II, C. 1660/1665

WRIGHT, John Michael. *King Charles II.* 1660/1665. Oil on canvas, 126.4 cm × 101 cm. National Portrait Gallery, London, UK.

ALLAN RAMSAY, KING GEORGE III, C.1761/1762

RAMSAY, Allan. *King George III.* 1761/1762. Oil on canvas, 147.3 cm × 106.7 cm. National Portrait Gallery, London, UK.

VELAZQUEZ, PORTRAIT OF PHILIP IV, 1628

VELÁZQUEZ, Diego. *Philip IV, King of Spain.* 1628. Oil on canvas, 205 cm × 117 cm. J&M Ringling Museum of Art, Sarasota, Florida, USA.

5. Answer the following questions about the painting described in activity 4.

a. What is the name of the picture?

____

b. What is the name of the painter? When was the picture painted?

____

6. Read the description from activity 4, again. Who do you think would need this kind of description?

____

7. Underline the correct options to complete the text about the present continuous.

In the description in activity 4, the verbs in bold are in the present continuous form. We use the present continuous to talk about an action that is happening **at the moment/before** we speak. To form the present continuous in the affirmative form, we use the verb **can/ to be** + the main verb in the **-ing/-ed** form.

8. Look at the following picture for one minute. Then cover the picture and write three sentences describing what the people are doing.

DANIEL CYMBALISTA/PULSAR IMAGENS

Villa-Lobos Park, São Paulo, SP, 2009.

____

____

____

HANDS ON!

In pairs, mime actions for a classmate to guess. The student who tries to guess the actions has to use the present continuous. You can say: *You're skateboarding. You're playing golf.* Take turns.

Regular and irregular plurals

Regular plurals		
For most nouns, just add an **-s** to the word.	For most nouns that end in **-s**, **-x**, **-z**, **-ch**, **-sh**, **-o**, make the plural by adding **-es**.	If the noun ends in **-y** preceded by a consonant, make the plural by substituting the **-y** by **-ies**.
car – car**s** house – house**s** book – book**s**	bus – bus**es** fox – fox**es** buzz – buzz**es** match – match**es** wish – wish**es** tomato – tomato**es** potato – potato**es**	baby – bab**ies** city – cit**ies**

Irregular plurals		
Some nouns do not follow any of the rules mentioned for regular plurals. Some do not change, some have different spellings. Consult a dictionary if necessary.		
child – children foot – feet knife – knives man – men	mouse – mice parenthesis – parentheses person – people	quiz – quizzes sheep – sheep tooth – teeth woman – women

Imperative

Forms and some uses	
To form the imperative in affirmative sentences, we use the **base form** of the verbs. To form the imperative in negative sentences, we use the auxiliary verb **do**, followed by **not** and the **base form** of the verbs.	
We use the imperative to give orders.	**Sit** down, students. **Open** your books.
We use the imperative to give instructions.	First, **insert** the batteries. **Do not open** the slot. Then, **turn** it on.
We use the imperative to give warnings.	**Look out!** **Do not park** here. **Mind** the gap.

Present continuous

Affirmative sentences	subject + verb to be (am/is/are) + verb ending in **-ing**	**I am playing** video games. **You are listening** to music. **He is walking** the dog.

1. Write the correct plural forms of the words below.

a. police – ______________
b. fish – ______________
c. half – ______________
d. video – ______________
e. pencil – ______________
f. wife – ______________
g. boy – ______________
h. goose – ______________
i. information – ______________
j. homework – ______________

2. Complete the following sentences with an appropriate verb from the box. Use the affirmative or negative forms.

close	come	eat	forget	get	pass
sit	take	touch	wait		

a. ______________________ behind the yellow line, please.

b. ______________________ it. It's hot.

c. ______________________ out of here!

d. ______________________ the door when you leave.

e. ______________________ two pills every 8 hours.

f. ______________________ in and ______________ down, please.

g. ______________________ that. You are allergic to it.

h. ______________________ the salt, please.

i. ______________________ your coat. It's freezing out there.

3. Use the verbs in parentheses to complete the affirmative sentences with the present continuous tense.

a. You ______________________ Math now. (to study)

b. She ______________________. (to sleep)

c. I ______________________ well. (to feel)

d. I think that he ______________________ the truth. (to tell)

e. They ______________________ their quizzes. (to answer)

f. We ______________________ to watch a movie. (to try)

g. She ______________________ something special for you. (to do)

h. I ______________________ a delicious Italian dish. (to cook)

i. He ______________________ at the bank now. (to work)

LISTENING COMPREHENSION

BEFORE LISTENING

1. The human body is present in many art works. According to an article in the website of the Museum of Modern Art (MoMA):

> The human body is central to how we understand facets of identity such as gender, sexuality, race, and ethnicity. People alter their bodies, hair, and clothing to align with or rebel against social conventions and to express messages to others around them.

Extracted from: <www.moma.org/learn/moma_learning/themes/investigating-identity/the-body-in-art>. Accessed on: May 19, 2016.

In your opinion, why do artists represent human bodies in their works of art?

a. ☐ To honor people who were important for society or for the artists themselves.

b. ☐ To show the beauty of the human body.

c. ☐ To make people identify with the human element in the picture.

d. ☐ To question and change conventions about the body.

e. ☐ To understand the body scientifically.

2. Artists also use many different media to represent the body. Look at the following pictures. Which one do you think is the most interesting? Why? Share your opinion with your classmates.

THE BRIDGEMAN ART/KEYSTONE BRASIL

☐

Augustus (Emperor from 27 BC to AD 14). c. 20 BC (head), first third of 2nd century BC (body). Marble, 207 cm. Musée du Louvre, Paris, France.

RAPHAEL, SAINT CATHERINE OF ALEXANDRIA, 1507

☐

Raphael. *Saint Catherine of Alexandria*. c. 1507. Oil on panel, 72.2 cm × 55.7 cm. The National Gallery, London, UK.

PAUL CEZANNE, THE GARDENER, 1906

☐

CÉZANNE, Paul. *The Old Gardener*. 1906. Oil on canvas, 65 cm × 54 cm. Foundation E. G. Bührle Collection, Zurich, Switzerland.

VIVIAN MAIER

☐

MAIER, Vivian. *Self-Portrait*. Undated.

ANDRE STEFANO/FOTOARENA

☐

KOBRA, Eduardo. *Graffiti mural tribute to Oscar Niemeyer*, 2013. Paulista Avenue, São Paulo.

ROBERT HARDING PICTURE LIBRARY/AGB PHOTO

☐

MUECK, Ron. *Boy*. 1999. Aros Aarhus Kunstmuseum, Aarhus, Demmark.

LISTENING

3. Listen to the verbal description of a sculpture and answer the questions.

3

a. Who is represented in the sculpture?

____

b. Where is this sculpture?

____

c. Why do you think this sculpture was built?

____

4. Listen again and check the correct answers.

4

a. Who built the sculpture?

- [ ] Beth C. Palmer.
- [ ] George Lober.

b. When was it installed?

- [ ] In 1956.
- [ ] In the 1800s.

5. Listen to the next part of the verbal description. Draw the sculpture as it is described.

5

AFTER LISTENING

6. Think of three people from your community you would like to honor with a sculpture. Write their names and why you chose them.

____

____

7. Do you know any works by Hans Christian Andersen? Look for his bibliography and write the titles you have already read or heard about.

____

____

SPEAKING

1. In small groups, play *Simon Says* using the parts of the body studied in this unit. Student A gives a command, for example: *Simon says: Touch your nose*. Students B, C, and D touch their noses. If student B, C, or D does another action, he/she is out of the game.

- **https://www.youtube.com/watch?v=gjgtiQcpKCk**

  Episode of the *Corpo em Movimento* series from the TV show *Fantástico* – TV Globo.

Reflecting on the theme

Bullying is still a common practice students face in schools. It might happen simply because someone has a different opinion or is too short or too tall, has acne, or is dyslexic, etc. Have you ever witnessed someone being bullied? Do you know what to do in this situation?

WRITING

BEFORE WRITING

1. In art catalogs, we find information about the works of art and about the artists that made them. Why do people who go to museums and art galleries read these catalogs?

2. Read the catalog and compare it to the one on page 14. Then check the true sentences about them.

Portage

WILLIAM KENTRIDGE, PORTAGE, 2000

KENTRIDGE, William. *Portage*. 2000. Collage, 27.5 cm × 422.9 cm (unfolded). Philadelphia Museum of Art, Philadelphia, USA.

William Kentridge
South African, born 1955

This image is a detail from a larger work of art—an accordion-fold book that is almost fourteen feet long [...]. To create it, the artist William Kentridge arranged small pieces of torn black paper into figures. He then glued the figures onto pages that he removed from a French dictionary.

While the dictionary definitions in the background represent precise, factual information, the procession of shadowy figures presents a narrative that is more open to interpretation. [...]

The poses of the four figures pictured here give us clues about their feelings. The woman on the left seems to stride forward confidently, while the person in front of her looks down, perhaps tired or lost in thought. The next person holds something above her head. What could it be? The figure on the far right seems especially burdened with a heavy load. Whoever they may be, they move forward together.

Extracted from: <www.philamuseum.org/doc_downloads/education/object_resources/306053.pdf>. Accessed on: May 19, 2016.

a. ☐ They are about works of art.

b. ☐ They say what people are doing in the works of art.

c. ☐ Both works of art have the same theme.

d. ☐ They present a physical description of the people in the works of art.

WRITING

3. In pairs, you are going to write a description of a work of art to be published in a catalog.
   - Choose and describe a work of art that is depicting people. You may search the website of Brazilian artist Portinari, which offers a wide variety of works depicting people (children and adults).

     Portal Portinari: <www.portinari.org.br/>
   - Then, write down the name of the piece of art. Observe its details.
   - Describe the people, the colors, the place where they are and what they are doing.
   - Make a list of words related to the piece of art. If necessary, consult a dictionary.
   - Write on your notebook a rough draft introducing the piece. Make sure that the text contains a description of the people, vocabulary related to body parts, and the use of the present continuous tense, to indicate what they are doing.
   - Show your draft to the teacher.

AFTER WRITING

- After you finish your draft, exchange it with another pair of students and check if:
  - the title, date and artist were listed;
  - there is a description of the people, vocabulary related to body parts, and the use of the present continuous tense.
- Make any necessary corrections and organize together a catalog of the descriptions of the works of art selected by you. If possible, make the texts available to other students or people who are interested in art.

SELF-EVALUATION

Check the true sentences about your learning in Unit 1.
In this unit you have learned to:

- [ ] identify body parts;
- [ ] use the present continuous tense to indicate actions that are in progress at or around the time of speaking;
- [ ] read and write art catalogs.

Reflecting...

- **What did I learn about the use of the present continuous tense?**
- **What did I learn about the description of works of art?**
- **What did I learn about the changes that occur in adolescence?**

UNIT

2

What are you wearing?

JUM NAKAO/DIVULGAÇÃO

The image on this page is from a fashion show by the Brazilian stylist Jum Nakao, who was born in São Paulo, in 1966. The show took place in 2004 and was named *Sewing the Invisible.* The clothing of this collection were made with a very creative material, the vegetable paper. In the end of the show, the models tore up their clothes.

This is how Nakao explained the use of paper in his clothes:

"Paper is the first material. Fragile, fleeting, ephemeral. Easily affected by time. It embodies the writing, the poetry, the dreams. The lightness that is necessary for art to flow."

Translated from: <www.proec.ufg.br/revista_ufg/dezembro2009/jum_nakao_19.pdf>. Accessed on: May 19, 2016

Your learning objectives for this unit are...

- to recognize and describe physical characteristics and parts of the body;
- to ask questions about what is happening at the moment;
- to read and produce a campaign ad.

EXCHANGING IDEAS

1. By tearing up his creations, Nakao shocked the audience. Why were people surprised by his action during one of the most important fashion events in Brazil?
2. What is the connection between the stylist attitude and the type of material he chose to use for the fashion show?

- ***A costura do invisível***
  Jum Nakao. São Paulo: Editora Senac, 2005.
  Book and DVD about the nearly 700-hour creation process of the 2004 fashion show for the São Paulo Fashion Week. In end of the show, the models tore up their clothes.

- **www.jumnakao.com/portfolios/a-costura-do-invisivel/**
  A description and a video of *A costura do invisível* fashion show, by Jum Nakao.

Model wearing an outfit made with laser-cut vegetable paper by stylist Jum Nakao, during a fashion show for the São Paulo Fashion Week 2004.

2 What are you wearing?

READING COMPREHENSION

TEXT 1

BEFORE READING

1. Read the definition of a conscious consumer.

"Besides the price and the brand, the conscious consumer also takes into account the environment, human and animal well-being, and fair trade when choosing a product to buy."

Translated from: <www.mma.gov.br/responsabilidade-socioambiental/producao-e-consumo-sustentavel/consumo-consciente-de-embalagem/quem-e-o-consumidor-consciente>. Accessed on: May 19, 2016.

Are you a conscious consumer? Give examples of actions that are representative of a conscious consumer behavior.

2. Look at the text below and answer the questions.

a. Where can you find texts similar to this one? ____________________

b. What is the purpose of this text? ____________________

READING

3. Read the advertisement (ad) below and answer: What is it about?

____

PETER HOLST

Be attentive to images that illustrate a text because they can give us clues about the content of the text and help us infer information.

• **www.ecofashion-week.com**
Website of the non-profit organization Eco Fashion Week.

waste: desperdício
textile: tecido

Pound is a unit of mass which is defined as 0.454 kilogram.

4. Look at the ad on page 30 again and check what you can identify.

a. ☐ a model
b. ☐ clear, blue sky
c. ☐ clothes
d. ☐ date and place of the event
e. ☐ name of the event
f. ☐ time of the event
g. ☐ audience
h. ☐ houses and buildings

DANNY E. MARTINDALE/GETTY IMAGES/AFP

5. Answer the questions below.

catwalk: passarela

a. Why are there many clothes around the long catwalk?

____
____
____

b. Why is there so much gray in the ad?

____
____
____

c. How much water can we save if we recycle one pound of textile?

____

d. A campaign usually has a sponsor, that is, a person, an organization, or a company that provides funds for a project. Is there any sponsor in this advertisement campaign? If so, who?

____
____

e. A slogan is an impacting sentence that expresses a goal or an ideal. What is the slogan of this campaign?

____

AFTER READING

- How do you choose your clothes and decide what to buy?
- Do you think it is possible to make conscious choices when shopping? How?
- Can the choices people make when shopping influence the way products are manufactured?

TEXT 2

BEFORE READING

1. Read the title and subtitles of the text and check the information you expect to read.

a. [ ] How to save money when shopping for clothes.

b. [ ] How to mend clothes.

c. [ ] How to shop for expensive clothes.

READING

2. Read the text and check if your predictions in activity 1 are correct.

www.recyclenow.com/reduce/love-your-clothes

recyclenow

About us | Events | News | Contact us

Search

WHAT TO DO WITH... | REDUCE | RE-USE | RECYCLE | FACTS & FIGURES

Love Your Clothes

[...]

We can all save money and help the environment by making simple changes to the way we buy, use and get rid of our clothing.

Buying Clothes

We spend £1,800 on average each year on clothes. There are lots of ways we can make the most of this money by checking our wardrobes and making a list before we go shopping, choosing clothing designed to last longer and buying second hand.

Getting More out of Our Existing Clothes

The reason some of our clothes remain unworn is because they no longer fit, need repairing, or they don't suit our style or taste anymore. To overcome this you can:

- look for shops nearby which offer repair and alteration services
- wear clothes in new combinations and use accessories to give clothing a new lease of life

[...]

Extracted from: <www.recyclenow.com/reduce/love-your-clothes>. Accessed on: Jan. 7, 2015.

get rid of: nos livramos de
wardrobes: guarda-roupas
unworn: sem uso

The **£** symbol refers to the **pound**, which is the basic monetary unit of the United Kingdom (England, Scotland, Wales and Northern Ireland).

3. Match the questions to their corresponding answers.

a. How can people help the environment?

b. What can we do to save money before going shopping?

c. Why are many of our clothes unworn?

[ ] We can check our wardrobe, make a list, and choose clothes that last longer.

[ ] Because they don't fit anymore, need some repair, or are no longer our style.

[ ] By changing the way they buy and getting rid of clothes properly.

4. Read the text on page 32 again and check the pictures that describe what you can do to take more advantage of your clothes.

ILUSTRAÇÕES: ZUBARTES

A

[ ]

B

[ ]

C

[ ]

AFTER READING

- Recycling can help the planet. What is the connection between the reuse of materials and the conservation of the planet?
- What can you do at school and at home to avoid the waste of natural resources?

FOCUS ON VOCABULARY

1. Unscramble the letters and find words from the texts on pages 30 and 32. Label the pictures.

A

THINKSTOCK/GETTY IMAGES

C Y R E G I N L C

____

B

THINKSTOCK/GETTY IMAGES

L I E X T E T

____

C

THINKSTOCK/GETTY IMAGES

A V E S

____

D

THINKSTOCK/GETTY IMAGES

P A I R E R

____

2. Go back to text 2 on page 32 and find **last longer**, **look for**, and **a new lease of life**. Read the sentences they are in and try to understand their meanings. Then use them to complete the sentences below.

a. ____________ mentors who take joy in the success of others and want them to get ahead. Self-absorbed people never make good mentors (beyond observable narrow skills).

Extracted from: <www.linkedin.com/pulse/finding-great-mentor-what-look-joel-peterson>. Accessed on: May 20, 2016.

b. The average family in the US wastes up to $2,000 annually on food that never gets eaten. Don't let that be you! Here are some creative tips for making fresh food ________________.

Extracted from: <foodrevolution.org/blog/make-fresh-food-last/>. Accessed on: May 20, 2016.

c. A PORTSMOUTH post office is to be given ________________________.
The Post Office is to modernise its branch at One-Stop Stores in Allaway Avenue, Paulsgrove.

Extracted from: <www.portsmouth.co.uk/news/business/local-business/city-post-office-to-get-a-new-lease-of-life-1-6597012>. Accessed on: May 20, 2016.

Physical descriptive adjectives

3. Read an excerpt from *The Hitchhiker's Guide to the Galaxy*, by Douglas Adams. Which actress fits the description of the character Trillian best?

> She was slim, darkish, humanoid, with long waves of black hair, a full mouth, an odd little knob of a nose and ridiculously brown eyes.
>
> *The Hitchhiker's Guide to the Galaxy*, by Douglas Adams. p. 26.

TOUCHSTONE PICTURES/EVERETT COLLECTION/KEYSTONE BRASIL

Zooey Deschanel

BBC

Sandra Dickinson

4. Read the following headline and check the best meaning for the expression **ridiculously brown eyes** from Trillian's description.

www.facebook.com/TELEGRAPH.CO.UK/posts/10153119948584749

10 ridiculously cool things Taylor Swift has done for her fans

Surprise visits, home-made cookies and a very merry 'Swiftmas' – we round up the reasons Taylor Swift is one celebrity that's earned her dedicated fanbase

Extracted from: <www.facebook.com/TELEGRAPH.CO.UK/posts/10153119948584749>. Accessed on: Jan. 18, 2016.

a. ☐ Brown eyes that look bad.

b. ☐ Brown eyes that are ridiculous.

c. ☐ Eyes that are extremely brown and look good.

5. Zooey Deschanel and Sandra Dickinson are both different from Trillian's description. Complete the table and compare.

	Trillian	Sandra Dickinson	Zooey Deschanel
hair		blond	brown
eyes		green	blue
build		slim	slim

IT'S YOUR TURN!

In your notebook, write the physical description of any person you admire. It can be a friend, a family member, or someone famous. Then share it with a classmate. If possible, bring a picture to show him/her.

LANGUAGE IN USE

Verb to be

1. Complete the following description with the verb **to be**. Then check who Gabriel is in the picture.

– Gi, what does Gabriel look like?

– What do you mean?

– His face, for example...

– Let me see. Gabriel? He has dark hair... He _______ about my height... He has light skin... curly hair, you know? He has big eyes, he _______ thin, _______ arriving...

Transcripted from: <www.youtube.com/watch?v=1Wav5KjBHbI>. Accessed on: May 20, 2016.

LACUNA FILMES

2. Write a description of the two other characters: Leonardo and Giovana. Remember to write about their hair, build, height, and skin color.

a. Leonardo: ______________________________

b. Giovana: ______________________________

Present continuous (negative and interrogative forms)

3. Read the title and an excerpt from an article from Refinery29 website and answer: What is the full article probably about?

5 Editors + $50 = 5 Outfits You Have To See

Our fashion team took a little road trip to Long Island to hit up our favorite thrift store and see what we could find there in one hour and under $50. [...]

Extracted from: <www.refinery29.com/69506#page-1>. Accessed on: May 20, 2016.

4. Look at the pictures and match the questions to the correct answers.

ERIN YAMAGATA

ERIN YAMAGATA

a. What is Connie wearing?

b. What is Annie wearing?

c. Are Annie and Connie wearing similar outfits?

☐ No, they are not wearing similar outfits.

☐ She's wearing a T-shirt, a skirt, and holding a clutch.

☐ She's wearing a shirt, jeans, a belt, and holding a bag.

- **www.oeco.org.br/reportagens/24862-moda-feita-com-reciclagem**
  A text about the use of recycled material in the clothing industry.

5. Complete the sentences about activity 4 using the words from the box.

are	-ing	invert	negative	time

a. The sentences refer to actions that are happening at or around the ____________ of speaking.

b. The present continuous is formed by the verb form **am**, ____________, or **is** + the main verb in the ____________ form.

c. In the ____________ form, we use **not** between the verb **to be** and the main verb.

d. In the interrogative form, we ____________ the position of the verb **to be** and the subject.

PRONUNCIATION PRACTICE

6 Listen and practice the **-ing** endings in the following verbs. Then choose the correct option to complete the pronunciation rule.

smile: smil**ing**
talk: talk**ing**
run: runn**ing**
listen: listen**ing**

We pronounce the **-ing** ending as
☐ /ing/.
☐ /in/.

6. Form questions using the present continuous. Then read the cartoon and answer the questions.

MIKE FLANAGAN/CARTOONSTOCK

a. the man / wear / a raincoat

Is the man wearing a raincoat?

No, he isn't wearing a raincoat.

b. it / rain / outside

______

______

c. the boy / wear / glasses

______

______

d. the man and the boy / smile

______

______

HANDS ON!

In pairs, take turns describing your classmates without saying their names. Your partner has to guess who you are describing. You can use:

She's tall and chubby. Her hair is short and brown. Her eyes are blue.

Verb to be

We use the verb **to be** to describe physical features, such as height and build.

My father **isn't** tall but he **is** very thin.

Claire and Jenny **are** about the same height.

Watch out! To describe someone's hair, eyes and skin, we use the verb **to have**.

He **has** short hair and dark skin.

The Shimabukuro sisters **have** black eyes and long straight hair.

Present continuous

Negative sentences	subject + negative verb to be (am not/isn't/aren't) + main verb ending in **-ing**	**I'm not playing** video games. **You aren't listening** to music. **Rodrigo isn't walking** the dog. **The dancers aren't practicing** today.
Interrogative sentences	verb to be (am/is/are) + subject + main verb ending in **-ing**	**Am I driving** too fast? **Are you listening** to the radio? **Is Walter feeding** the cat? **Are the teachers working** right now?

1. Complete the descriptions according to the images and your opinion.

ISTOCKPHOTO/GETTY IMAGES

FMB PHOTO/GETTY IMAGES

a. My neighbor Fred ________________ very short and he ________________ red hair. He ________________ handsome in my opinion.

b. Timothy has light skin, long hair and he is quite thin. He ________________ beautiful eyes.

2. Use the prompts to write questions and answers about what the people in the images are doing. Follow the example.

SHUTTERSTOCK

(sleep) *Is he sleeping?*

No, he isn't sleeping. He is studying.

INGOLF POMPE/LOOK-FOTO/GETTY IMAGES

a. (dance) ________________________________

____

MONKEY BUSINESS IMAGES/SHUTTERSTOCK

b. (drive) ________________________________

____

LISTENING COMPREHENSION

BEFORE LISTENING

1. Read the words/expressions below and match them to their definitions.

   a. NGO

   b. volunteer work

   ☐ Work you do for free, to help other people

   ☐ Non-Governmental Organization

2. How is volunteer work related to NGOs?

   ____

   ____

   ____

3. Write **T** (true) or **F** (false) according to the information presented in the text below.

Starting as a freelance journalist, Anshu left a corporate job in 1998 and founded GOONJ with a mission to make clothing a matter of concern and to bring it among the list of subjects for the development sector. [...] Anshu is creating a mass movement for recycling and reuse of tones of waste material by channelising it from the cities to the villages, as a resource for rural development. [...]

Recently Anshu has been awarded the **'Social entrepreneur of the year award'** by the Schwab Foundation, sister concern of the World Economic Forum.

TEAM GOONJ

Extracted from: <https://www.startupgrind.com/events/details/startup-grind-delhi-ncr-presents-anshu-gupta-goonj#/>. Accessed on: Jan. 18, 2016.

a. ☐ Anshu Gupta created GOONJ.

b. ☐ GOONJ is an important news company.

c. ☐ His recycling program aims to develop cities, not rural areas.

d. ☐ He was named India's Social Entrepreneur of the Year.

e. ☐ GOONJ aims to sell low cost food to people in need.

• **goonj.org**
Website from the organization GOONJ, which recycles fabric and clothes in order to donate them.

LISTENING

4. Listen to Anshu Gupta talking about his organization. Check the sentences you hear.

7

a. ☐ Clothes cannot be reused.

b. ☐ I initiated this organization called GOONJ in 1998.

c. ☐ I am from Pakistan.

d. ☐ First thing you see is a T-shirt which you don't need.

e. ☐ People do not need food, clothes, and shelter.

f. ☐ My name is Anshu Gupta.

g. ☐ It is impossible to reuse or recycle clothes.

h. ☐ I am a fashion news reporter.

5. Complete this extract with the expressions from the box. Then listen and check your answers.

8

cannot use	is not usable	repair it

"Anything which ____________________, if it is repairable, we will ____________________, and then it will be utilized, but even if there is a cloth which is, which is like we ____________________ for anything, we can work it into two different products."

AFTER LISTENING

6. How can we reduce our textile waste? Talk to your classmates and list some suggestions.

____

____

____

____

7. In pairs, write two or three tips about how to recycle clothes in a creative way. Then tell your suggestions to your classmates.

____

____

____

____

SPEAKING

1. Choose one person from the ones illustrated below and describe him/her to a classmate. He/She has to guess who you are talking about.

Thelma

Leah

ILUSTRAÇÕES: ZUBARTES

Justin

Martin

Mrs. Bing

Michael

- ***The Magic Barber***

  John Milne. Macmillan Readers, Starter Level. 1. ed. São Paulo: Macmillan ELT, 2005.

  Crossways is a peaceful place where everyone wears a hat. Everything changes when a barber comes to town.

Reflecting on the theme

- Do you usually buy second-hand clothes or recycle the ones you have? If so, how do you usually do that? If not, why?
- Imagine you are organizing a flea market for clothes. How would you convince your family and friends to take part in this event?

WRITING

BEFORE WRITING

1. Read the ad and answer the questions.

a. What is the purpose of this ad?

☐ To tell people they have more than they need.

☐ To ask for donations of clothing.

b. Why should you donate clothes?

☐ Because you want to buy new ones.

☐ Because people in need can wear them.

c. Who launched the campaign?

☐ Kata Sea Breeze.

☐ The Mirror Foundation.

PHUKET'S KATA SEA BREEZE RESORT

2. Join the parts and form sentences.

a. The intention of the ad is to

b. The text and images in the ad

c. The text in the ad is

d. Anyone that wants to help people

☐ clear, direct, and objective, with persuasive words.

☐ call the readers' attention to the message.

☐ can be interested in the ad.

☐ convince the readers to donate.

3. Go back to the ad on pages 30 and compare it to the ad on this page. Pay attention to the pictures. Why are they important? Check the correct answers.

a. ☐ To engage the reader's attention.

b. ☐ To create a visual impact.

c. ☐ To remind the readers about the sponsors.

> • **www.ted.com/talks/maya_penn_meet_a_young_entrepreneur_cartoonist_designer_activist?language=en**
> Maya Penn's TED talk. Maya is a girl who has an eco-friendly clothing line and accessories.

WRITING

4. In pairs, create your own campaign ad. Follow the steps.
    - In pairs, plan a campaign ad for collecting used clothes, shoes and toys to be donated to the community and to charity.
    - Write a draft of the ad in your notebook.
    - Use objective language and sentences that can impact the reader.
    - Show your draft to your teacher and other classmates and ask them for suggestions on how to improve your text and adjust it accordingly.
    - Select some images to illustrate the ad.
    - Write the final version of your ad on poster boards and add the images.

AFTER WRITING

- Spread the posters around the school. Underneath the posters, place a big cardboard box where people can leave their donations.
- Ask teachers and the school staff about charities that can benefit from the donations.
- If possible, using a cell phone or a digital camera, make a video of the process of making the campaign poster as well as of the donations being delivered at the charitable organization, and post it on the school website.

SELF-EVALUATION

Check the true sentences about your learning in Unit 2.
In this unit you have learned to:

- [ ] recognize and describe physical characteristics and parts of the body;
- [ ] ask questions about what is happening at the moment;
- [ ] read and produce a campaign ad.

Reflecting...

- **What did I learn about being a conscious consumer?**
- **What did I learn about asking questions using the present continuous?**
- **What questions do I still have about creating a campaign ad?**
- **What questions do I still have about describing physical characteristics?**

Imperial vs. Metric System

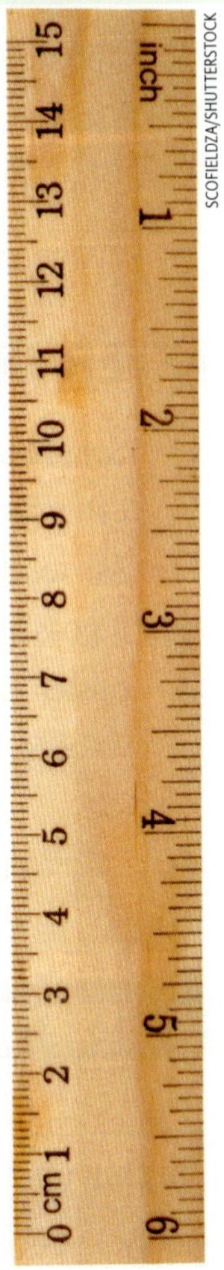
SCOFIELDZA/SHUTTERSTOCK

There are two main systems for measuring distances and weight, the Imperial System of Measurement and the Metric System of Measurement. Most countries use the Metric System, which uses the measuring units such as meters and grams and adds prefixes like kilo, milli and centi to count orders of magnitude. In the United States, we use the older Imperial System, where things are measured in feet, inches and pounds. It might be confusing if you are living in the US for the first time and are not used to this system. If you ask someone for directions, they will probably tell you something is a certain number of miles away. Or you may be told to move a few feet... But whose feet?

The Imperial System is also called The British Imperial because it came from the British Empire that ruled many parts of the world from the 16th to the 19th century. After the US gained independence from Britain, the new American government decided to keep this type of measurement, even though the Metric System was gaining in popularity at the time.

We are one of the few countries in the world that still use this system, and first time visitors may find it confusing. Here are a few things to remember that will come in handy day to day:

- 1 mile equals 1.6 kilometers.
- 1 inch is about 25 millimeters or 2.54 centimeters.
- A 3-foot measurement is almost exactly 1 meter.
- 1 kilogram is just over 2 pounds.
- 1 pound is about 454 grams.

[...]

By the way, the temperature scales are different too. We didn't want to make things too easy for you! Though not technically part of the Metric System, Americans measure temperature in Fahrenheit, not Celsius. You may turn on the television and listen for the weather and hear that it is 70 degrees outside. No, you won't pass out and be vaporized by the sun; 70 degrees Fahrenheit is actually very pleasant, about 21 degrees Celsius. Celsius has been used around the world from the mid 20th century, but, again, Americans held fast to the original Fahrenheit system.

Here are some more handy conversions for temperature:

- 0 degrees Celsius is equal to 32 degrees Fahrenheit (the freezing point).
- 24 degrees Celsius is equal to 75 degrees Fahrenheit (a very pleasant day).
- To convert Celsius (C) to Fahrenheit (F), use the formula F = (C x 1.8) + 32.

There is no reason to expect that we will change over to the Metric System and Celsius anytime soon. The chances that we will make the switch during your short-term stay in the United States are slim, so your best bet is to try to adjust as much as possible. Or, if you have a smartphone, you can do what I do when I travel – download a conversion app. [...]

Adapted from: <www.interexchange.org/articles/career-training-usa/2012/05/24/imperial-vs-metric-system/>. Accessed on: May 20, 2016.

1. Based on the information provided in the text, what are your measurements (height and weight) in the Imperial System?

____

2. What is the average temperature in your region during summer time? Answer in Fahrenheit.

____

3. When did Brazil adopt the Metric System?

____

____

4. Make the conversions of the following information from the Imperial System to the Metric System.

in: inch(es) **ft**: foot(feet) **lb(s)**: pound(s)	**Imperial System**	**Metric System**
 Usain Bolt	Height: 6 ft 5 in Weight: 207 lb	Height: ____________ Weight: ____________
 Serena Williams	Height: 5 ft 9 in Weight: 155 lb	Height: ____________ Weight: ____________
 Cristiano Ronaldo	Height: 6 ft 1 in Weight: 176 lb	Height: ____________ Weight: ____________
	Distance: 99 miles	Distance: ____________
	Temperature: 114° F	Temperature: ____________

MICHAEL KAPPELER/DPA/CORBIS/FOTOARENA
OSCAR GONZALEZ/WENN.COM/EASYPIX
MARCOS MESA SAM WORDLEY/SHUTTERSTOCK
BUDDY MAYS/ALAMY STOCK PHOTO/FOTOARENA
AP PHOTO/RICHARD VOGEL/GLOW IMAGES

UNIT

3

Houses around the world

Cildo Meireles is one of the most important Brazilian contemporary artists. His work was displayed in important exhibits such as the retrospectives at the New Museum of Contemporary Art, in New York, and at the Tate Modern, in London. His work was also shown at the Museum of Modern Art in Rio de Janeiro and in São Paulo.

MEIRELES, Cildo. *Desvio para o vermelho*. 1967-1984. Several materials. Inhotim, Brumadinho, Brazil.

Your learning objectives for this unit are...

- to identify and describe types of housing;
- to name the parts of a house, some furniture and appliances;
- to read and write an ad for a house for rent.

EXCHANGING IDEAS

1. Look at the opening image of this unit. This is a photo of an installation created by the artist. What is it?
2. This installation is part of a collection from a museum. People can walk into the room. What effect does the use of colors have on the visitor?
3. If you could choose a new place to live in, where would it be? What kind of housing would you like to have?

CILDO MEIRELES. DESVIO PARA O VERMELHO: I. IMPREGNAÇÃO, 1967-1984

- **enciclopedia.itaucultural.org.br/pessoa10593/cildo-meireles**
  Information about the artist Cildo Meireles and his artworks.
- **www.tate.org.uk/node/237205/about.shtm**
  Information, images and videos about Cildo Meireles' exhibit at the Tate Modern in London, England.

3 Houses around the world

READING COMPREHENSION

TEXT 1

BEFORE READING

1. "Adequate housing is a fundamental right since 1948, with the Universal Declaration of Human Rights, making it a human right universally accepted and applicable in all parts of the world as a fundamental right to life of people."

Translated from: <direitoamoradia.org/page_id=46&lang=pt>. Accessed on: May 20, 2016.

Why is it so important for human beings to have a house in your opinion? Justify.

READING

2. Scan the following text and answer: What is it about? Talk to a classmate and compare your answers.

Types of Houses around the World

Many unique houses exist across the world.

They are different according to the varying history, geographical factors and sciences applied in building them at different places.

Here's a quick look at some of these interesting types of houses. [...]

Snow House

- Snow houses are made up of snow blocks built up into the shape of a dome.
- These houses are also sometimes referred to as an 'igloo'.
- Temperatures inside a snow house can be raised up to around 15 degrees Celsius when the outside temperature is –40 degrees Celsius! [...]

Snow houses can be found in **the areas around the Arctic Circle**, in places such as **Alaska** and **Greenland**.

THINKSTOCK/GETTY IMAGES

Stilt House

- Instead of being at ground level, some houses are raised above ground with stilts.
- This protects them from floods, and also from the wild animals that roam around. The elevation also keeps the house cool. Stilt houses can be found at coastal areas where it is easily flooded, but can also be found inland.

They are common in parts of Southeast Asia.

THINKSTOCK/GETTY IMAGES

Extracted from: <www.nlb.gov.sg/sure/wp-content/uploads/2013/11/Cheatsheet_house_Final_lowres.pdf>. Accessed on: May 20, 2016.

dome: cúpula
stilt: estaca
ground level: térreo
floods: enchentes

3. Join the parts to make questions. Then match questions and answers.

a. Where can we	☐ a stilt house raised?	☐ They can be found at coastal areas, but also inland.
b. What is another word	☐ for a snow house?	☐ Around the Arctic Circle.
c. What is the temperature	☐ be found?	☐ Around 15 degrees Celsius.
d. To which level is	☐ inside an igloo?	☐ Above the ground.
e. Where can stilt houses	☐ find snow houses?	☐ It's also called an igloo.

4. Which pieces of information are NOT mentioned in the text?

a. ☐ An igloo is made of ice blocks.

b. ☐ It is easy to construct a stilt house.

c. ☐ Stilt houses built inland are different from those built above water.

- **hagafoto.jp/templates/hagahaga/topics/house/house-e.html**
  Images of different kinds of houses around the world.

5. Answer the questions below.

a. Greenland, an island located in the Arctic Ocean, has a population of around 57 thousand people. Brazil has a population of 202 million inhabitants, according to the Brazilian Geography and Statistics Institute (IBGE).

In your opinion, why is the population of Greenland so small?

____

____

____

____

b. What might be the advantages and disadvantages of living on a stilt house?

____

____

____

____

AFTER READING

- Did you know these types of housing?
- Have you ever been to a type of housing different from yours? If so, which one? If not, what type of housing would you like to visit? Why?
- What is the most common type of housing in your region? Is it similar to any of the types presented earlier?

TEXT 2

BEFORE READING

1. How do you imagine living on a boat is?

2. Read the ad quickly and check what kind of information about this type of housing you can find.

READING

3. Read the text and then check the correct sentences according to it.

Summit Houseboat

The Summit houseboat is perfect for ten, cozy and cooled by two air conditioners – cozy never becomes sweltering. The cabin is very nice and quite large, and pull out beds that can easily sleep two are in the living area. There are plenty of closets for storage space.

The kitchen is excellent, fully equipped with utensils and plates as well as a good-sized stove, microwave, blender, toaster and coffeemaker. With a refrigerator and a large ice chest, you'll always be able to keep your food fresh.

For fun in the sun, enjoy the massive upper deck and its large sun deck. [...]

2002-2015 HOUSEBOATS.COM

DOUGLAS HAUCK

Season	3 days	4 days	5 days	6 days
value	$1,150	$1,350	$1,500	$1,750
summer	$1,350	$1,700	$1,950	$2,200

Extracted from: <www.houseboating.org/Summit-Houseboat>. Accessed on: Jan. 18, 2016.

a. ☐ The boat is ideal for 10 people.

b. ☐ The boat does not have air-conditioning.

c. ☐ The boat rent is lower in summer.

d. ☐ The boat has a fully equipped kitchen.

e. ☐ There are places on the boat where you can enjoy the sunlight.

AFTER READING

- On the common areas, there are rules that regulate the daily routine. What rules do you think are necessary for a harmonious coexistence between people on a small space such as a boat?
- Would you like to live on a boat for some time? Why?

FOCUS ON VOCABULARY

1. Match the pictures to the sentences.

THINKSTOCK/GETTY IMAGES

The USA

GARETH MCCORMACK/GETTY IMAGES

Ireland

SPENCER WILTON/GETTY IMAGES

India

THINKSTOCK/GETTY IMAGES

Scotland

☐ Yosemite Creek has 75 campsites and is open from July to early September.

Extracted from: <www.campingatyosemite.com/yosemite_creek_campground.htm>. Accessed on: May 20, 2016.

☐ From Unst to St Abb's Head National Nature Reserve and from the islands of St Kilda and Iona to the mountains of Glencoe and Mar Lodge Estate, we look after some of Scotland's finest landscapes and wildlife.

Extracted from: <www.nts.org.uk/Countryside/>. Accessed on: May 20, 2016.

☐ Since the 1730s, the gardens at Powerscourt have been on a remarkable journey. Hundreds of people worked to create the views we enjoy today and many of them never lived to see the completion of a lifetime's work.

Extracted from: <powerscourt.com/gardens/our-gardeners>. Accessed on: May 20, 2016.

☐ Mumbai, formerly called as Bombay, is the financial and the entertainment capital of India. More than 20 million people reside in this city.

Extracted from: <grabhouse.com/urbancocktail/10-best-residential-areas-mumbai/>. Accessed on: May 20, 2016.

2. Check the appropriate alternatives to complete the sentences. Then write the answers in the spaces provided.

a. The number of U.S. households heating with ______________ rose 34% nationwide from 1.8 million in 2000 to 2.4 million in 2010.

Extracted from: <usatoday30.usatoday.com/money/industries/energy/story/2011-11-10/woodstoves-regulations-heating-pollution/51160192/1>. Accessed on: May 20, 2016.

☐ wood ☐ stone

b. Before any fibrous raw material – wood, ______________, bamboo – can be used for paper manufacture, it has to be converted into pulp by disintegrating the fibres, which is also true in fibreboard production.

Extracted from: <www.fao.org/docrep/l2015e/l2015e03.htm>. Accessed on: May 20, 2016.

☐ blocks ☐ straw

c. Kitchen

noun kitch•en \'ki-chən\: a ______________ in which food is cooked.

Extracted from: <www.merriam-webster.com/dictionary/kitchen>. Accessed on: May 20, 2016.

☐ storey ☐ room

d. National Weather Service issues a winter weather advisory for ______________, freezing rain, icy conditions, flooding and advises to 'keep a winter survival kit'.

Extracted from: <www.theguardian.com/us-news/2015/jan/03/winter-weather-advisory-us-snow-tornadoes>. Accessed on: May 20, 2016.

☐ snow ☐ mud

Parts of the house, furniture and appliances

3. Listen and check. Which house is being described?

A

TIME LIFE/GETTY IMAGES

Casa das Canoas

B

ACERVO SÍTIO ROBERTO BURLE MARX

Sítio Roberto Burle Marx

C

ACERVO EDUARDO LONGO

Casa-Bola 2

4. Listen again and complete the floor plan with the rooms that are mentioned.

10

5. Look at the pictures and complete the chart.

bed

table and chairs

sofa

TV

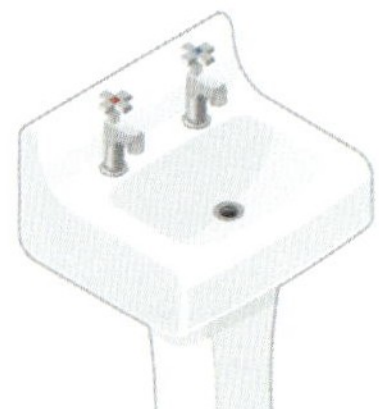
sink

IMAGENS: SHUTTERSTOCK

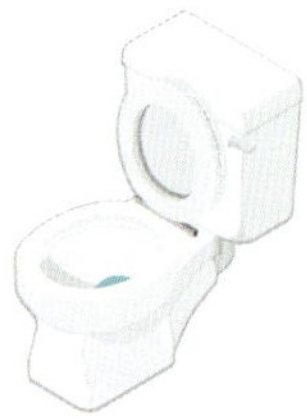
toilet

shower

THINKSTOCK/GETTY IMAGES

microwave oven

fridge

THINKSTOCK/GETTY IMAGES

Living room	Bedroom	Bathroom	Kitchen	Dining room
__________	__________	__________	__________	__________
__________	__________	__________	__________	__________
__________	__________	__________	__________	__________

IT'S YOUR TURN!

Bring a picture, make a video or a drawing of your house. Show it to a classmate and talk about it. Use the words from activities 4 and 5, and a dictionary to help you.

There to be

1. Look at the floor plan of Casa-Bola 2 and write **T** (true) or **F** (false). Then correct the false statements.

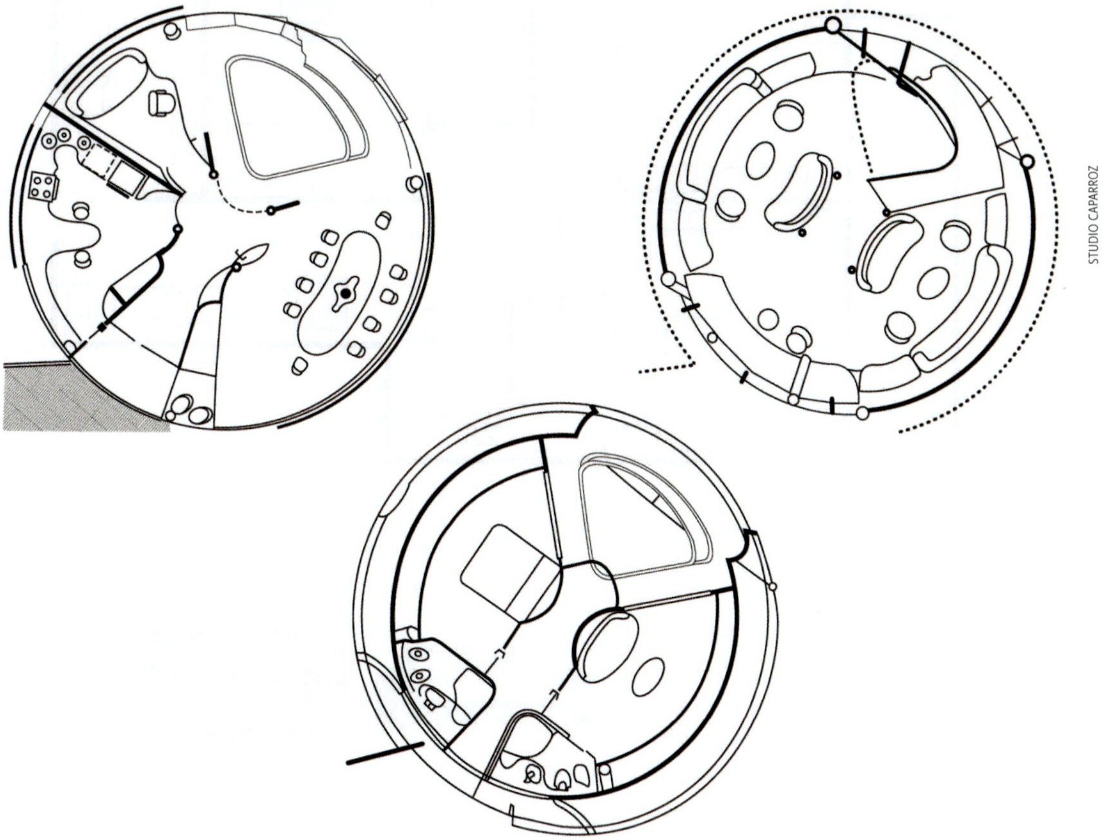

In this house:

a. ☐ There is only one bedroom.

____

b. ☐ There is one bathroom in each bedroom.

____

c. ☐ There are two kitchens.

____

d. ☐ There is a sink in the kitchen.

____

e. ☐ There isn't a dining room.

____

2. Read the following rental house description and answer the questions.

www.bucknell.edu/x4874.xml

Rental House Descriptions

221 S. 6th Street, Gross Sq. Ft. 3071, Three story house with 4 bedrooms, living room, dining room, kitchen with stove and refrigerator, laundry room, 2 bathrooms, oil heat, electric hot water. Grass mowed by Facilities.

GETTY IMAGES

Extracted from: <www.bucknell.edu/x4874.xml>. Accessed on: May 20, 2016.

a. Is there a bathroom for every bedroom?

____

b. Are there any appliances already in the house? If so, which ones?

____

c. Is there a place to do the laundry in the house?

____

d. Are there 2 stories in the house?

____

How many...?

3. Read the description in activity 2 again and answer the questions.

a. How many bedrooms are there in the house?

____

b. How many living rooms are there?

____

4. Underline the appropriate options in the following sentences.
We use **How many** to ask about the **quantity** / **size** of things or people in a place. **How many** is used before a **singular** / **plural** noun.

Demonstrative pronouns

5. Look at the pictures and read the speech bubbles. Then match the columns.

ILUSTRAÇÕES: VICENTE MENDONÇA

a. **This** and **these** refer to	☐	people or things that are far from the speaker.
b. **That** and **those** refer to	☐	are used with the plural form.
c. **This** and **that**	☐	things or people that are near the speaker.
d. **These** and **those**	☐	are used with the singular form.

HANDS ON!

Take a classroom survey. Ask six classmates different questions about their houses. You can use: *How many rooms are there in your house? Are the bedrooms big? Is there a garden? Which part of your house do you like most?* Then report the results of the survey to your classmates and teacher. You can say, for example: *Tony and Sabrina like the TV room most.*

There to be

We use **there to be** to say or ask about the existence of something.

	Singular	Plural
affirmative	**There is** one wrong answer in the test.	**There are** two correct answers in this exercise.
negative The is / are + not	**There is not / isn't** one wrong answer in the test.	**There are not / aren't** two correct answers in this exercise.
interrogative Is / Are there	**Is there** one wrong answer in the test?	**Are there** two correct answers in this exercise?

How many

We use **how many** to ask about quantity. It is used with plural nouns.
Examples:
How many books are there in your bag?
How many alternatives are there in this exercise?

Demonstrative pronouns

Singular nouns	Plural nouns
this (for things that are near the speaker)  **This** is my favorite T-shirt.	**these** (for things that are near the speaker)  **These** sneakers are new.
that (for things that are far from the speaker)  **That** is my house on the corner.	**those** (for things that are far from the speaker)  I want to try **those** shoes over there.

ANDREI SHUMSKIY/SHUTTERSTOCK
SOLOVIOVA LIUDMYLA/SHUTTERSTOCK
SUZANNE TUCKER/SHUTTERSTOCK
THINKSTOCK/GETTY IMAGES

1. Look at the images and answer the questions.

PRESSMASTER/SHUTTERSTOCK

NONCHANON/SHUTTERSTOCK

CAR CULTURE/GETTY IMAGES

HEMIS/ALAMY STOCK PHOTO/FOTOARENA

JEFF GYNANE/SHUTTERSTOCK

BINH THANH BUI/SHUTTERSTOCK

a. How many hands are there?

____

b. How many belts are there?

____

c. How many cars are there?

____

d. How many dogs are there?

____

e. How many pencils are there?

____

f. How many cookies are there?

____

2. Complete these sentences with **this**, **these**, **that**, or **those**.

HARTCREATIONS/GETTY IMAGES

RADIUS IMAGES/GETTY IMAGES

SASWELL/SHUTTERSTOCK

WAVEBREAKMEDIA/SHUTTERSTOCK

a. ______________ grapes are delicious!

b. I don't like ______________ sneakers because they are very uncomfortable.

c. ______________ is my cat, Whiskers. Isn't she wonderful?

d. Do you remember the name of ______________ book about a man with his dragon?

LISTENING COMPREHENSION

BEFORE LISTENING

1. Use the words from the box to complete the rental ad.

bathroom	bed	desk	fridge	microwave	table	TV

North Melbourne fully furnished one bedroom apartment located at Arden Street.

This apartment has security entrance. 10 minutes walk to Melbourne University, RMIT and Queen Victoria Market, 5 minutes walk to all major hospitals, a short walk to shopping precincts and public transport (tram 57, 55 and 59) to CBD.

NORTH MELBOURNE HOTEL

This one bedroom apartment comprises of a double ____________, 32" Digital ____________ with remote control, study ____________ and computer chair, dining ____________ and chairs. Kitchen comes with cordless kettle, ____________, toaster, rice cooker and ____________. You also get your own private ____________.

Rent is $350/week with gas and water usage included.
AVAILABLE 13/03/15
Please feel free to contact me to arrange a time for an inspection.

Extracted from: <www.gumtree.com.au/s-ad/north-melbourne/property-for-rent/fully-furnished-one-bedroom-apartment-for-rent/1071953882>. Accessed on: Mar. 6, 2015.

LISTENING

2. Listen to the description of another rental apartment. Check the floor plan that corresponds to the description. 11

ILUSTRAÇÕES: ZUBARTES

A

☐

B

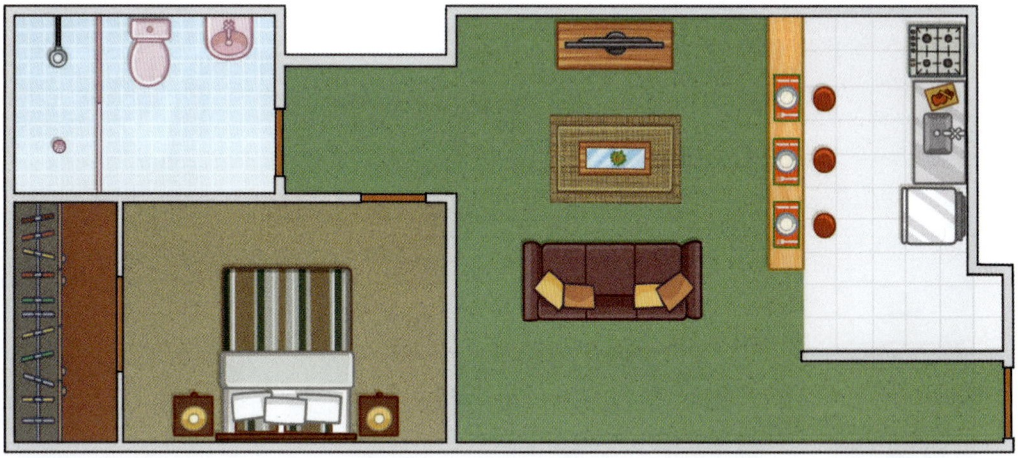

☐

C

☐

AFTER LISTENING

3. On page 58 you talked to some classmates about the part of the house you like most. In your notebook, draw the furniture you have there and write sentences. You can use a dictionary to help you.

SPEAKING

1. Describe the house of your dreams to a classmate. He/She has to draw the floor plan of this house in the space below. Check if the drawing corresponds to your description. Then change roles.

Reflecting on the theme

What makes the house that you have just described the house of your dreams?

WRITING

BEFORE WRITING

1. There are many ways you can advertise a house for rent or sale on the internet. What kind of information do you think ads should have to get the reader's attention?

2. Read the text below and check the correct sentences.

www.brazilrentmyhouse.com/to-rent/property/brazil/?houseid=6217&pageno=0&from=search&strBeds=2&strType=house

RENT MY 2 BED HOUSE DURING RIO 2016 OLYMPIC GAMES

FLORIANÓPOLIS, BRAZIL. 2 BEDROOM,
2 BATH, GARDEN
RIO TAVARES, SOUTH FLORIANÓPOLIS

$400USD | per night

OPÇÃO BRASIL

A very comfortable 2 bed, 2 bathroom house with a very nice garden and view to Novo Campeche beach.

It is close to south beaches, the city center and Lagoa da Conceição. Also close to the airport.

I lived in this lovely house for 5 years until I decided to move to London. Each double bedroom features a double bed and the living room also has a couch-bed, the garden is lovely and you will be very close to the beaches.

There's a barbecue in the garden and parking space for up to 3 cars.

I'm looking for someone or a family that would like to exchange home for a year and would take care of our lovely house as if it was its own.

Extracted from: <www.brazilrentmyhouse.com/to-rent/property/brazil/?houseid=6217&pageno=0&from=search&strBeds=2&strType=house>. Accessed on: May 21, 2016.

In this text:

a. ☐ there is a picture of the house.

b. ☐ there is the location of the house.

c. ☐ there is the rent of the house.

d. ☐ there is a description of the house.

e. ☐ there are adjectives to describe the house.

f. ☐ there are descriptions of the people.

- ***The Girl in the Mirror***

  Paul Davies. Hotshot Puzzles 1. 6. ed. Oxford: Oxford University Press, 2002.

  A teenager, Martin, and his mother move to an old house in a village called Westborne. Martin feels bad about leaving Cathy and all his friends. One day, Martin looks in the mirror in his new bedroom: his life changes and he is happy again.

WRITING

3. Imagine you work for a company that rents houses for foreigners. Write a rental ad of a house for people who want to live in Brazil for a few months.
   - Choose a place that might be interesting for a tourist.
   - Think about the qualities that might be attractive to this tourist.
   - Consider the aspects that might be interesting for different tourists: culture, business, adventure, leisure, relaxation, history, etc.
   - Describe the house and its parts.
   - Highlight the qualities of the place using adjectives.
   - Consider the information that might help the reader of the ad: price, location, photos.
   - Write a draft of the ad on your notebook.
   - If necessary, consult a dictionary.
   - Show your draft to the teacher.
   - Make the necessary corrections to your ad.

AFTER WRITING

- Exchange ads with a classmate and check if the ad:
  - is attractive to the reader;
  - describes the parts of the house;
  - highlights the qualities of the place;
  - brings the necessary information for the reader.
- Display the ads so that everybody in the class can read them.

SELF-EVALUATION

Check the true sentences about your learning in Unit 3.
In this unit you have learned to:

- [ ] identify and describe types of housing;
- [ ] name the parts of a house, some furniture and appliances;
- [ ] read and write an ad for a house for rent.

Reflecting...

- What did I learn about types of housing?
- What did I learn about the characteristics of ads?
- What questions do I have about there to be?

Tiny houses can help save the planet

What are tiny houses?

RICK WILKING/REUTERS/LATINSTOCK

AP PHOTO/CHARLES KRUPA/GLOW IMAGES

RICK WILKING/REUTERS/LATINSTOCK

AP PHOTO/CHARLES KRUPA/GLOW IMAGES

The typical American home is around 241.5 square meters, whereas the typical small or tiny house is between 9.3 and 37 square meters. Tiny houses come in all shapes, sizes, and forms, but they enable simpler living in a smaller, more efficient space.

Why do people choose to live in a tiny house?

People are choosing to live in tiny houses for many reasons, but the most popular reasons include environmental concerns, financial concerns, and the desire for more time and freedom. For most Americans 1/3 to 1/2 of their income is dedicated to having and maintaining a house or an apartment; this means 15 working years of your lifetime just to pay for your home.

What is the main barrier people encounter when they decide to live in a tiny house?

Besides the obvious fact that people need to learn to live with less, the main barrier might still be social pressure. In our society today, bigger is better, more is better, we are conditioned to want more and more stuff. These cultural norms are very strong in our society and tiny houses go against this current, questioning much of what people hold dear.

Why are tiny houses sustainable?

Because the natural resources you need to build and maintain a tiny house are reduced to a minimum. During construction of the average sized house, nearly 7 trucks of wood products are used whereas in a tiny house, only about half of that is needed. The pollution associated with an average house is significant (about 14 tons of CO_2 emissions each year). In contrast, a tiny house only generates about 907 kilos. Besides, many tiny houses are solar-powered and have a rainwater collection systems.

1. Complete the chart below using information about your own house. Ask your parents to help you.

	Information about your house
size	
electricity consumption	
number of light bulbs	

2. Now, calculate how much electricity your own house consumes a year. How is your house consumption compared to a tiny house's?

____

____

3. What can you and your family do to reduce the consumption of your house and make it more sustainable?

____

____

4. Would you like to live in a tiny house? Why?

____

____

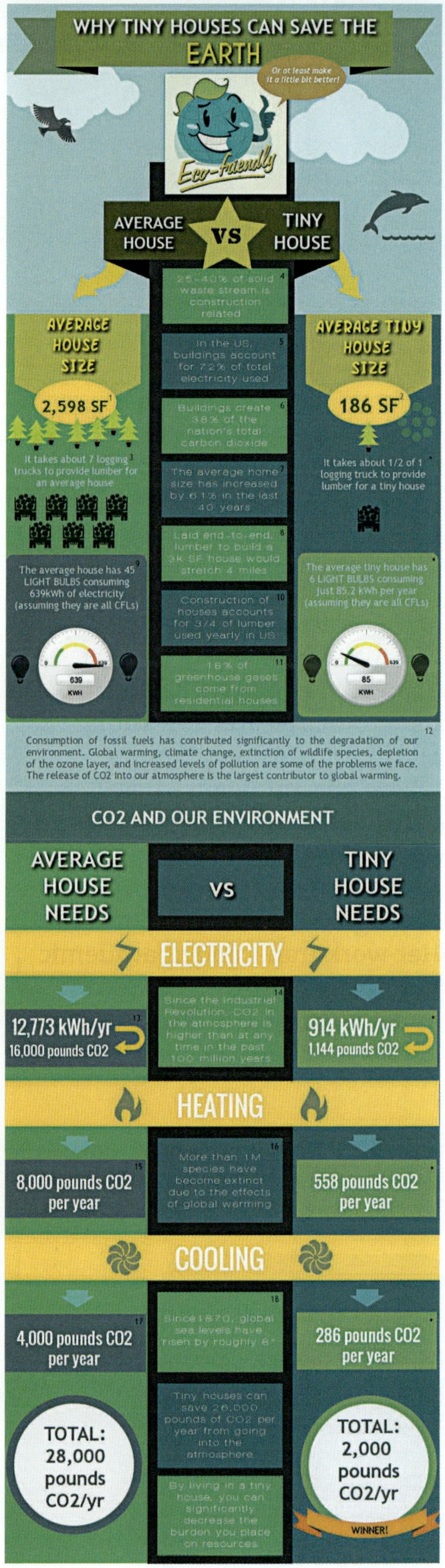

WWW.TINYHOUSEB.JILD.COM

Adapted from: <thetinylife.com/what-is-the-tiny-house-movement/>. Accessed on: May 20, 2016.

UNIT

4

What's your favorite festivity?

Anita Malfatti was born in São Paulo in 1889. She began her studies in arts at a young age and traveled to Europe, where she got involved with the modernist movements. Back in Brazil, she took part in the Modern Art Week in 1922 among other artists and poets. Her work transcended academic painting and stirred controversy at the time.

Your learning objectives for this unit are...

- to talk about festivities in Brazil and other countries;
- to identify characteristics of a travel guide;
- to read and write a travel guide page.

EXCHANGING IDEAS

1. Look at the opening image of this unit. It depicts a very popular event in Brazil: June parties. Which elements in the painting are typical of these parties?
2. Describe the place in the painting.
3. What are other traditional festivals and parties in Brazil?
4. Do you know traditional festivals from other countries? Which ones?

FESTA DE SÃO JOÃO COM GUIRLANDAS, ANITA MALFATTI, S.D. COLEÇÃO PARTICULAR

MALFATTI, Anita. *Festa de São João com Guirlandas.* Date unknown. Oil on canvas, 50 cm × 61 cm. Private collection, São Paulo.

- **www.institutoanitamalfatti.com.br/**
  Painter Anita Malfatti's official website, featuring her biography and artwork.

4 What's your favorite festivity?

READING COMPREHENSION

TEXT 1

BEFORE READING

1. What are the most important traditional festivals or parties in your city?
2. Do you usually attend traditional festivals or parties in your city? What activities usually take place in these festivals or parties?

- **www.cnfcp.gov.br/**
Website of the Centro Nacional de Folclore e Cultura Popular.

READING

3. Skim the text and answer: Which popular Brazilian festivity is it about?

www.johninbrazil.org/festas-juninas

Hi all,

WWW.JOHNINBRAZIL.ORG

Brazilians love a party, and in June you'll find here a slew of parties collectively called the "festas juninas", or June parties.

These parties originated in Brazil's colonial days. [...]

Kids, and often adults, dress as country rubes, with straw hats and patched clothes. Often – I'm not sure why – attendees add fake freckles on their cheeks.

At the parties you'll find traditional food and drink, including a kind of cider. Music is country-themed, kind of reminiscent of square dance music but incorporating that most noxious of instruments, the accordion.

In the northeast and the north, the celebrations can be very elaborate. [...]

There are dances at night in which the girls dress in elaborate costumes and perform in large groups for the spectators.

Some of the songs tell the story of the Boi Bumbá. *Boi* means cow. [...]

Brazil is a culturally diverse and rich country. So much more than Carnaval. I hope you make time to visit here. [...]

Até mais, guys.

John

Still in Brazil

Extracted from: <www.johninbrazil.org/festas-juninas>. Accessed on: May 21, 2016.

fake freckles: sardas falsas

4. Read the text and answer the questions.

a. Who writes the text?

____

b. Where is the author writing from?

____

____

c. Is the author Brazilian?

____

____

5. In the first sentence of the text, John writes: "Brazilians love a party". Is this affirmation a fact or an opinion?

____

6. Look at the following sentences from the text and write **O** (opinion) or **F** (fact).

a. ☐ "These parties originated in Brazil's colonial days."

b. ☐ "Kids, and often adults, dress as country rubes"

c. ☐ "At the parties you'll find traditional food and drink"

d. ☐ "Music is country-themed, kind of reminiscent of square dance music but incorporating that most noxious of instruments, the accordion."

7. Overall, is the author's point of view of Brazil positive or negative? Find in the text the extract that justifies your answer and write it below.

____

____

____

8. Why do you think the author mixes opinions and facts?

____

____

____

AFTER READING

- Music, dance, stories and festivals are some of the ways a culture is expressed. These manifestations preserve the cultural richness that survived to this day thanks to our ancestors.

  What are the cultural manifestations in your city like? Do they preserve a tradition? Did they change over time? Did they disappear? Give examples to justify your answer.

TEXT 2

BEFORE READING

1. The text you are about to read was published in an online travel guide. What kind of information does the reader find in a travel guide?

2. Who are the probable readers of a travel guide?

READING

3. Read the text, join the parts and write meaningful sentences.

Día de los Muertos

AIZAR RALDES/AFP

If visitors know just one Mexican holiday, it's probably the **Day of the Dead**, when families honour and remember those who have died. Actually taking place over two days, November 1 and 2, it's an indigenous tradition unique to Mexico. With a few exceptions [...], it's usually a private rite. In every home and many businesses people set up *ofrendas* (altars) for the deceased: the centrepiece is always a photograph, lit by candles. In addition to the photo, the person's favourite foods are also placed on the altar, as a way of luring the soul back to this world. [...]

On the streets, market stalls brim with eggy, orange-scented *pan de muertos* and colourfully iced sugar skulls. Families usually gather to eat dinner on the night of November 1, then visit gravesites, which are also cleaned and decorated. Far from being a sad time, the **Day of the Dead** is an occasion for telling funny stories, bonding with family and generally celebrating life.

Extracted from: <www.roughguides.com/destinations/north-america/mexico/festivals/d%C3%ADa-los-muertos/>. Accessed on: May 23, 2015.

a. During *Día de los Muertos*
b. This indigenous tradition
c. People put candles,
d. *Día de los Muertos* is not

happens only in Mexico.
people remember their dead relatives.
a sad day, actually, it's a celebration of life.
pictures and food on the altars.

a. ______________________________.

b. ______________________________.

c. ______________________________.

d. ______________________________.

- **http://www.placesto seeinyourlifetime.com/top-10-celebrations-around-the-world-1937/**
  Information about famous festivals and festivities around the world.

AFTER READING

- Research about other popular festivals around the world. Learn about where and when they take place, the typical clothes, the traditional music, the dances and the food. Share your findings with your classmates.

FOCUS ON VOCABULARY

1. Use the words from the box to label the following images.

accordion	patched clothes	square dance	straw hat

A

G. EVANGELISTA/OPÇÃO BRASIL IMAGENS

____

B

ISABEL SÓ/OPÇÃO BRASIL IMAGENS

____

C

JOE FOX/AGE FOTOSTOCK/KEYSTONE BRASIL

____

D

MOURÃO PANDA/FOTOARENA

____

Days of the week

2. Listen to part of *The Lego Movie* (2014) and check what event they talk about.

12

A

REPRODUÇÃO

☐

B
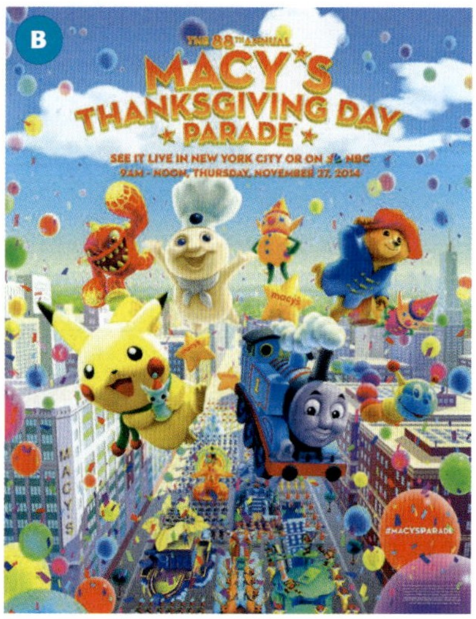

REPRODUÇÃO

☐

C

ABC/OSCAR.COM

☐

3. Complete the schedule with the days of the week. Use the posters from activity 2 to help you.

______________	The Oscars
Monday	
______________	Taco Tuesday
Wednesday	
______________	Thanksgiving
Friday	
Saturday	

4. Now complete the schedule with activities you usually do on Mondays, Wednesdays, Fridays, and Saturdays.

Months of the year

5. Read about Thanksgiving Day in the USA and answer the questions.

Thanksgiving Day is celebrated on the fourth Thursday in November.

In the fall of 1621, the Pilgrims held a three-day feast to celebrate a bountiful harvest. Many regard this event as the first Thanksgiving in the United States.

Adapted from: <http://www.usa.gov.edgesuite-staging.net/citizens/holidays.shtml>. Accessed on: Jan. 21, 2016.

Pilgrims: peregrinos

a. Is Thanksgiving Day always celebrated on the same date?

____

b. In what month is Thanksgiving Day celebrated in the USA?

____

c. Canada also celebrates Thanksgiving Day, but it's in October. Is it before or after Thanksgiving Day in the USA?

____

6. Festivals celebrating the harvest are common not only in the USA and Canada. Look at some other festivals that celebrate the harvest throughout the year and answer.

calendar

January	February	March	April	May	June
Incwala (Swaziland) Blessing of Waters (Greece)	Vendimia (Argentina)		Madeira Flower Festival (Portugal)	Chanthaburi Fruit Fair (Thailand) Rice Harvest Festival (Indonesia)	Chanthaburi Fruit Fair (Thailand)

July	August	September	October	November	December
Lammas Festival (United Kingdom)		Sukkot (Israel)	Sukkot (Israel)	Olivagando (Italy)	Incwala (Swaziland)

- Why are harvest festivals celebrated on different dates?

____

____

7. In pairs, find out the missing words and complete the sequences.

a. Monday, ________________, Wednesday

b. Sunday, Wednesday, ________________

c. ________________, Wednesday, Sunday

d. ________________, June, November

e. November, February, May, ________________

f. October, February, June, ________________, ________________

- **www.timeanddate.com/holidays/**
  Dates and information about holidays and celebrations around the world.

- ***Festivals – Portfolio***
  Susan Holden. São Paulo: Macmillan, 2004.
  The book brings information about the most important international celebrations.

PRONUNCIATION PRACTICE

13 Listen to the months of the year and pay attention to the stress.

January	**A**pril	Ju**ly**	Oc**to**ber
February	May	**Au**gust	No**vem**ber
March	June	Sep**tem**ber	De**cem**ber

IT'S YOUR TURN!

In your notebook, create your own schedule for the following week. Write your main activities for every single day. Then compare it to a classmate's schedule.

Wh-questions

1. International Human Rights Day is celebrated every year all around the world. Look at the poster and answer the questions.

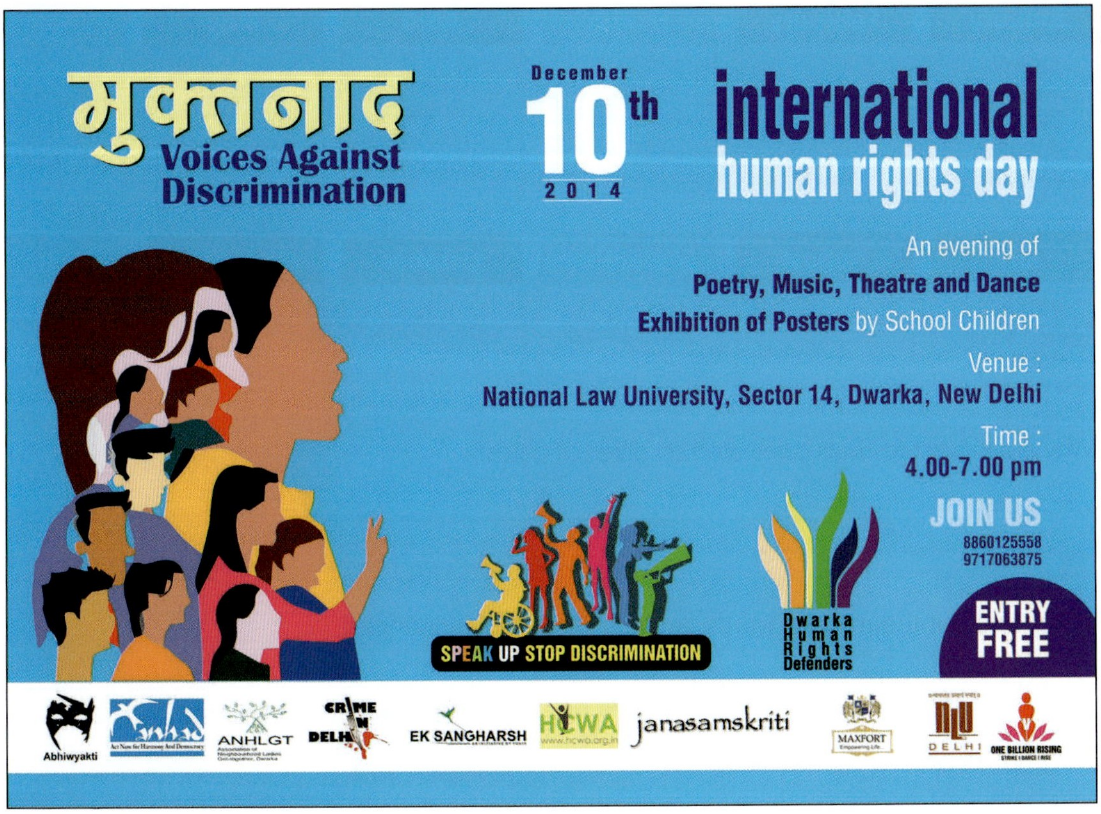

DWARKA HUMAN RIGHTS DEFENDERS

a. What is the event? ______

b. What are the event attractions? ______

c. When is the event? ______

d. Where is the event? ______

e. How much does it cost to enter the event? ______

2. Check the true statements about the poster in activity 1.

a. ☐ The event is scheduled for the morning.

b. ☐ Information such as date, time, and place are mentioned.

c. ☐ There is a short description of the event.

d. ☐ The theme of the event is Voices Against Discrimination.

e. ☐ Contact information is mentioned.

Why? Because...

3. Choose the correct alternative to explain the strip.

a. ☐ Calvin and his friend Hobbes are talking about the forest.

b. ☐ Calvin wants to know the reason they are on Earth.

Earth: planeta Terra
anywhere: em qualquer lugar

4. Complete these sentences using **why** and **because**.

a. We use _______________ to ask for reasons, causes, or purposes.

b. We use _______________ to explain reasons, causes, or purposes.

Prepositions of time: in, on

5. Read the following sentences. Pay attention to the prepositions of time **in** and **on**. Then write examples to complete the chart.

Closing a gap of 46 years, the state of Bahia resumed in 2014 its Biennale of visual arts as a continuity of the 1966 and 1968 editions.

Extracted from: <www.biennialfoundation.org/biennials/bahia-biennale-brazil/>. Accessed on: May 21, 2016.

The 3rd Bahia Biennale (Bienal da Bahia) announces the opening of its second season, adding a new set of exhibitions, debates and public actions to the extensive program initiated on May 29, 2014.

Extracted from: <www.biennialfoundation.org/2014/07/the-3rd-bahia-biennale-bienal-da-bahia-announces-the-opening-of-its-second-season-adding-a-new-set-of-exhibitions-debates-and-public-actions-to-the-extensive-program-initiated-on-may-29-2014/>. Accessed on: May 21, 2016.

Alexia Riner *was one of several students selected to travel with Berklee's Interdisciplinary Arts Institute Ensemble to Salvador da Bahia, Brazil in July 2014. [...]*

On the first day in Brazil we arrived around 2:30 pm on Sunday (July 13th 2014) at the Salvador Airport. [...]

We all met up in the afternoon and decided to visit the Smetak museum. [...]

Extracted from: <www.berklee-blogs.com/2014/09/my-trip-to-brazil-performing-at-the-3rd-biennale-of-bahia/>. Accessed on: May 21, 2016.

IN	ON
Period of the day: *in the afternoon*	**Day of the week:** _______________
Month: _______________	**Date:** _______________
Year: _______________	

Simple present (affirmative form)

6. Read about the Spanish celebration *La Tomatina* and circle the correct alternatives to complete the rules of the simple present.

La Tomatina, Buñol, Spain

Held on the last Wednesday of August, the celebration **attracts** many locals as well as tourists, who **throw** tomatoes just for fun! The city **becomes** entirely covered with tomato paste.

JOSÉ FUSTE RAGA/AGE FOTOSTOCK/KEYSTONE BRASIL

Extracted from: <www.placestoseeinyourlifetime.com/top-10-celebrations-around-the-world-1937>. Accessed on: May 21, 2016.

a. The verbs **attracts**, **throw**, and **becomes** are in the **negative/affirmative** form of the simple present. We often use the simple present to talk about **actions in progress/permanent situations**, habits, hobbies, routines, and repeated actions.

b. The verb **attracts** refers to **the celebration** and the verb **becomes** refers to **the city**. Both verbs get an **-s** at the end because they refer to the third person **singular/plural**.

c. The verb **throw** refers to "many locals as well as tourists". The verb does not get an **-s** at the end because it refers to the third person **singular/plural**.

7. Complete the text about Carnival in Venice with the simple present of the verbs in parentheses.

The Carnival of Venice, Italy

The colorful fest ________________ (take) place just the day before Ash Wednesday. Its roots ________________ (go back) to 1162. Venetian masks ________________ (define) the carnival, which also attracts many theaters troupes to participate in it.

THINKSTOCK/GETTY IMAGES

Extracted from: <www.placestoseeinyourlifetime.com/top-10-celebrations-around-the-world-1937>. Accessed on: May 21, 2016.

HANDS ON!

Tell your partner about your routine as he/she takes notes. Change roles. Then report your notes to the class. You can use:

My friend... wakes up early, has breakfast with his/her family, and goes to school. In the afternoon, he/she comes back home and does his/her homework. In the evening, he/she watches TV and goes to bed.

WH-questions

We use **wh-questions** to ask for specific information. The wh-words (**who**, **what**, **where**, **how**, **when**, **why**) come before the verb **to be** or the auxiliary verb.

Who is that boy?
What are you doing?
Where is the book?
How are you?
How much is this blue shirt?
When is the party?
Why are you crying?

Why/Because...

We use **why** to ask questions and **because** in answers.

Why are you crying?
Because the story is so sad!

GPOINTSTUDIO/SHUTTERSTOCK

Prepositions of time: in/on

We use **in** for	• period of the day; • month; • year.	I go to school **in the morning**. My birthday is **in February**. World War II started **in 1939**.
We use **on** for	• day of the week; • date.	We have English class **on Tuesdays**. The celebration is **on September 14**.

Simple present (affirmative form)

We use the simple present to talk about permanent situations, like hobbies, habits, routines and repeated actions.

Subject (**I, you, we, you, they**) + verb + complement	I **swim** at the club every Saturday. You **need** to study hard. We **play** video games together. They frequently **travel** to Rio.
Subject (**he, she, it**) + verb + complement	She **travels** every weekend. He **needs** a new computer. It **tells** the story of a famous rock band.

Besides adding the **-s**, for some verbs you need to add or remove other letters in the third person.

If the verb ends in **-s**, **-x**, **-ch**, **-sh** or **-o**, we add **-es**.	Marcia **goes** to school everyday. Junior **watches** too much TV.
If the verb ends in a **consonant** + **y**, remove **-y** and add **-ies**.	Cynthia **studies** hard. The dog **carries** his own bag.

1. Complete the questions with appropriate question words.

a. ____________ old are you?
I'm 12.

b. ____________ is the celebration?
At a restaurant.

c. ____________ are you reading?
A comic book.

d. ____________ is his birthday?
On January 19.

e. ____________ aren't they here?
I don't know.

f. ____________ much is this?
It's 14 dollars.

2. What is the boy asking his dad? What does the dad answer? Use **why** and **because** to write their dialogue in the speech bubbles. Be creative!

LISA PINES/GETTY IMAGES

3. Use the verbs from the box to complete the paragraph below. You will use one of the verbs more than once.

do	drink	finish	get up	go	have	leave	love	prefer	take

My brother and I ____________ to school in the morning so we ____________ very early. I like to eat a big breakfast, with yogurt, toast, cheese and fruits, but my brother ____________ to eat later so he just ____________ a glass of milk before school. We ____________ the bus and arrive at school at about 7 o'clock. I ____________ school at 12:10 pm and go home for lunch. My brother is in high school and his classes ____________ at 1:50 pm, so he ____________ lunch at school. He ____________ the food at school.

In the afternoon we both ____________ our homework. On Mondays and Wednesdays we ____________ English classes and my brother ____________ soccer practice afterwards.

LISTENING COMPREHENSION

BEFORE LISTENING

1. Look at the graph about New Year's Day and write **T** (true) or **F** (false).

www.vox.com/2015/1/1/7475805/new-year-calendar-2014

**Not everyone celebrates the New Year on January 1.
Here's when other cultures do it.**

Updated by *Susannah Locke* on January 1, 2014, 12:30 p.m. ET

January 1 is far from the only New Year's Day. Many cultures have other New Year's spread throughout the seasons:

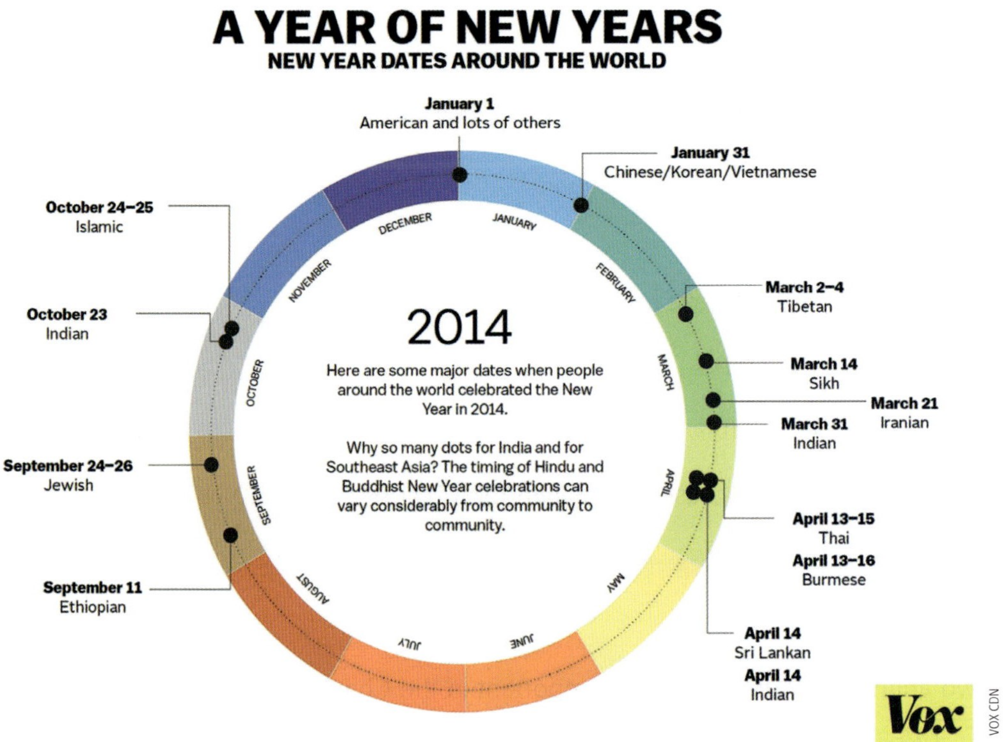

[...]

Extracted from: <www.vox.com/2015/1/1/7475805/new-year-calendar-2014>. Accessed on: May 21, 2016.

a. ☐ According to the graph, there isn't any New Year celebration in months such as May, June, July, and August.

b. ☐ China is the only country that celebrates the New Year at the end of January.

c. ☐ In Thailand, the New Year celebration lasts three days.

d. ☐ In India, the New Year is celebrated only on March 31.

e. ☐ The Tibetan New Year is celebrated at the beginning of March.

LISTENING

2. Listen about the Chinese New Year celebration. Number the facts in the sequence they are mentioned.

14

- [ ] Lunar New Year or Spring Festival are other names for the Chinese New Year.
- [ ] The Chinese New Year celebration lasts 15 days.
- [1] Every winter, more than 1 billion Chinese citizens celebrate the Chinese New Year.
- [ ] The Chinese New Year is the country's most important social and economic holiday.

3. In pairs, check the correct alternatives to complete the sentences. Then listen again and check your answers.

15

a. The Chinese New Year is celebrated

- [ ] only in China.
- [ ] all over the world.

b. The biggest celebration of the Chinese New Year outside of China is in

- [ ] all of North America.
- [ ] the United States.

c. In 1840s and 50s Chinese immigrant workers went to

- [ ] Northern California.
- [ ] Southern California.

d. The number of animals associated with the Chinese zodiac is

- [ ] twelve.
- [ ] two.

e. Two animals that are particularly important in the Chinese New Year celebration are

- [ ] the dog and the tiger.
- [ ] the dragon and the rabbit.

AFTER LISTENING

4. Write about how you and your family celebrate New Year's Day. Are there any special traditions? Report to the class.

____

____

____

____

SPEAKING

1. Look at the pictures below and ask a classmate if he/she knows or has been to any of these festivities.

Festa da Uva in Caxias do Sul.

Festa de Parintins in Amazonas.

As Cavalhadas de Pirenópolis in Goiás.

Congada in Minas Gerais.

2. In small groups, research festivities in Brazil and around the world. In your notebook, make notes of your findings.

3. Select some of the questions you would like to ask another group. Then add two questions of your own.

- [ ] Where is it celebrated?
- [ ] When is it celebrated?
- [ ] What is the origin of this festivity?
- [ ] Is it a religious festivity?
- [ ] Are there special foods connected with the celebration?
- [ ] What are some of the things that are done during this festivity?
- [ ] ____?
- [ ] ____?

4. Now join another group from your class to talk about festivities. Which one was your favorite? Why?

Reflecting on the theme

Brazil has a vast cultural diversity. Why is that so? How is it reflected in the festivities around the country?

WRITING

BEFORE WRITING

1. Look at the text on page 72 again and compare it to the text below. What do they have in common?

____

2. Read the online travel guide tips about a Japanese tradition and answer the questions.

www.lonelyplanet.com/japan/kansai/yoshino/travel-tips-and-articles/76349#ixzz3atJHLb5L

Hanami: a guide to cherry blossom viewing in Japan

Location: throughout Japan, but especially good at Yoshino.

Dates: cherry blossoms can begin to appear in Okinawa as early as January and not until May in Hokkaido, but through the bulk of the country they're usually in flower near the end of March.

BUDDHIKA WEERASINGHE/GETTY IMAGES/AFP

[...] Hanami tradition is to have a picnic party amid the blooming trees, and parties begin with the arrival of the earliest buds and endure to the last clinging blossoms. [...] You can enjoy Hanami anywhere there's a cherry tree in blossom, but a few places have become favourites over the centuries.

[...] Japan's top cherry-blossom destination, however, is the mountain-top Kansai town of Yoshino, where the blossoms of thousands of cherry trees form a floral carpet gradually ascending the mountainsides. [...]

Extracted from: <www.lonelyplanet.com/japan/kansai/yoshino/travel-tips-and-articles/76349#ixzz3atJHLb5L>. Accessed on: May 21, 2016.

a. What is Hanami? ____

b. When does it happen? ____

3. Choose the alternatives that show characteristics of a travel guide, like the ones you saw above and on page 72.

a. ☐ They bring the date of events.

b. ☐ They bring the name of people who participate in the events.

c. ☐ They bring information about the location of the event.

d. ☐ They bring information about how people celebrate the events and what they eat.

e. ☐ They show interviews with people at the event.

WRITING

4. You're going to write a tip about a traditional party to be published in a travel guide made by your class.
    - Choose a traditional festival or party in your country or in another place in the world.
    - Prefer festivals or parties that are not famous so that everybody gains further knowledge.
    - Research websites, books, and magazines.
    - You can also ask people from other countries who know different festivals or parties.
    - Organize the information about the festival or party: where and when it happens, how do people celebrate it, typical clothes, food, dances, or music.
    - Write your text and introduce each item of the festival or party as a subtitle.
    - Choose images to illustrate your text.
    - Write a draft of your tip about a festival or party on your notebook.
    - Consult a dictionary if necessary.
    - Show the draft to your teacher.

AFTER WRITING

- Exchange your text with a classmate and check if:
    - the tip about the festival or party is attractive to the reader;
    - the tip offers all the necessary information about the festival or party;
    - the image is eye-catching.
- Put together a guide with the tips from all students. The guide should be available in an accessible place so all interested readers can consult it.

SELF-EVALUATION

Check the true sentences about your learning in Unit 4.
In this unit you have learned to:

- ☐ talk about festivities in Brazil and other countries;
- ☐ identify characteristics of a travel guide;
- ☐ read and write a travel guide page.

Reflecting...

- **What did I learn about traditional festivals and parties?**
- **What did I learn about reading and writing tips for traditional festivals and parties?**
- **What questions do I still have about prepositions of time?**

UNIT

5

Let's have fun!

THINKSTOCK/GETTY IMAGES

CLAUDIO CAPUCHO/FOTOARENA

According to the Article 71 of the Child and Adolescent Statute (*Estatuto da Criança e do Adolescente*), "the child and the adolescent have the right to information, culture, entertainment, leisure and products that respect their developmental stage."

Translated from: <www.planalto.gov.br/ccivil_03/Leis/l8069.htm>. Accessed on: May 21, 2016.

According to the Article 27 of the Universal Declaration of Human Rights, "everyone has the right freely to participate in the cultural life of the community, to enjoy the arts and to share in scientific advancement and its benefits."

Extracted from: <www.un.org/en/universal-declaration-human-rights/>. Accessed on: May 21, 2016.

Your learning objectives for this unit are...

- to read, comprehend and identify characteristics of movie synopsis;
- to recognize different movie genres and leisure activities;
- to discuss and reflect about the importance of museums, movies, shows, etc. for education;
- to discuss the benefits of leisure activities;
- to write a movie synopsis and set up a movie catalog.

POPOVA VALERIYA/SHUTTERSTOCK

OPÇÃO BRASIL

EXCHANGING IDEAS

1. Why do you think that the right to culture and entertainment are claimed in these documents?
2. Look at the images on these two pages. What leisure activities do they represent?
3. Do you have easy access to leisure activities? If so, exemplify. If not, what needs to be done in order to change this situation?

5 Let's have fun!

READING COMPREHENSION

TEXT 1

- **www.rottentomatoes.com**
Website with information and reviews of movies.

BEFORE READING

1. Which activities are leisure activities, in your opinion?
2. Do you watch movies during your free time? If so, what are your favorite genres?
3. In your opinion, what makes a movie stand out and be critically acclaimed?

READING

4. Scan the synopsis and answer: Who is the main character?

While you are reading a text or a book, practice the strategy of **active reading**: highlight or underline words, expressions and important ideas.

www.rottentomatoes.com/m/paddington_2014/

Rotten Tomatoes

PADDINGTON (2015)

MOVIE INFO

TOMATOMETER
98%
Average Rating: 7.9/10
Reviews Counted: 125
Fresh: 122
Rotten: 3

From the beloved novels by Michael Bond and producer David Heyman (HARRY POTTER), PADDINGTON tells the story of the comic misadventures of a young Peruvian bear (voiced by Firth) who travels to the city in search of a home. Finding himself lost and alone, he begins to realize that city life is not all he had imagined – until he meets the kindly Brown family who read the label around his neck that says "Please look after this bear. Thank you," and offer him a temporary haven. It looks as though his luck has changed until this rarest of bears catches the eye of a museum taxidermist. [...]

STUDIOCANAL

Rating: PG (for mild action and rude humor)
Genre: Comedy, Kids & Family
Directed By: Paul King
Written By: Paul King
In Theaters: Jan 16, 2015 Wide
US Box Office: $19.3M
Runtime: 1 hr. 35 min.
[...]

Extracted from: <www.rottentomatoes.com/m/paddington_2014>. Accessed on: May 21, 2016.

novels: romances
look after: cuide
catches the eye: chama a atenção
taxidermist: taxidermista (especialista na arte de empalhar animais)

PG stands for **Parental Guidance**. When a movie is rated PG in the United States, it means that some material in the movie may not be suitable for young children.

5. Read the movie review and check the phrase that best summarizes the story.

a. ☐ The adventures of a nice family that lives in a big city.

b. ☐ The adventures of a bear that tries to find a home in the city.

c. ☐ The adventures of a bear that is captured by a museum taxidermist.

d. ☐ The adventures of a rare Peruvian bear in the jungle.

e. ☐ The adventures of a bear who travels to Peru.

6. Underline the wrong information in the sentences below. Then rewrite these sentences with the correct information.

a. The bear is American.

____

b. A museum taxidermist offers to help the bear.

____

c. The movie lasts 2 hours.

____

d. The critics' consensus about the movie is negative.

____

e. David Heyman is the movie director.

____

f. The novels by Michael Bond are based on the movie.

____

7. Check the true statements. If necessary, read the synopsis once again.

a. ☐ The text presents basic facts about the story of the movie.

b. ☐ There are many technical movie-making words in the movie review.

c. ☐ The text doesn't reveal the end of the story.

d. ☐ The *Tomatometer* represents the percentage of favorable reviews that the movie receives.

e. ☐ Ratings show the appropriate audience for a movie.

AFTER READING

- In your opinion, what are the benefits of free time?
- Does the city or community where you live provide free leisure activities?
- Which free leisure activity would you like to have available for people in your community? Why?

TEXT 2

BEFORE READING

1. Read the title of the text and look at the images. What do you think the text refers to?

- **www.malba.org.ar/en/**
  Museo de Arte Latinoamericano de Buenos Aires (MALBA) official website.
- **www.eravirtual.org/**
  Website that offers virtual tours of Brazilian museums, exhibits and cultural heritage sites.

READING

2. Read the text and check if your predictions in activity 1 are correct.

theonearmedcrab.com/malba

MALBA

Excellent collection of modern art from Latin America

One of the newer museums in Buenos Aires is the MALBA (Museo de Arte Latinoamericano de Buenos Aires), established in 2001. The museum has a really nice collection of modern Latin American art works, a category that is often underrepresented in museums across the world. A variety of paintings and sculptures from the 20th Century show that quite a few South Americans could compete quite well with their more famous colleagues in Europe. Mexicans Diego Rivera and Frida Kahlo and Cuban Wilfredo Lam are perhaps the best known artists represented in the MALBA, but the works of a host of in Europe lesser-known Argentinean, Brazilian and Uruguayan artists are also well worth a visit to this museum.

A small sample of the collection, in pictures – nothing compared to the real thing, of course.

MALBA, BUENOS AIRES, ARGENTINA

RIVERA, Diego. *Portrait of Ramón Gómez de la Serna*. 1915. Oil on canvas. 110.5 cm × 90.5 cm.

MALBA, BUENOS AIRES, ARGENTINA

PETTORUTI, Emilio. *The Song of the People*. 1927. Oil on wood. 73.8 cm × 64.7 cm.

Extracted from: <theonearmedcrab.com/malba>. Accessed on: May 21, 2016.

underrepresented: pouco representada

3. Match the questions to their corresponding answers.

a. What does MALBA mean?

b. What kind of collection is there at MALBA?

c. Who are Diego Rivera, Frida Kahlo and Wilfredo Lam?

d. Where is MALBA?

e. When was MALBA established?

☐ They are well-known Latin American artists.

☐ Latin American artworks.

☐ Museo de Arte Latinoamericano de Buenos Aires.

☐ It was established in 2001.

☐ It is in Argentina.

4. Find in the text the extracts that prove the statements below. Write the extracts here.

a. The Latin American art is not usually well-represented around the world.

____

____

b. Art produced in Latin America by less-known artists have similar quality to the ones produced by Europeans.

____

____

5. Check the best alternative to complete the statement.

The author's point of view about MALBA and Latin American art is

a. ☐ negative.

b. ☐ positive.

c. ☐ neutral.

d. ☐ not mentioned.

• ***Night at the Museum***

Direction: Shawn Levy. USA: 20th Century Fox, 2006. 105 min.

A recently hired night security guard working at the American Museum of Natural History in New York City discovers that an ancient curse causes the animals and exhibits on display to come to life at night. The movie was followed by *Night at the Museum*: Battle of the Smithsonian (2009) and *Night at the Museum*: Secret of the Tomb (2014).

AFTER READING

- What is a museum? What kind of museums are there? Why are people attracted to them?
- Have you ever been to a museum? If so, which one(s)? If not, which one would you like to visit?
- Some museum websites offer virtual tours online. Have you ever done a virtual tour on a museum? If so, which one?

FOCUS ON VOCABULARY

1. Go back to the texts on pages 88 and 90. Find the words listed below and read the sentences they are in again. Then choose the best definition for each of them.

a. novel

☐ a kind of thin book with a paper cover that is published regularly

☐ a long written story about imaginary or partly imaginary characters and events

b. producer

☐ someone that writes books, stories, articles, etc.

☐ someone that controls how a movie, a program, a musical, or a play is made

c. collection

☐ a group of objects put together as a hobby in order to exhibit or study them

☐ a picture made using paint

Leisure activities

2. Match the pictures to the sentences.

THINKSTOCK/GETTY IMAGES

hang out

THINKSTOCK/GETTY IMAGES

listen to music

- ***Lights, Camera, Action! On Location***

  Kerry Powell. São Paulo: Macmillan ELT, 2013.

  Students find out how movies are made and make their own movie.

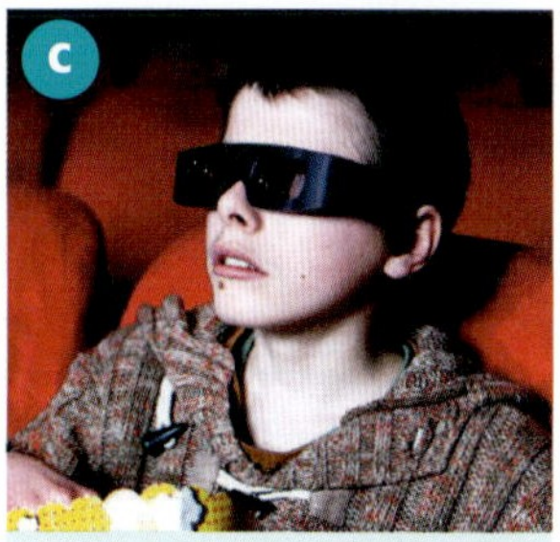

THINKSTOCK/GETTY IMAGES

watch movies

THINKSTOCK/GETTY IMAGES

read books

BLEND / DIOMEDIA

practice sports

☐ Andy wants to be a filmmaker. He watches movies all the time.

☐ Johnny reads books at the library during his break. He likes mystery books.

☐ Carina and her friends usually hang out after school.

☐ Jayden and his brother practice sports every day. They prefer to play basketball and soccer.

☐ Melissa listens to music every day during her free time. She likes romantic songs.

Movie genres

3. Label the pictures with the words from the box. Then read the movie characteristics and write the corresponding movie genre. Use a dictionary if necessary.

comedy	documentary	horror	musical	romantic comedy	~~science fiction (sci-fi)~~

A

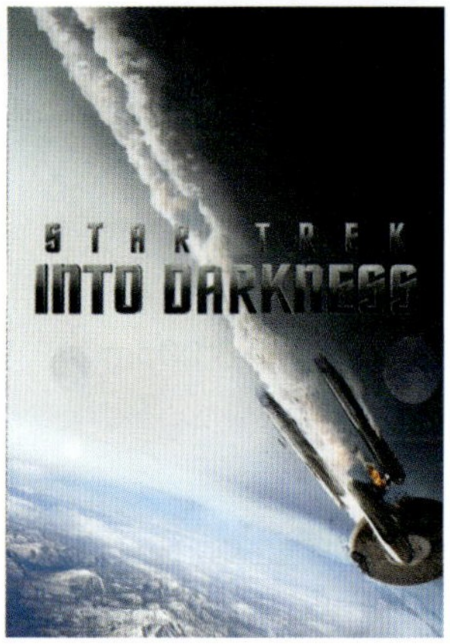

PARAMOUNT PICTURES

science fiction (sci-fi)

B

ARTHOUSE FILMS

____

C

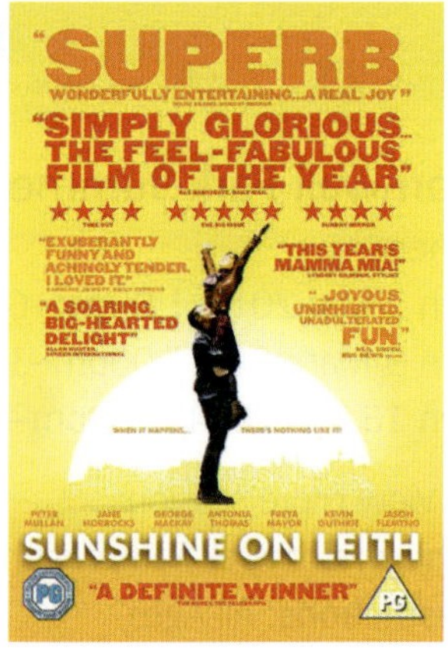

EIV STUDIO

____

D

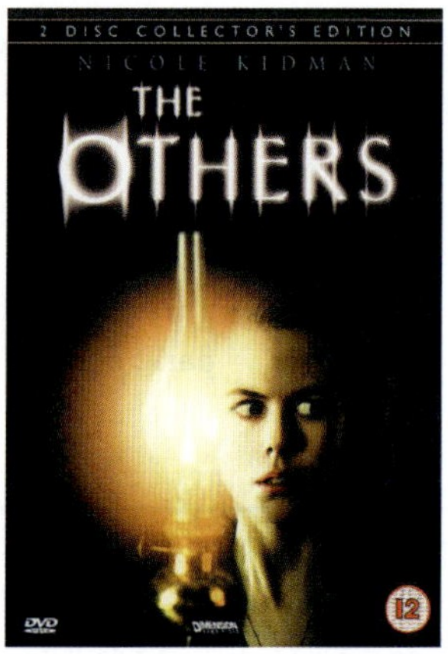

DIMENSION FILMS

____

E

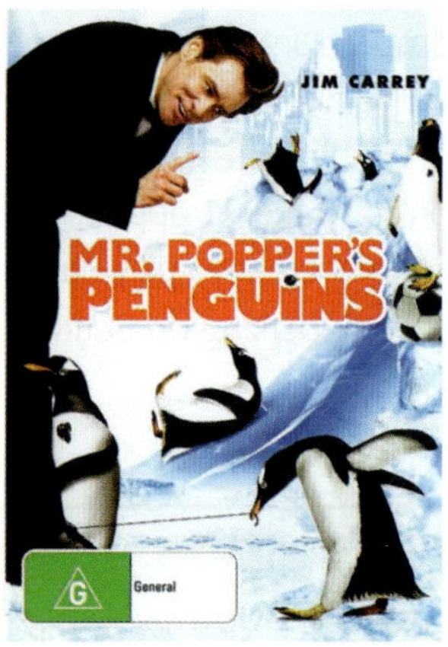

20TH CENTURY FOX FILM CORP

____

F

UNIVERSAL STUDIO

____

Movie characteristics	Movie genres
a. This is about space and aliens.	
b. The movie brings situations that make you laugh.	
c. This movie shows romantic and funny scenes.	
d. It's a movie that tries to document reality.	
e. This kind of movie shows scary scenes.	
f. There is a lot of singing and dancing in this kind of movie.	

IT'S YOUR TURN!

In pairs, play a mime game. Student A chooses a movie genre and mimes it to student B. Student B has to guess the movie genre. Take turns.

Remember that the dictionary is a valuable learning tool. Besides learning the meaning of a word and examples of its use in context, you can also use a dictionary to check spelling, pronunciation and find synonyms to improve your vocabulary.

Simple present (negative and interrogative forms)

1. Read the schedule for Cornwall Park Summer Music Concerts and check the correct answers.

www.eventfinder.co.nz/2014/cornwall-park-summer-music-concert-series/auckland/epsom

Cornwall Park Summer Music Concerts

When:

Sun 2 Mar 2014, 1:00pm–6:00pm
Sun 9 Mar 2014, 1:00pm–3:00pm
Sun 16 Mar 2014, 1:00pm–3:00pm
Sun 23 Mar 2014, 1:00pm–3:00pm
Sun 30 Mar 2014, 1:00pm–3:00pm

➤ View more sessions

Where: Cornwall Park, Greenlane Rd, Auckland
Restrictions: All Ages
Ticket Information: Admission: Free
Website: www.cornwallpark.co.nz
Listed by: Cornwall Park

Cornwall Park's summer music concerts are back.
Join us from 1-3pm every Sunday from January 19th to March 30th for free music at the Band Rotunda. Also featuring two early evening concerts 4-6pm on the 2nd February and the 2nd March.
[...]
For rain-affected concerts, a decision is made at approximately 11am on the day; please contact the Cornwall Park Information Centre for the alternative play date.
Parking in the Park? Consider carpooling or parking on Puriri Drive.

parking: estacionar
park: parque

Extracted from: <www.eventfinder.co.nz/2014/cornwall-park-summer-music-concert-series/auckland/epsom>. Accessed on: May 21, 2016.

Carpooling is a kind of group ride. It is when a group of car owners agree to travel together to work, school, etc., so that only one car is used each time.

a. Does the Sunday 2nd concert end at 6:00pm?

☐ Yes, it does.

☐ No, it doesn't. It ends at 3:00pm.

b. Do viewers need to download a special app to see the times and dates of the concerts?

☐ Yes, they do.

☐ No, they don't. They just have to click on the **View more sessions**.

2. Based on activity 1, complete the rules of the negative and interrogative forms of the simple present.

a. In the interrogative form, we use ____________ with the third person singular (it/Sunday) and ____________ with the third person plural (they/the viewers). After **do** and **does**, we use the subject and then the main verb.

b. In the negative form, we use the subject, **does not**, or **do not**, and the main verb. The contracted forms are ____________ and ____________.

c. We do not use the main ____________ in short answers.

Likes and dislikes

3. Kyle, Katia, Dominic, and Marcus are expressing their opinions about some movie genres. Read the sentences and write **P** (positive) or **N** (negative) for each opinion.

a. ☐ **Kyle:** I **like** horror movies because they're scary and funny at the same time.

b. ☐ **Katia:** I **love** action and adventure movies. The stories are full of action. It's exciting to watch them.

c. ☐ **Dominic:** I **don't like** science fiction. The idea of future science and technology is boring.

d. ☐ **Marcus:** I **hate** war movies because they show too much suffering.

4. Use the verb forms from the box to complete the sentences.

do	doesn't like	don't like	love	prefers

a. My mom ________________ movies with sad endings. She ________________ comedies.

b. My sister and I ________________ art exhibitions. We love to see the sculptures.

c. **A:** Why ________________ you hate concerts at the park?

B: Oh, I don't hate them. I just ________________ them because there aren't comfortable seatings.

Would you like to...? / Which...? / How much...?

5. Gary and his friend Jay are planning to go to the movies. Order the sentences and form a meaningful dialogue.

☐ **Gary: I'd like to** watch *Paddington*, the animated movie about a young Peruvian bear that goes to London.

1 **Gary:** Hi, Jay! **Would you like to** go to the movies tonight?

☐ **Gary:** Say, in front of the Cineworld Cinema around 11:30? We can buy the tickets and hang out. The first exhibition starts at 12:00.

☐ **Jay:** Right. See you there!

☐ **Jay:** Oh, that seems to be a good movie. I like animated movies. Where do we meet?

☐ **Gary:** It's £8.60.

☐ **Gary:** See you there, Jay!

☐ **Jay:** Sure. **Which** movie **would you like to** watch?

☐ **Jay:** All right. And **how much** is the ticket?

6. Go back to the dialogue on page 95 and pay attention to the words and expressions in bold. Read the sentences they are in to guess what they mean. Then circle the correct answers to complete the following sentences.

a. When we want to ask a question that requires a choice between a limited number of items, we use **which/how much**.

b. We use **how many/how much** to ask about prices.

c. **I don't like to/Would you like to** + the base form of the verb is a polite way of making an invitation or offering something.

d. **I'd like to (= I would like to)/I don't like to (= I do not like to)** is a polite way to say we want to do something.

7. Match questions and answers.

ANTON GVOZDIKOV/SHUTTERSTOCK

a. What kind of music do you like?
b. Which book genre do you prefer, adventure or sci-fi?
c. How much are the movie apps?
d. Would you like to meet me at the park?
e. How much is the movie ticket for adults on the weekends?
f. How much is the student discount?
g. Would you like to go to the museum?

☐ Actually I like both of them.
☐ Good idea. Let's have a picnic.
☐ They're free. They don't cost a thing. Just download the apps and you can use then.
☐ It's £12.00.
☐ I like pop music a lot.
☐ Sure! I really want to see the new exhibit.
☐ It is a fifty percent discount.

HANDS ON!

In pairs, take turns making invitations. Use the expression *Would you like to + verb*. Then report to the class the invitations that are accepted. Here are some suggestions of answers you can use.

Accepting	Declining
Thanks, I'd love to.	I'm sorry, I can't.
Sure!	That's very kind of you, but...
Great idea!	I'd like to, but...
That would be very nice.	I don't think I can.

Simple present (negative and interrogative)

Negative	
Subject (**I, you, we, you, they**) + **do** + **not** + **verb** + complement	I **do not/don't play** soccer. You **do not/don't speak** Spanish. We **do not/don't know** the answer. They **do not/don't live** here.
Subject (**he, she, it**) + **does** + **not** + **verb** + complement	He **does not/doesn't play** soccer. She **does not/doesn't like** hot dogs. It **does not/doesn't work**.

Interrogative	
Do + subject (**I, you, we, you, they**) + **verb** + complement	**Do** I **wait** here? **Do** you **speak** Spanish? **Do** we **know** the answer? **Do** they **live** here?
Does + subject (**he, she, it**) + **verb** + complement	**Does** he **play** soccer? **Does** she **like** hot dogs? **Does** it **work**?

What…?/Which...?

We use **what** in a question when there is an unknown number of answers or many possible answers.	**What** is your favorite color? (There are many colors.)
We use **which** in a question if there is a limited number of possible answers.	I don't have a red pen. I have a blue and a black pen. **Which** one do you prefer? (Now there are only two options.)

How much...?

We use **how much** in a question to know about prices. It is used with singular and plural nouns.

How much is this book?

How much are those sandals?

Would… like to...?

We use subject + **would like to** + **the base form of the verb** in affirmative sentences. It is a polite way to say that we want to do something.	I **would like to see** your vacation photos. He **would like to come** to your party.
We use **Would** + subject + **like to** + **the base form of the verb** in questions. It is a polite way to make an invitation or offer something.	**Would** you **like to see** my vacation photos? **Would** he **like to come** to my party?

1. Rewrite these sentences according to the instructions in parentheses.

MAISANT LUDOVIC / HEMIS.FR/ALAMY STOCK PHOTO/FOTOARENA

GABRIEL ROSSI/STF/GETTY IMAGES

TASS/ITAR-TASS PHOTO/CORBIS/FOTOARENA

VECTORLIFESTYLEPIC/SHUTTERSTOCK

20THCENTFOX/COURTESY EVERETT COLLECTION/FOTOARENA

DANIEL M ERNST/SHUTTERSTOCK

a. The museum has a nice collection of modern Latin American art works. (interrogative)

____

b. Does MALBA mean "Museo de Arte Latinoamericano de Buenos Aires"? (affirmative)

____

c. My brother wants to be a filmmaker. (negative)

____

d. Carina doesn't read books at the library during her break. (affirmative)

____

e. His movies show romantic and funny scenes. (interrogative)

____

f. Do viewers need to download a special app to see the times and dates of the concerts? (affirmative)

____

2. Complete the questions in these dialogues appropriately.

a. **A:** ______________ the tickets on Wednesdays?
B: On Wednesdays the tickets are 50% cheaper.

b. **A:** ______________ students ______________ there in your class?
B: 23.

c. **A:** There are two movies starting now: *Alvin and the Chipmunks* and *Star Wars*. ______________ one do you prefer?
B: *Star Wars*, of course!

d. **A:** ______________ buy some popcorn before the movie starts?
B: No, thanks. I'm not hungry.

LISTENING COMPREHENSION

BEFORE LISTENING

1. Read the movie review of *Back to the Future* and check the correct alternatives.

www.metacritic.com/movie/back-to-the-future

Back to the Future

Universal Pictures | Release Date: Jul. 3, 1985

Your Score 0

UNIVERSAL PICTURES

86 **Metascore**
Universal acclaim
based on 12 critics
What's this?

9.0 **User Score**
Universal acclaim
based on 242 ratings

Starring: Christopher Lloyd, Michael J. Fox

Summary: Marty McFly goes back in time, in a DeLorean invented by his friend, Dr. Emmett Brown, and must make sure his high-school-age parents get together, so he doesn't cease to exist.

See the trailer

Director: Robert Zemeckis
Genre(s): Adventure, Sci-Fi, Comedy
Rating: PG
Runtime: 116 min
More details and credits »

Critic Reviews

Positive: 11
Mixed: 1
Negative: 0

[...]

40 **Los Angeles Times**
Sheila Benson
Feb 7, 2013

It's big, cartoonish and empty, with an interesting premise that is underdeveloped and overproduced. [3 July 1985, p. Calendar 6]

[...]

Extracted from: <www.metacritic.com/movie/back-to-the-future>. Accessed on: May 21, 2016.

a. In the movie, Marty McFly goes back in time to:

- [ ] get his parents together.
- [ ] get his friend Dr. Emmett Brown.

b. The director of the movie is:

- [ ] Christopher Lloyd.
- [ ] Robert Zemeckis.

c. The critics' reviews are predominantly:

- [ ] positive.
- [ ] mixed.

premise: ideia
underdeveloped: subdesenvolvida
overproduced: superproduzida

LISTENING

16 **2.** Listen to an extract of the movie *Back to the Future* and underline the correct options.

Back to the Future

> **doc:** doctor
> **gonna:** going to
> **wanna:** want to

Marty: Doc?

Doc: Don't say a word.

Marty: Doc.

Doc: I don't wanna **know/get** your name. I don't wanna know anything about you.

Marty: Listen, Doc.

Doc: Quiet!

Marty: Doc, Doc, it's me, Marty.

Doc: Don't tell me anything.

Marty: Doc, you gotta help...

Doc: Quiet. Quiet. I'm gonna read your thoughts. Let's **go/see** now, you've come here from a great distance?

Marty: Yeah, exactly.

Doc: Uh, don't tell me. Uh, you **would/want** me to buy a subscription to the *Saturday Evening Post*?

Marty: No.

Doc: Not a word, not a word, not a word now. Quiet, uh, donations. You want me to **give/make** a donation to the Coast Guard Youth Auxiliary.

Marty: Doc, I'm from the **past/future**. I came here in a time machine that you invented. Now, I need your help to get back to the year 1985.

Doc: My God!

Transcripted from: <www.youtube.com/watch?v=SR5BfQ4rEqQ>. Accessed on: May 21, 2016.

3. Listen to the dialogue between Marty and Doc Brown again. Write **T** (true) or **F** (false).

17 a. ☐ Marty asks the doctor to help him.

b. ☐ Marty comes from the past.

c. ☐ Doc Brown invented a time machine.

d. ☐ The doctor gives Marty an aspirin.

4. The tone of voice of the characters can reveal feelings and emotions. Check the correct alternatives to answer the questions.

a. How is Doc Brown feeling?

☐ He is calm. ☐ He is nervous.

b. How is Marty McFly feeling?

☐ He is anxious. ☐ He is happy.

AFTER LISTENING

5. How do you choose a movie you want to watch? Check what you take into consideration to choose it. Explain your choices to a classmate.

a. [ ] the actors and actresses

b. [ ] the story

c. [ ] my friends' opinions

d. [ ] the genre of the movie

e. [ ] the movie reviews available on the internet or in newspapers

f. [ ] others: ______________________

SPEAKING

1. Answer the questions below about your favorite movie. The answers will be used in the conversation task in activity 2.

What's the title of the movie? ______________________

What genre of movie is it? ______________________

Which actors and actresses are in this movie? ______________________

What happens in the movie? ______________________

Where and when does the story take place? ______________________

What do you like most about the movie? ______________________

2. In pairs, ask a classmate about his/her favorite movie and guess what movie it is. You can ask some of the questions below.

- Is it an old movie?
- Is it a franchise?
- Is it a foreign movie?
- What kind of movie is it?
- Why do you like it so much?
- Who acts in the movie?
- Who is your favorite character? Why?
- Where/When does the story take place?

3. Report to the class the information you got from your classmate.

Reflecting on the theme

Besides entertainment, what other benefits do good movies offer?

WRITING

BEFORE WRITING

1. Read the synopsis about *Into the Woods* and answer the questions.

www.rottentomatoes.com/m/into_the_woods_2014

Into the Woods (2014)

WALT DISNEY STUDIOS MOTION PICTURES

TOMATOMETER

71%

Average Rating: 6,6/10
Reviews Counted: 186
Fresh: 132
Rotten: 54

All Critics | Top Critics

Critics Consensus: On the whole, this Disney adaptation of the Sondheim classic sits comfortably at the corner of Hollywood and Broadway even if it darkens to its detriment in the final act.

AUDIENCE SCORE

52%
liked it

Average Rating: 3.2/5
User Ratings: 88,634

WWW.ROTTENTOMATOES.COM

MOVIE INFO

"Into the Woods" is a modern twist on several of the beloved Brothers Grimm fairy tales, intertwining the plots of a few choice stories and exploring the consequences of the characters' wishes and quests. This humorous and heartfelt musical follows the classic tales of Cinderella (Anna Kendrick), Little Red Riding Hood (Lilla Crawford), Jack and the Beanstalk (Daniel Huttlestone), and Rapunzel (MacKenzie Mauzy) – all tied together by an original story involving a baker and his wife (James Corden & Emily Blunt), their wish to begin a family and their interaction with the witch (Meryl Streep) who has put a curse on them. (C) Disney

Rating: PG (for thematic elements, fantasy action and peril, and some suggestive material)
Genre: Musical & Performing Arts, Kids & Family
Directed By: Rob Marshall
Written By: James Lapine

In Theaters: Dec. 25, 2014 Wide
US Box Office: $114.3M
Runtime: 2 hr. 5 min.
Walt Disney Pictures

Extracted from: <www.rottentomatoes.com/m/into_the_woods_2014>. Accessed on: May 21, 2016.

woods: floresta
intertwining: intercalando
quests: aventuras
tied together: unidos
put a curse on: amaldiçoou

a. What ties together Meryl Streep's character, the baker, and his wife?

____

b. Based on the Tomatometer, what is the audience score?

____

2. Go back to page 88 and read *Paddington* synopsis again. Compare it to the *Into the Woods* synopsis. Then check the true statements.

a. ☐ A synopsis describes what the movie is about, so it helps people decide to watch it or not.

b. ☐ Synopses don't present the writer's opinion.

c. ☐ Synopses usually present the title of the movie, its genre, and the name of the actors and actresses.

WRITING

3. In pairs, follow the steps to create a synopsis of your favorite movie.
   - Do some research and find basic information (genre, runtime, director's name, etc.) about your favorite movie.
   - Write a draft of the movie synopsis.
   - If necessary, use a dictionary.
   - Show your draft to your teacher and ask him/her for suggestions on how to improve your text.
   - Adjust it accordingly and write it down on an A4 sheet of paper.

AFTER WRITING

- Collect all the synopses written by the class, organize them by movie genre and set up a movie catalog.
- Leave the movie catalog at the school library or in another accessible place so other students can read it. Promote the catalog in the school website, if possible.

SELF-EVALUATION

Check the true sentences about your learning in Unit 5.
In this unit you have learned to:

☐ read, comprehend and identify characteristics of a movie synopsis;

☐ recognize different movie genres and leisure activities;

☐ discuss and reflect about the importance of museums, movies, shows, etc. for education;

☐ discuss the benefits of leisure activities;

☐ write a movie synopsis and set up a movie catalog.

Reflecting...

- **What did I learn about the characteristics of a movie synopsis?**
- **What did I learn about leisure activities?**
- **What else would I like to know about the topics that I studied in this unit?**

Latin American artists: Fernando Botero

ROLF HAID/DPA/CORBIS/FOTOARENA

Name: Fernando Botero
Occupation: Painter, Sculptor
Birth date: April 19, 1932
Place of birth: Medellín, Colombia

Fernando Botero is a Colombian artist known for creating bloated, oversized depictions of people, animals and elements of the natural world. [...]

THE BRIDGEMAN ART LIBRARY/KEYSTONE

BOTERO, Fernando. *Los músicos*. 1986. Oil on canvas, 177 cm × 137 cm. Private collection.

BOTERO, FERNANDO. WOMAN WITH UMBRELLA, 1977.

BOTERO, Fernando. *Mujer con sombrilla*. 1977. Bronze with brown patina, 228.6 cm. Private collection.

Fernando Botero was born in Medellín, Colombia, on April 19, 1932. He attended a matador school for several years in his youth, and then left the bull ring behind to pursue an artistic career. Botero's paintings were first exhibited in 1948, when he was 16 years old, and he had his first one-man show two years later in Bogotá. [...]

Throughout the 1950s, Botero experimented with proportion and size, and he began developing his trademark style, the "Boterismo", depicting people and figures in large, exaggerated volume. The inflated proportions of his figures suggest an element of political satire, and are depicted using flat, bright color and prominently outlined forms—a nod to Latin American folk art. And while his work includes still-lifes and landscapes, Botero has typically concentrated on his emblematic situational portraiture. [...]

Extracted from: <www.biography.com/people/fernando-botero-241190>. Accessed on: Jan. 13, 2016.

1. Look at the painting and answer the questions.

a. What is the couple doing?

b. How does the painting make you feel?

c. Describe the painting.

BOTERO, FERNANDO. PAREJA BAILANDO, 1987.

BOTERO, Fernando. *Pareja bailando*. 1987. Oil on canvas, 195 cm × 130 cm. Museo de Arte del Banco de la República, Bogotá, Colombia.

2. Now, look at this other Botero's artwork and answer.

a. Who is presented in the painting?

b. How did you get to this conclusion?

FERNANDO BOTERO, MATADOR, 2006.

BOTERO, Fernando. *Matador*. 2006. Oil on canvas, 180 cm × 128 cm. Private collection.

3. Why do you think Botero used volume in his work?

UNIT

6

Let's go to the theater

Your learning objectives for this unit are...

- to talk about leisure time activities;
- to discuss the importance of cultural activities;
- to read and write a flyer.

Theater has many origins and formats. Ancient civilizations had rituals which involved staging scenes. The origins of the theater date back to Ancient Greece. Poem reading and storytelling were part of festivals in honor of the Greek god Dionysus. The art of drama has since developed and improved, incorporating new elements throughout the centuries.

The European-style theater was brought to Brazil by Portuguese colonizers to teach their culture and religion to native inhabitants. At that time, Father Anchieta was one of those responsible for teaching the art of drama and writing theater plays as well.

According to the article "The importance of role-playing in the child's development": "Role-playing contributes to the development of communication and favors the collective production of culture knowledge, in both aesthetic and educational values."

ARCOVERDE, Silmara Lídia Moraes. *A importância do teatro na formação da criança*. Translated from: <www.pucpr.edu.br/eventos/educere/educere2008/anais/pdf/629_639.pdf>. Accessed on: Mar. 21, 2016.

LEONARDO PAPINI/SAMBAPHOTO

ANNA JURKOVSKA/SHUTTERSTOCK

EXCHANGING IDEAS

1. Look at the images on the left and answer: What are the similarities and differences between them?
2. Theater has existed since ancient times. In your opinion, why has this artistic expression been around for so long?

6 Let's go to the theater

READING COMPREHENSION

TEXT 1

BEFORE READING

1. The art of theater is part of the history of mankind as one of the oldest artistic manifestations. Have you ever been to a theater? If so, what did you watch? If not, would you like to?

READING

2. Scan the flyer and check what kind of show it is about.

☐ A movie. ☐ A musical. ☐ A ballet performance.

> • ***História mundial do teatro***
> Margot Berthold. São Paulo: Perspectiva, 2004.
> A book about the different origins and styles of theater.

3. Read the flyer and write the appropriate questions from the box for the corresponding answers.

What is the name of the musical?
Who is the musical director?
What is the name of the theater company?
How many people are considered a group?
When are there shows?

a. ______________________________

On Mondays, Tuesdays, Wednesdays, Thursdays, Fridays, and Saturdays.

b. ______________________________

The Really Useful Theatre Company.

c. ______________________________

The Phantom of the Opera.

d. ______________________________

Ten or more.

e. ______________________________

Harold Prince.

4. Read the flyer again and check the sentences that present characteristics of this flyer.

a. ☐ It presents the names of the characters.

b. ☐ It presents a sentence that is not finished.

c. ☐ It informs that you can get further information about the musical on the internet.

d. ☐ It presents information in more than one language.

e. ☐ It presents the ticket price.

5. Considering this flyer is about a musical staged in New York City, what can you infer about the information in many languages on the flyer?

____

____

____

AFTER READING

- How can attending cultural events such as a performance of a play reflect on your school, family and social life?

TEXT 2

BEFORE READING

1. Look at the two admission tickets. Are these two museums in the same country?

READING

2. Read the tickets below and check the correct answer to the question.

AMERICAN MUSEUM of NATURAL HISTORY
Adult
WEDNESDAY
07/09/2014
Museum Adm
Turn today's visit into years of wonder. Become a Member!

Item M Trans 24180439 Cust 1135300A $110.00
Bat1209510 Ord 4080157 CM

REPRODUÇÃO

Museu da Língua Portuguesa x 2013
12/04/2013 10:00
Museu da Língua Portuguesa 2013
Museu da Língua Portuguesa
MEIA ENTRADA
Entrada Principal

FILA	ASSENTO	SUBSETOR	INTEIRA
-	254	MEIA	R$3,00

MLP20104121010 3570631-30/6

56871423

FINEPHOTO

Why are tickets necessary to get into some places?

a. ☐ Because they prove visitors have permission to enter.

b. ☐ Because they prove visitors like museums.

c. ☐ Because visitors can't buy them online.

3. Read the sentences and check the appropriate columns.

	American Museum of Natural History	Museu da Língua Portuguesa
a. You can learn a lot about the Portuguese language and literature.		
b. You can see specimens of plants, fossils, ancient human artifacts, etc.		
c. Many people interested in Science visit the museum.		
d. You can read about Brazilian poets and writers.		

4. Read the tickets on page 110 once again and answer the questions.

a. Which museum was visited in April?

____

b. Which ticket presents admission (adm) prices?

____

c. What was the time of the visit according to the ticket for the Museu da Língua Portuguesa?

____

d. What is the visitor's seat number at the Museu da Língua Portuguesa?

____

5. Match the pictures to the museums they are related to.

a. American Museum of Natural History

b. Museu da Língua Portuguesa

FUNDAÇÃO CASA DE JORGE AMADO

J. MIERS

AFTER READING

- Have you ever been on a school tour to a museum? If so, talk about your experience. If not, which one would you like to visit and why?

- **www.museudalinguaportuguesa.org.br/index.php**
  Museu da Língua Portuguesa's official website.
- **www.amnh.org/**
  American Museum of Natural History's official website.

FOCUS ON VOCABULARY

1. Julia and Charlie are talking about going to the school play. Read their conversation and circle the correct words.

THINKSTOCK/GETTY IMAGES

DON MASON/BLEND/DIOMEDIA

Julia: Charlie, what about going to the school play tonight? *Romeo and Juliet* is on.

Charlie: Good idea! My friend Susannah is the **leading/second** actress. She plays Juliet.

Julia: I know. I love her! She's a great actress. Her **character/performance** is excellent.

Charlie: Yes, it's true. The **audience/actor** usually applauds her for minutes!

Julia: So, let's buy the **CD/tickets**, then.

Charlie: Hold on a second, Julia! What time is it now?

Julia: Four o'clock.

Charlie: Oh, I can't go to school now. I have a guitar lesson. Can you buy the ticket for me?

Julia: Sure!

Telling the time

2. Match the times to their corresponding clocks. Then listen and repeat.

18 What time is it?

a. It's eight-oh-five.

b. It's eleven o'clock.

c. It's three thirty.

d. It's four fifteen.

e. It's midday.

f. It's midnight.

IMAGENS: SHUTTERSTOCK

Ordinal numbers

3. Look at the number chart below and write the missing ordinal numbers. Then listen and repeat.

19

1st first	______ sixth	11th ______	16th sixteenth	______ twenty-first
2nd second	7th ______	12th twelfth	17th ______	22nd ______
3rd third	______ eighth	______ thirteenth	18th eighteenth	23rd ______
______ ______	9th ninth	14th ______	19th ______	30th thirtieth
5th fifth	10th ______	15th fifteenth	20th twentieth	31st ______

PRONUNCIATION PRACTICE

20 Underline the correct numbers according to what you hear.

a. 13th 13
b. 21st 21
c. 10th 10
d. 4th 4
e. 15th 15
f. 17th 17
g. 30th 30

Dates

4. Look at the pictures and complete the sentences using expressions from the box.

in September	on November 19th

PRESIDÊNCIA DA REPÚBLICA

Brazilian Flag Day is ______________________.

Brazilian Independence Day is ______________________.

EDSON SATO/PULSAR IMAGENS

IT'S YOUR TURN!

In pairs, ask a classmate about the time he/she does things. Use: *What time do you…?* and the cues given. Take notes of his/her answers. Then report the information you get to the class.

do homework	go to bed	study	watch TV

LANGUAGE IN USE

Adverbs of frequency / How often...?

1. Read the dialogue between two classmates and pay attention to the words in bold. Then check the correct alternatives to complete the sentences.

THINKSTOCK/GETTY IMAGES

Will: What do you do in your free time, Doug?

Doug: I **usually** hang out with my brothers. We like to go to the beach, play soccer, and ride our bikes.

Will: You guys love sports! **How often** do you take part in cultural activities like visiting museums, for example?

Doug: To be honest, we **never** do that! We are **always** involved in sports in our free time. And you?

Will: In fact, I **rarely** take part in cultural activities either. In my free time, I prefer to stay home, read books, and watch some movies. I **sometimes** volunteer at an orphanage, too.

Doug: Hey, that's something I would like to do. **How often** do you volunteer?

Will: **Four times a month**. I'll call you next time I go there.

a. We use the words **usually**, **never**, **always**, **rarely**, and **sometimes** and a verb in the simple present to talk about:

☐ things we are doing now. ☐ habits and routines.

b. We use **How often** to ask questions about the:

☐ places people go. ☐ frequency people do things.

c. Adverbs come before the main verbs. However, in sentences with the verb **to be**, the adverbs are:

☐ placed after the verb. ☐ placed before the verb.

2. Use the words from the box to complete the frequency adverbs stairs. Then answer the questions about yourself.

rarely	sometimes	usually

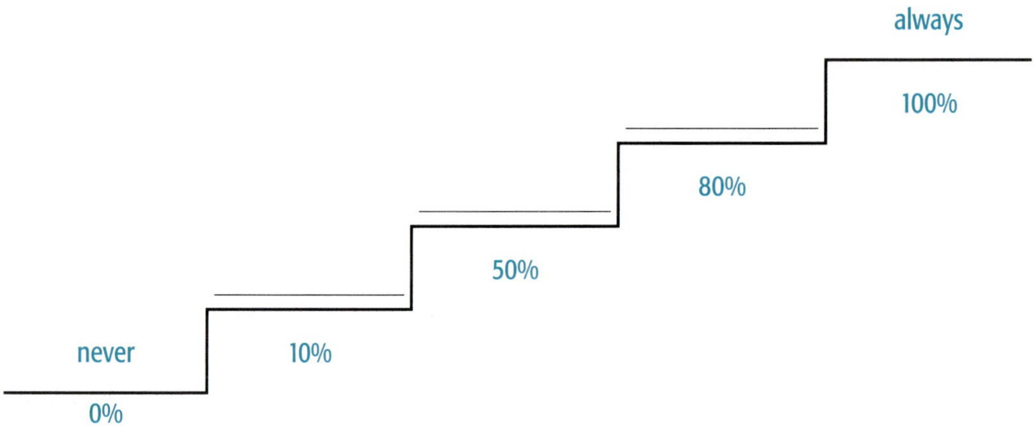

a. How often do you hang out with your friends?

____

b. How often do you take part in cultural activities?

____

Simple present × Present continuous

3. Circle the correct form of the verbs to complete the dialogue.

Mrs. Collins: What **do you do/are you doing** here, guys?

Brian: **We're waiting/We wait** for Debbie, Mrs. Collins.

Mrs. Collins: Oh, I see. You usually **are going/go** home together, right?

Lucy: Yeah, we all live on the same street. She **isn't having/doesn't have** a lot of friends around here, so we **are always walking/always walk** back home together.

Mrs. Collins: Look! Debbie **is coming/comes**. Bye, everyone!

Sarah: See you tomorrow, Mrs. Collins.

THINKSTOCK/GETTY IMAGES

4. Use the verbs in parentheses in the simple present or present continuous to complete what the tour 21 guide says during a tour. Then listen and check.

We __________ (be) in front of the City Museum. This museum ______________ (exhibit) the works of man from prehistoric to modern times. Today they ______________ (display) three different exhibitions. See that artist over there? He ______________ (paint) a canvas to show his technique to the visitors. In some museums, that's a routine: an artist ______________ (demonstrate) his abilities to visitors. Most exhibitions here ______________ (not require) tickets, but some do. Let's go and enjoy your visit.

Let's

5. Go back to activity 4 and read the tour guide's last sentence again. Then write **T** (true) or **F** (false).

a. ☐ We use **Let's** to make suggestions or invitations.

b. ☐ After **Let's** we use a verb in the **-ing** form.

6. What would people say in these situations? Unscramble the words to find out their suggestions.

a. The Browns are going to the movie theater now. Mrs. Brown is ready to start the car so she says:

(go, / guys / Let's / !) ______________________________

b. Your friend Paddy is late for work, and you are leaving home right now. You tell her:

(taxi / share / Let's / a / !) ______________________________

c. You and the other tourists don't know which way to go when you leave the theater. You look at them and say:

(map / city / the / Let's / check / !) ______________________________

d. Your friend insists that he is very hungry. He turns to you and says:

(snack bar / a / Let's / at / stop / !) ______________________________

HANDS ON!

Think about three simple situations and write them down. Read them to a classmate. He/She makes up suggestions using *Let's*. Change roles. You can use:
A: It's very hot here.
B: Let's open the windows!

Adverbs of frequency / How often...?

We use adverbs of frequency to describe the frequency of our actions and they are used before the **main verbs** or after the verb **to be**. We ask about frequency using **How often**.

A: **How often** are you at home in the afternoon?
B: I **am always** at home in the afternoon.

A: **How often** does the teacher ask for a research?
B: He **usually asks** for a research.

A: **How often** do they play at the club?
B: They **sometimes play** at the club.

A: **How often** do you go to the movies?
B: I **rarely go** to the movies.

A: **How often** is your sister late?
B: She **is never** late.

Simple present × Present continuous

We use the **simple present** to talk about permanent situations (for example: hobbies, habits, routines and repeated actions) and the **present continuous** to talk about temporary situations (for example: what is happening right now).

PHOTOALTO/ERIC AUDRAS/GETTY IMAGES

Adam studies Spanish at school. He is studying irregular verbs.

ROBERT NIEDRING/CORBIS/FOTOARENA

Ellie and Ariana don't eat meat. They are making a vegetable soup for dinner.

Let's

We use **let's** to make suggestions and invitations. After **let's**, we use the base form of the main verb.

LEONARDO PATRIZI/GETTY IMAGES

Wow, look at the time, it's late! **Let's** go home!

BLEND IMAGES/SHUTTERSTOCK

I'm so hungry. **Let's** stop at that Italian restaurant!

1. Order the words in "B" to form sentences. Then, make a question using **how often** for each corresponding sentence.

a. A: How often ______________________________
B: and / I / on / weekends / museums / sometimes / family / My / visit
____

b. A: How often ______________________________
B: takes part / Lola / cultural activities / in / always/ because / rarely / is / very busy / she
____

c. A: How often ______________________________
B: usually / my / on / grandparents / I / Sunday / see
____

d. A: How often ______________________________
B: never / these vitamins, / takes / father / but my mother / My / takes / them / sometimes
____

2. Use the verbs and prompts in parentheses to write sentences about you or about a friend using the simple present or present continuous.

a. (temporary situation) study:
____

b. (permanent situation) not/like:
____

c. (temporary situation) not/read:
____

d. (permanent situation) live:
____

3. Analyze the images and complete the speech bubbles with a suggestion or invitation using **let's**.

a.

KRIS UBACH AND QUIM ROSER/GETTY IMAGES

b.

SHUTTERSTOCK

LISTENING COMPREHENSION

BEFORE LISTENING

1. Read about São Paulo's Football Museum and write **T** (true) or **F** (false).

Football Museum

Even for non-football fans, São Paulo's Museu do Futebol (Football Museum) is a must-see tourist attraction. The Brazilian team has been unquestionably the most delightful and successful national team in football's history [...]. The beauty of São Paulo's Football Museum, housed within the Pacaembu Stadium (which is itself an icon of the city), is that it takes a modern, interactive approach toward its exhibitions, with holographic displays, touch-screen information panels, and various other multimedia installations. [...]

CAIO PIMENTA/DIVULGAÇÃO/MUSEU DO FUTEBOL

Be sure to budget at least two or three hours for the museum, as there's a lot to see.

Address: Estádio do Pacaembu, Praça Charles Miller 1, São Paulo

Extracted from: <www.wordtravels.com/Attractions/3410>. Accessed on: May 21, 2016.

a. ☐ The Brazilian team has not been very successful in the history of football.

b. ☐ The Football Museum is a nice attraction even for people that do not love football.

c. ☐ The exhibitions in the Football Museum do not use technology. They present only photos and profiles of famous players.

2. Match the parts to form meaningful sentences.

football (UK) – soccer (USA)

a. The exhibitions in the Football Museum are

b. São Paulo's Football Museum is located

c. The Brazilian team is

d. Pacaembu Stadium is

☐ the most successful national team in football's history.

☐ a tourist attraction itself.

☐ modern, interactive, and present holographic displays.

☐ inside the stadium.

- **www.funarte.gov.br/**
  Fundação Nacional de Artes' official website, with information about cultural events all around Brazil.

LISTENING

3. Listen to a reporter talking about the Football Museum and answer the questions.

22

a. How many years of football are there in the museum?

____

b. Who welcomes visitors in the museum?

____

c. How many languages does he speak to welcome the visitors?

____

d. What does the number 1,000 (one thousand) refer to?

____

4. Read the first part of the reporter's speech and complete it using the words from the box. Then listen and check.

23

football	museum	stadiums

Reporter: Over one hundred years of _______________ history in one of the most emblematic _______________ in the world; after visiting this _______________ you'll understand why Brazilians live and breathe this sport.

5. Read the extract in activity 4 again. Do you agree that Brazilians live and breathe football? Why?

____

____

____

AFTER LISTENING

6. If you went to the Football Museum, what would you like to find out? Check. Then compare your answers to a classmate's. Add one more item to the list.

- [ ] The greatest players' careers.
- [ ] The history of my favorite soccer team.
- [ ] The history of the World Cup.
- [ ] The most exciting matches in past World Cups.

____

____

SPEAKING

1. Look at the pictures and choose your top three free time activities. Number them from the first to the third according to your preferences.

THINKSTOCK/GETTY IMAGES

practice sports

THINKSTOCK/GETTY IMAGES

hang out with friends

THINKSTOCK/GETTY IMAGES

watch TV

MINT IMAGES/ALAMY/LATINSTOCK

read books

ALFRED ABAD/AGE FOTOSTOCK/KEYSTONE BRASIL

go to the movies

CESAR DINIZ / PULSAR IMAGENS

visit museums

2. Explain your choices in activity 1 to a classmate and ask him or her to do the same. Take notes and report them to the class. You can say: "Diego likes to practice sports during his free time because he...".

____

____

____

Reflecting on the theme

- Do your favorite activities chosen in activity 1 promote a more sedentary or more active routine?
- How do leisure and appreciation of cultural events positively contribute to your health?

WRITING

BEFORE WRITING

1. Compare the flyer on page 108 to the one below and check the true statements about them.

a. ☐ The messages in the flyers are short and objective.

b. ☐ The images on the flyers are clearly related to the events.

c. ☐ The flyers are printed on multiple pages.

d. ☐ They aren't addressed to the same audience.

INSTITUTE OF JAMAICA

Jamaica is a sovereign nation since 1962, but because it was colonized by England, English is the official language of Jamaica. The majority of the population speaks the Jamaican Patois dialect though.

centre (UK) – center (USA)
programme (UK) – program (USA)

2. Match the questions to their corresponding answers.

a. What is the flyer about?

b. What activities are available to children in the program?

c. What do children have to do if they want to take part in the program?

d. Who is responsible for the program?

☐ The Ministry of Youth, Sports and Culture of Jamaica.

☐ A program of visual and performing arts for children.

☐ Call one of the telephone numbers on the flyer and register.

☐ Drumming, reading and counselling, dancing, art and craft.

WRITING

3. With your classmates, create your own flyers for a Talent Show in your school. Follow the steps below.
   - Talk to your classmates about the skills they have and what they would like to perform in a school event. These skills might be related to dance, music, arts, drama, handcraft, etc.
   - Select a date, time and place for the presentation.
   - In pairs, gather all the information and write a draft flyer with the event schedule in your notebook.
   - All data about day, time and place of the event must be informed in the flyer.
   - If necessary, consult a dictionary.
   - Show your draft to your teacher.
   - Make any necessary corrections according to your teacher's suggestions.
   - Rewrite the text in the flyer on an A4 sheet of paper.
   - Paste images to illustrate the flyer.

AFTER WRITING

- With your classmates, decide on the number of copies of the flyer that is necessary to promote the Talent Show and where to distribute them.
- If possible, include the flyer on your school website and/or on your class' pages on social networks.

SELF-EVALUATION

Check the true sentences about your learning in Unit 6.
In this unit you have learned to:

- [ ] talk about leisure time activities;
- [ ] discuss the importance of cultural activities;
- [ ] read and write a flyer.

Reflecting...

- **What questions do I still have about the production of flyers?**
- **What did I learn about the use of adverbs of frequency?**
- **Which leisure time activities would I like to start doing?**
- **In which cultural activities would I like to actively participate?**

UNIT

7

What internet activities do you do?

Barrett Lyon is an artist who uses his knowledge about technology in his work. His images are digital drawings. The Opte Project, from 2003, is an example of this kind of art. Lyon made a representation of the internet connections.

In 2010, Lyon created the image on the right for the same project, which was later exhibited at MoMA (The Museum of Modern Art) in New York City. The brightest colors in the image represent the places where most people are connected to the internet in a computer.

Your learning objectives for this unit are...

- to talk about events that happened in the past;
- to discuss changes in the use of the internet;
- to read and write tips.

THE OPTE PROJECT

EXCHANGING IDEAS

1. The images of the Opte Project represent the use of the internet. What differences do you think the images from 2003 and the one from 2010 (on the left) may show?
2. In your opinion, what is probably the reason why the artist wanted to show different representations in different years?

The Opte Project. *The Internet 2010.*

7 What internet activities do you do?

READING COMPREHENSION

TEXT 1

BEFORE READING

1. The Brazilian Institute of Geography and Statistics (IBGE) reports that half of the population of Brazil had access to the internet in 2013. How did the school, social and professional life change because of the internet?

READING

2. Skim the tips and check the best alternative to complete the sentence.
The tips are about:

☐ cyberbullying. ☐ internet safety. ☐ online ethics.

www.nypl.org/help/about-nypl/legal-notices/internet-safety-tips

Internet Safety Tips for Children and Teens

- **Personal Information.** Don't give out personal information without your parents' permission. [...]
- **Screen Name.** When creating your screen name, do not include personal information like your last name or date of birth.
- **Passwords.** Don't share your password with anyone but your parents. [...]
- **Photos.** Don't post photos or videos online without getting your parents' permission.
- **Online Friends.** Don't agree to meet an online friend unless you have your parents' permission. [...]
- **Online Ads.** Don't buy anything online without talking to your parents first. [...]
- **Downloading.** Talk to your parents before you open an email attachment or download software. [...]
- **Bullying.** Don't send or respond to mean or insulting messages. Tell your parents if you receive one. [...]

Extracted from: <www.nypl.org/help/about-nypl/legal-notices/internet-safety-tips>. Accessed on: May 21, 2016.

attachment: anexo
mean: maldosas

- **http://internetsegura.br/dicas-jovens-criancas/**
This website offers tips for children and teenagers about how to use the internet safely.

3. Read the text again and find the tips that correspond to the pictures below and write them down.

MICHAEL JUNG/DEPOSIT PHOTOS/GLOW IMAGES

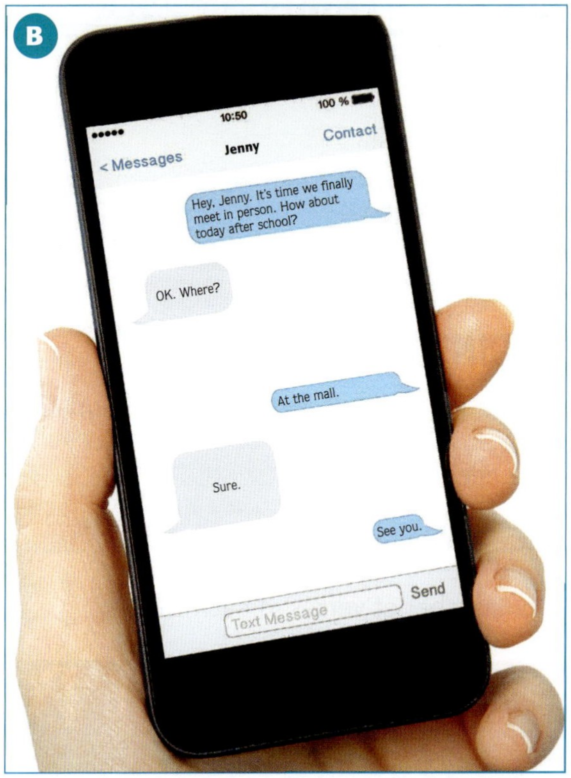

SHUTTERSTOCK

4. Read the text on page 126 again and check the true sentences.

a. ☐ There is a cue for every tip, so we know what we are going to read about.

b. ☐ There is a bullet for every single tip.

c. ☐ Some tips aren't about internet safety.

d. ☐ Most tips begin with the negative form of the imperative.

e. ☐ The tips present formal language.

f. ☐ The tips are for kids and teenagers.

AFTER READING

- Read the "Internet Safety Tips for Children and Teens" again. Evaluate your own safety online based on those tips. Do you have a safe attitude towards the use of the internet? Do you usually follow those tips?
- What can you do to be safer when using the internet?

TEXT 2

BEFORE READING

1. Look at the text below. What text genre is it?

a. ☐ A note.

b. ☐ A poem.

c. ☐ An ad.

READING

2. Read the text and complete the information.

a. title ________________________________

b. number of stanzas ______________________

c. number of verses in each stanza __________

Each line of a poem is called **verse**. A group of verses make up a **stanza**.

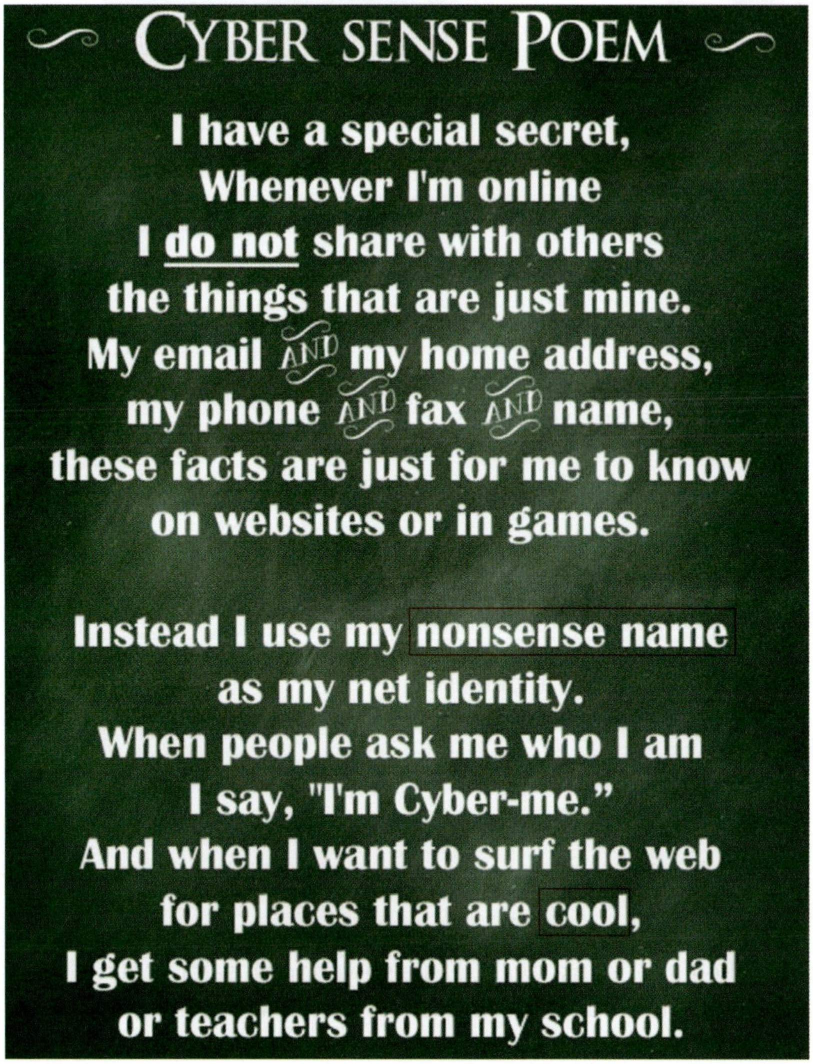

THINKSTOCK/GETTY IMAGES

nonsense name: apelido bobo
cool: legais

- ***Meu computador, a internet... E EU!***

Jérôme Colombain. São Paulo: Escala, 2008.

This book offers simple advice to children and teenagers about how to better manage a computer, focusing on how it can be used cautiously and for their development.

3. Match the parts and make meaningful sentences.

a. The poem shows different forms of being

b. A good piece of advice is not to

☐ share your e-mail and home address with people you don't know.

☐ protected when using the internet.

4. What does the verse "the things that are just mine" refer to?

a. ☐ School information.

b. ☐ Personal information.

c. ☐ Personal preferences.

d. ☐ Personal computer.

e. ☐ Websites and games.

5. Copy the verses that justify your answer in activity 4.

____

____

6. Answer these questions. If necessary, go back to the poem.

a. What is the nonsense name used in the poem as a Net identity?

____

____

b. Who are the people mentioned that can help when necessary?

____

____

c. Are there words that rhyme? What are they? Write them below.

____

____

____

d. What do the text on page 126 and the poem on page 128 have in common?

____

____

AFTER READING

- What tips would you give people who do not know how to protect their safety online?
- Where can you find information about safety online? Who can you talk to about that?

FOCUS ON VOCABULARY

1. Complete the mini-dialogues using the words from the box.

online ad	password	personal information	screen name

a.

Greg: Hey, Layla, I can't remember my Cyberspace page ____________. Can I use yours?

Layla: I'm sorry, Greg. It's my secret word. Why don't you open the Cyberspace page and click on the help icon? I'm sure they can solve your problem.

Greg: You're right. I'll do it now.

b.

Chris: Mom, I want to buy a new pair of sneakers. There is an ____________ selling them 50% off the original price. Can I buy them?

Mom: Wait a minute, Chris. Let's check if it's a safe site.

Chris: All right, Mom!

c.

Alexis: I'm creating my blog page and I need to decide what my ____________ will be. Can you help me?

Olivia: Well, I don't have any idea. But watch out! Don't give any kind of ____________ on the net.

2. Match the columns. Use a dictionary if necessary.

a. to be connected to the internet

b. the location of one or more webpages

c. to request a file from another computer and to receive it

d. a nickname to be used when you are connected to the internet

e. a secret word or expression used by authorized persons to prove their right to access, information, etc.

☐ net identity

☐ to be online

☐ password

☐ website

☐ to download

SHUTTERSTOCK

Computer parts

3. Unscramble the letters and find out the words that correspond to the images below.

A

THINKSTOCK/GETTY IMAGES

LHAFS REDIV

f__________ d__________

B

THINKSTOCK/GETTY IMAGES

OKEDYBAR

k__________

C

THINKSTOCK/GETTY IMAGES

SAHEDPOHNE

h__________

D

THINKSTOCK/GETTY IMAGES

RRINTEP

p__________

E

THINKSTOCK/GETTY IMAGES

RONIMOT

m__________

4. Complete the sentences using the words from activity 3. Make changes to the words if necessary.

a. I have to print my History report today and my __________ is not working.

b. I prefer LED __________. They're thin and have great resolution.

c. Our Geography teacher saves his lessons at home on his __________. Then he plugs it into the classroom computer before classes start.

d. Joey has lost his __________ again. Now he cannot listen to music when he walks home from school.

e. Lucca wants to buy a special ergonomic __________ to play his new computer game.

> To help you learn the names of objects, write their names on tags or removable sticky notes and stick them on the objects. You will see the words frequently and it will help you memorize them.

IT'S YOUR TURN!

Take a survey with three classmates. Ask them questions like these: *How many text messages do you send every day? Do you like chatting online with your friends? What do you use your cell phone for? How often do you play computer games?* Then report the results to your class and discuss them with the whole group.

LANGUAGE IN USE

Simple past (verb to be)

1. Read the text about Mike Krieger and answer the questions.

www.therichest.com/celebnetworth/celebrity-business/tech-millionaire/mike-krieger-net-worth/

Mike Krieger Net Worth

C. FLANIGAN/GETTY IMAGES

Net Worth:
$100 Million

Source of Wealth	Instagram
Birth Place	São Paulo, São Paulo, Brazil
Marital Status	Single
Full Name	Michel Krieger
Nationality	Brazilian
Date of Birth	March 4, 1986
More Stats	View More

About Mike Krieger

Brazilian software engineer and internet entrepreneur Mike Krieger has an estimated net worth of $100 million in 2013. Krieger is best known as the founder of Instagram, an online video-sharing, photosharing and social networking service that allows its users to take videos and pictures, and share them on various social networking platforms such as Flickr, Tumblr, Twitter and Facebook.
Michel "Mike" Krieger was born on March 4, 1986 in São Paulo, São Paulo, Brazil. He studied Symbolic Systems at Stanford University. While studying at the university, he met Kevin Systrom. Together, the two founded Instagram in 2010.

Adapted from: <www.therichest.com/celebnetworth/celebrity-business/tech-millionaire/mike-krieger-net-worth>. Accessed on: May 21, 2016.

a. What **was** Mike Krieger's estimated net worth in 2013? ____________________

b. When and where **was** Mike born? ____________________

c. **Were** Mike Krieger and Kevin Systrom students at the same university? ____________________

d. When **was** Instagram founded? ____________________

2. Look attentively at the verbs in bold in activity 1. Then use the words from the box to complete the rules below.

past	questions	was	were

a. We use **was** and **were** to talk about a situation in the ____________.

b. In "When **was** Instagram founded?" ____________ refers to **Instagram**, that is, third person singular.

c. In "**Were** Mike Krieger and Kevin Systrom students at the same university?" ____________ refers to **Mike and Kevin**, that is, third person plural.

d. When we ask ____________, the verb **to be** comes before the subject.

3. Check the alternative that best completes each text below. Then write the words in the spaces provided.

a. ☐ was / were / was not / was ☐ were / were / was not / was

Albert Einstein ______________ born to a middle-class German Jewish family. His parents ______________ concerned that he scarcely talked until the age of three, but he ______________ so much a backward as a quiet child. He would build tall houses of cards and hated playing soldier. At the age of twelve he ______________ fascinated by a geometry book.

[...]

FRED STEIN ARCHIVE/ARCHIVE PHOTOS/GETTY IMAGES

Extracted from: <www.aip.org./history/exhibits/einstein/inbrief.htm>. Accessed on: May 21, 2016.

b. ☐ were / were / was / was ☐ were / were / were / was

[...]

Auguste and Louis Lumière ______________ pioneers in the improvement of photographic materials and processes in the late 1800s and early 1900s. Using their scientific abilities and business talents, they ______________ responsible for developing existing ideas in still photography and motion pictures to produce higher quality products that ______________ practical enough to be of commercial value. [...] The best-known of the Lumières' achievements, however, ______________ the Cinematograph system of projected motion pictures.

[...]

GLASSHOUSE/ZUMA PRESS/GLOW IMAGES

Extracted from: <biography.yourdictionary.com/the-lumiere-brothers>. Accessed on: May 21, 2016.

c. ☐ were / was / were ☐ were / were / was

Jacob Ludwig Carl & Wilhelm Carl Grimm ______________ born in Hanau, Germany. The Grimm family had been living in Hanau for more than 100 years. Their father Philipp ______________ a lawyer and town clerk in Hanau, their mother Dorothea née Zimmer hailed from Kassel in North Hessen.

[...]

The original house where the brothers ______________ born in Hanau doesn't exist anymore, it was destroyed in 1945 during WWII. [...]

KURT GEIGER/PICTURE-ALLIANCE/GLOW IMAGES

Extracted from: <www.germany-insider-facts.com/grimm-brothers.html#.VNEHdGjF9il>. Accessed on: May 21, 2016.

4. Complete the dialogues with the simple past of the verb **to be**. Then match the dialogues to their corresponding pictures.

> **was not**: wasn't
> **were not**: weren't

a. A: __________ you at home this afternoon, Paulo?

B: No, Mom. I __________. I __________ at Mike's.

A: No problem, dear. But, please, don't forget to give me a call next time, OK?
B: All right, Mom.

b. A: Hey, Laura. Do you remember Lizandra?

B: Lizandra? __________ she that exchange student from Chile?

A: No, she's Brazilian. Don't you remember? She and her twin brother __________ on our soccer team.

B: Oh, yeah! And they played really well!

A: They're back!

THINKSTOCK/GETTY IMAGES

OLESYA FEKETA/SHUTTERSTOCK

HANDS ON!

Complete the text below with true information about yourself when you were a child. You can use the suggestions from the box or come up with other ideas. Share your text with a classmate. Then report your classmate's information to the class.

Your nickname	The name of your best friends	Your favorite color and TV programs

When I was a child, my nickname was... ______________________________

____

____

____

Simple past (verb to be)

Affirmative	
subject pronouns	**verb to be**
I	was
you	were
he/she/it	was
we/you/they	were

There are no contracted forms for the verb **to be** in the past in affirmative statements.

I was at school this morning.

They were happy to see me.

He was born in 2001.

Negative		
subject pronouns	**verb to be**	**contracted forms**
I	was not	wasn't
you	were not	weren't
he/she/it	was not	wasn't
we/you/they	were not	weren't

I was not/wasn't in Rio last week.

You were not/weren't a teacher two years ago.

He was not/wasn't sick.

Interrogative	
verb to be	**subject pronouns**
Was	I... ?
Were	you... ?
Was	he/she/it... ?
Were	we/you/they... ?

Were you late?

Was she the new teacher?

Was he French?

Short answers	
affirmative answer	**negative answer**
Yes, I was.	No, I was not/wasn't.
Yes, he/she/it was.	No, he/she/it was not/wasn't.
Yes, we/you/they were.	No, we/you/they were not/ weren't.

ANATOLII BABII/ALAMY/FOTOARENA

Sandra: Was it my phone?
Mary: Yes, it was.

IMAGE SOURCE/GETTY IMAGES

Bob: Were Craig and Billy at class today?
Jake: No, they weren't. They are sick.

1. Complete the text with the past form of the verb **to be**.

Who invented the mouse?

The mouse ____________ the standard way to control a desktop computer. It ____________ invented in the 1960s by a visionary man named Douglas C. Engelbart, who died at the age of 88 in 2013. He ____________ born in Portland, Ore., on Jan. 25, 1925.

He ____________ at home when he had the idea for the mouse. He ____________ at a computer graphics conference, thinking about ways to move an onscreen cursor. The first time Engelbart demonstrated the mouse ____________ in 1968 at the Fall Joint Computer Conference in San Francisco, California. At that time, the computer scientists ____________ using the keyboard to control computers.

____________ it a success? Yes, but the mouse ____________ a standard component of a computer. That changed when Apple released the Macintosh in 1984. The mouse that came with the computer ____________ actually an updated version of the mouse created for the Apple Lisa – a less popular personal computer that ____________ released a year earlier.

Engelbart's and Steve Jobs's opinions about the mouse ____________ very different. Engelbart imagined a mouse with many buttons in the future, but Jobs's Macintosh mouse had just one button for simplicity.

Modern mice are very different from the first Macintosh mouse, but most mice are still based on the same concept invented by Engelbart in 1964.

Adapted from: <appleinsider.com/articles/13/07/04/inventor-of-the-computer-mouse-dies-at-88>. Accessed on: May 21, 2016.

2. Circle the correct verb in each of the sentences below.

a. The weather **was/were** very cold last weekend.

b. Michael **was/were** in England last summer.

c. **Was/Were** you at home yesterday?

d. **Was/Were** you a good swimmer when you **was/were** a child?

e. **Was/Were** the History test difficult?

f. **Was/Were** Mrs. Robinson your teacher last year?

g. Tom and Carol **was/were** here five minutes ago.

h. I **was/were** in class this morning, but you **wasn't/weren't**. Where **was/were** you?

LISTENING COMPREHENSION

BEFORE LISTENING

1. Imagine you live in a place where there are no schools nearby. Check the devices you could use to attend a class in a quick and efficient way. Then match the words with the pictures.

a. ☐ an MP3 player

b. ☐ a tablet

c. ☐ a telephone

d. ☐ a computer

e. ☐ a smartphone

RALF KALYTTA/ALAMY/GLOW IMAGES

BONNINSTUDIO/SHUTTERSTOCK

ANTHONY BROWN/ALAMY/FOTOARENA

FOCUSDIGITAL/ALAMY/LATINSTOCK

THINKSTOCK/GETTY IMAGES

2. You are going to hear about Mr. Chandrakant Singh, an Indian who helps kids from distant areas to study. Check the expressions and sentences you might hear.

a. ☐ free computer online communication program

b. ☐ students get extra courses

c. ☐ via instant messages

d. ☐ providing top-rate schooling to youngsters

e. ☐ a projector allows the class to easily view the lesson

3. Number the following sentences in the order you will probably hear them.

a. ☐ "I like these lessons. It helps me understand things better."

b. ☐ "An Indian boarding school in Bihar State uses Skype to help enhance students' learning."

c. ☐ "Our sincere appreciation, Mr. Chandrakant Singh and dedicated instructors involved in this wonderful endeavor."

LISTENING

24 4. Listen to a reporter talking about Mr. Singh and check if your predictions in activity 3 are correct.

5. Listen to the reporter again and match the following questions to their appropriate answers.

25

a. Where is the school?

b. What technology do they use there to help enhance learning?

c. When do students have extra classes?

d. How old is Mr. Singh?

☐ In the evenings and on weekends.

☐ In India.

☐ He's 36.

☐ They use a projector and a free online communication program.

6. Write **T** (true) or **F** (false). Then listen to the reporter once again and check your answers.

26

a. ☐ Students are able to view the lesson through a projector.

b. ☐ One of the students says: "I don't like the lessons."

c. ☐ Chaitanya Gurukul is a public school.

d. ☐ Mr. Singh is involved in providing schooling to teens from remote areas.

e. ☐ Students get extra drawing courses.

f. ☐ Students have online lessons on Monday mornings.

g. ☐ Students are thankful for their teachers' dedication.

AFTER LISTENING

7. In pairs, write two questions you would like to ask Mr. Singh. Share them with your teacher and classmates. Explain why you would like to ask him these questions.

___

___

SPEAKING

1. Check the internet activities you often do. Compare your answers with a classmate's. Then share your results with the whole group. You can use the following:

I often play games, but I rarely shop online.
Roberto always writes messages using Twitter.
Tania always looks for information for her school work, but she never downloads music or movies.

SHUTTERSTOCK

a. ☐ download music and/or movies

b. ☐ look for information for your school work

c. ☐ play games

d. ☐ post photos, videos, and/or messages

e. ☐ read books

f. ☐ send and check e-mails

g. ☐ shop

h. ☐ upload home videos to YouTube

i. ☐ use Google to look for people and/or things

j. ☐ use Twitter, Facebook, Instagram, and Snapchat

k. ☐ write messages using Twitter

l. ☐ others: ____________________

- **www.youtube.com/watch?v=jOUiAr9-KSo&feature=youtu.be**
  Short movie about what happens when three friends can't access the internet for some minutes.
- **www.youtube.com/watch?v=d0mg9DxvfZE**
  Teenagers reacting to a video which explains how the internet worked in the 1990s.

Reflecting on the theme

In 10 years, how do you think technology will be affecting school and your life?

WRITING

BEFORE WRITING

1. Read the tips below and write **1** for Internet Safety Tips for Children and Teens and **2** for Netiquette Tips.

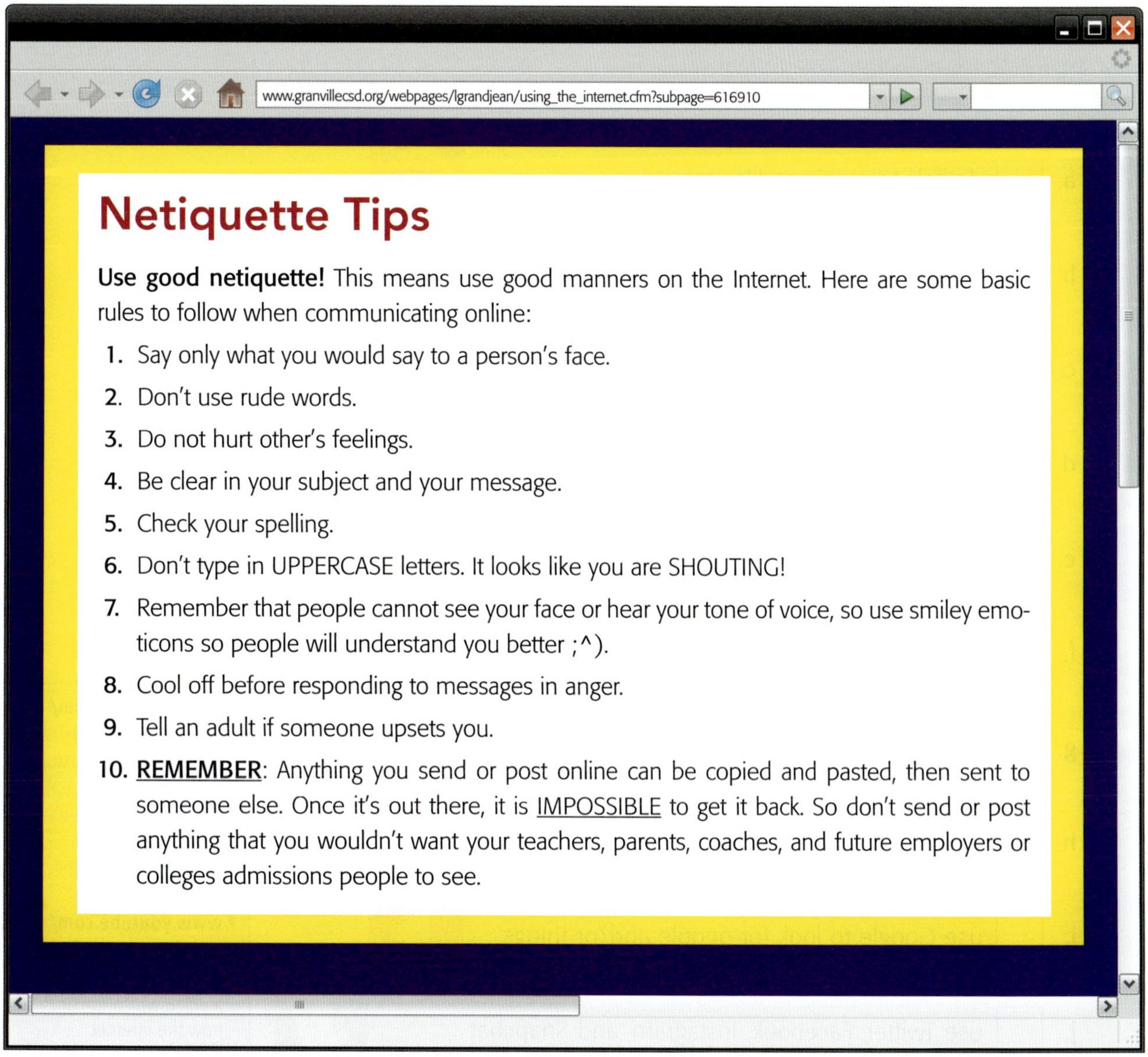

Netiquette Tips

Use good netiquette! This means use good manners on the Internet. Here are some basic rules to follow when communicating online:

1. Say only what you would say to a person's face.
2. Don't use rude words.
3. Do not hurt other's feelings.
4. Be clear in your subject and your message.
5. Check your spelling.
6. Don't type in UPPERCASE letters. It looks like you are SHOUTING!
7. Remember that people cannot see your face or hear your tone of voice, so use smiley emoticons so people will understand you better ;^).
8. Cool off before responding to messages in anger.
9. Tell an adult if someone upsets you.
10. REMEMBER: Anything you send or post online can be copied and pasted, then sent to someone else. Once it's out there, it is IMPOSSIBLE to get it back. So don't send or post anything that you wouldn't want your teachers, parents, coaches, and future employers or colleges admissions people to see.

Extracted from: <www.granvillecsd.org/webpages/lgrandjean/using_the_internet.cfm?subpage=616910>. Accessed on: May 21, 2016.

a. ☐ The tips are about good manners on the internet.

b. ☐ These tips have been especially written for internet users.

c. ☐ All of them begin with the imperative form of the verbs.

d. ☐ The tips are preceded by bullets and/or numbers.

e. ☐ The language used is informal.

WRITING

2. In pairs, create two or three new tips to add to the ones on page 140. Follow these steps.
   - Discuss with a classmate about other aspects of netiquette that you could talk about in your tips.
   - Some suggestions are:
     - how to end messages politely;
     - use of appropriate language;
     - use of capital letters and emoticons;
     - selection of content to be posted on social networks;
     - how long it is acceptable to wait before you answer a message.
   - Select the tips you wish to add.
   - Research about the topics you selected and write the tips.
   - If necessary, use a dictionary.
   - Make sure your text respects the characteristics of tips.
   - Write a draft in your notebook.
   - Show your draft to your teacher.
   - Ask your teacher for suggestions on how to improve your text and adjust it accordingly.

AFTER WRITING

- Compare your tips with your classmates'.
- Put together a section of tips using everyone's contribution. Make sure there are no repetitions.
- Ask your teacher to post the tips on the school website, blog or social network.

SELF-EVALUATION

Check the true sentences about your learning in Unit 7.
In this unit you have learned to:

- [ ] talk about events that happened in the past;
- [ ] discuss changes in the use of the internet;
- [ ] read and write tips.

Reflecting...

- **What did I learn about the use of the verb to be in the past?**
- **What did I learn about writing tips?**
- **What questions do I still have about the use of the verb to be in the past?**

Brazilian capitals with best internet connection

Brazil is a large country with a huge territory. It is not easy or cheap to provide internet access to the whole country, so it can vary greatly. Some locations have good broadband connections while others have no broadband at all. Substantial investments in the expansion of Brazil's internet infrastructure recently made by the Brazilian government and private initiatives may change that.

Fastest ISPs in Brazil

PC Magazine identified the fastest Internet Service Providers (ISPs) available by rating each one, using their Internet Speed Index. It is calculated from the average of 80% of the ISP's download speed and 20% of its upload speed. The broadband speeds are measured in megabits per second (mbps). They are highest in the most populated cities, so it is no surprise that the best internet connections are located in capitals such as São Paulo and Rio de Janeiro, as it can be seen in the rank below.

1. São Paulo (São Paulo)
   Speed Index: 16.7 mbps
   Average Download Speed: 19 mbps
   Average Upload Speed: 7 mbps
2. Curitiba (Paraná)
   Speed Index: 12 mbps
   Average Download Speed: 14 mbps
   Average Upload Speed: 5 mbps
3. Rio de Janeiro (Rio de Janeiro)
   Speed Index: 11.4 mbps
   Average Download Speed: 13.8 mbps
   Average Upload Speed: 4 mbps
4. Natal (Rio Grande do Norte)
   Speed Index: 10.8 mbps
   Average Download Speed: 13.6 mbps
   Average Upload Speed: 3 mbps
5. Porto Alegre (Rio Grande do Sul)
   Speed Index: 10.4 mbps
   Average Download Speed: 13.5 mbps
   Average Upload Speed: 2 mbps
6. Recife (Pernambuco)
   Speed Index: 8.9 mbps
   Average Download Speed: 10.5 mbps
   Average Upload Speed: 2 mbps
7. Fortaleza (Ceará)
   Speed Index: 8.2 mbps
   Average Download Speed: 10 mbps
   Average Upload Speed: 2.5 mbps
8. Belo Horizonte (Minas Gerais)
   Speed Index: 7.8 mbps
   Average Download Speed: 9.8 mbps
   Average Upload Speed: 2 mbps
9. Brasília (Federal District)
   Speed Index: 7.3 mbps
   Average Download Speed: 9.7 mbps
   Average Upload Speed: 2.1 mbps
10. Salvador (Bahia)
    Speed Index: 7.3 mbps
    Average Download Speed: 9.7 mbps
    Average Upload Speed: 2 mbps

broadband: banda larga **average:** média **megabits per second (mbps):** *megabits* por segundo

But the Olhar Digital website has found a different result. An extensive research from Agência Nacional de Telecomunicações (Anatel) included every telecommunication company available and compared mobile and broadband internet services. So, Anatel ranked the states with the best internet connection available, instead of a specific city. Here are the results.

1. Rio de Janeiro: 14.72 mbps
2. Federal District: 14.41 mbps
3. Alagoas: 13.93 mbps
4. Bahia: 13.86 mbps
5. São Paulo: 12.57 mbps
6. Espírito Santo: 12.34 mbps
7. Mato Grosso do Sul: 12.34 mbps
8. Santa Catarina: 12.27 mbps
9. Rio Grande do Sul: 11.92 mbps
10. Pernambuco: 11.33 mbps

It was found that Brazilian broadband connections have an average download speed of 9.9 mbps. That places Brazil in the 80th position out of 190 countries.

Adapted from: <thebrazilbusiness.com/article/brazilian-capitals-with-best-internet-connection>. Accessed on: May 20, 2016.

1. The article mentioned that "the broadband speeds [...] are highest in the most populated cities." Research the top 10 most populated cities in Brazil and write down the information on the table. Then compare it to the list of top 10 Brazilian capitals with best internet connection. It this affirmation true?

____

____

	State	City	Population
1.			
2.			
3.			
4.			
5.			
6.			
7.			
8.			
9.			
10.			

2. Locate and number the states mentioned in the ranking by Olhar Digital from 1 to 10 in the blank map of Brazil.

UNIT

8

Say no to cyberbullying!

Word clouds are visual representations of a concept or text. They are composed by words in different colors, sizes and orientation. Word clouds are used to illustrate news, articles, and other publications, since they have a strong visual impact.

REPRODUÇÃO

Your learning objectives for this unit are...

- to reflect and express your opinion about bullying and cyberbullying;
- to talk about events that happened in the past;
- to read and write posters.

EXCHANGING IDEAS

1. Look at the word cloud below. What shape does the word cloud form?
2. Which words from the cloud do you know? What do they mean?
3. Which word stands out in the cloud? Do you know what it means?
4. What connection do you make between the word that stands out and the others in the cloud?

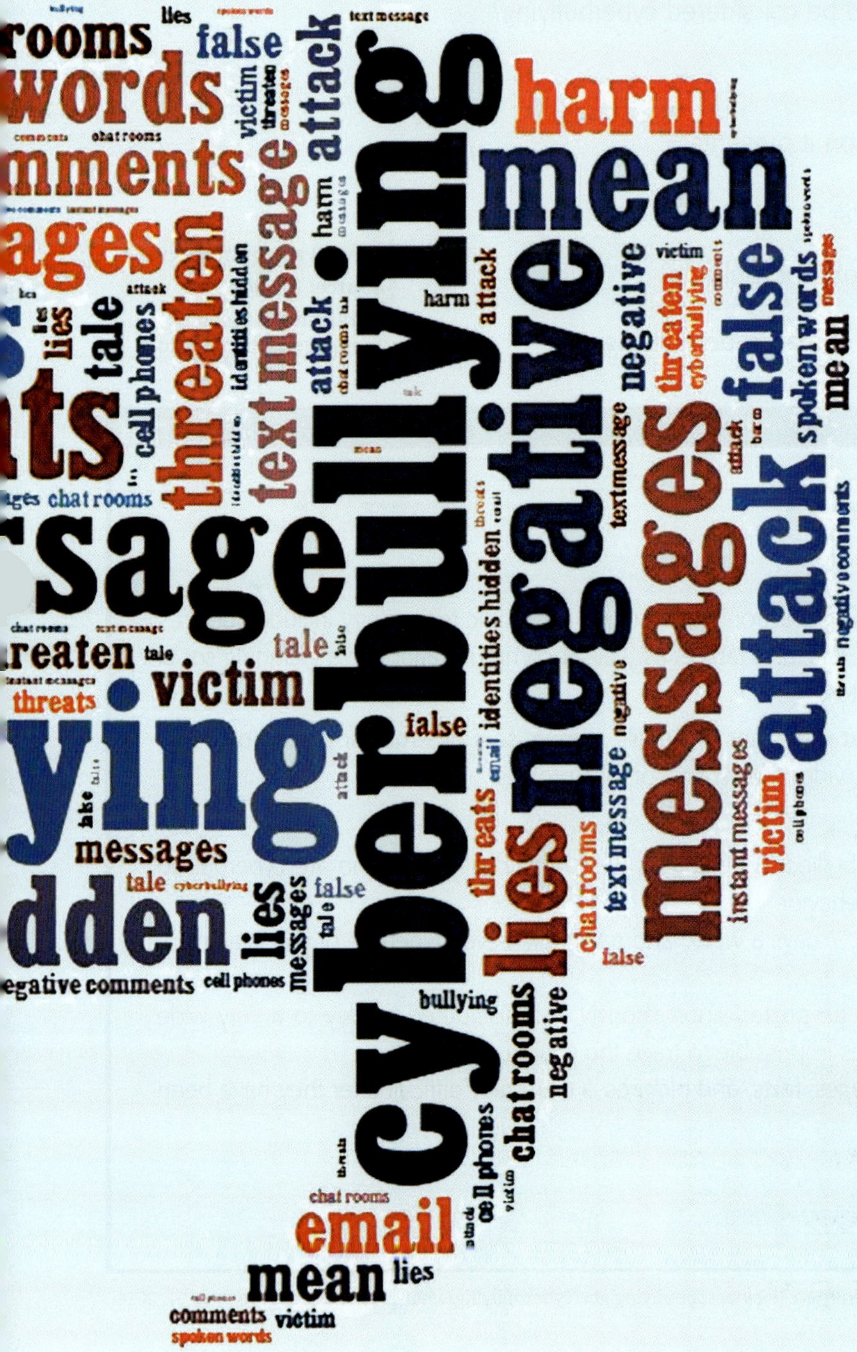

• **http://www.wordle.net/**
Free website to create word clouds.

8 Say no to cyberbullying!

READING COMPREHENSION

TEXT 1

BEFORE READING

1. Bullying is a type of repeated aggressive behavior which includes attacking someone physically or verbally.
   a. You will read a text about cyberbullying. What is the difference between bullying and cyberbullying?
   b. In your opinion, what actions could be considered cyberbullying?

READING

2. Skim the text and check the information it presents.
   a. ☐ The definition of cyberbullying.
   b. ☐ Reasons and consequences of cyberbullying.
   c. ☐ Examples of devices used to spread cyberbullying.

as well as: assim como
source: fonte
harassing messages: mensagens de assédio

www.stopbullying.gov/cyberbullying/what-is-it

What Is Cyberbullying

Cyberbullying is bullying that takes place using electronic technology. Electronic technology includes devices and equipment such as cell phones, computers, and tablets as well as communication tools including social media sites, text messages, chat, and websites.

Examples of cyberbullying include mean text messages or emails, rumors sent by email or posted on social networking sites, and embarrassing pictures, videos, websites, or fake profiles.

Why Cyberbullying Is Different

Kids who are being cyberbullied are often bullied in person as well. Additionally, kids who are cyberbullied have a harder time getting away from the behavior.

- Cyberbullying can happen 24 hours a day, 7 days a week, and reach a kid even when he or she is alone. It can happen any time of the day or night.
- Cyberbullying messages and images can be posted anonymously and distributed quickly to a very wide audience. It can be difficult and sometimes impossible to trace the source.
- Deleting inappropriate or harassing messages, texts, and pictures is extremely difficult after they have been posted or sent.

[...]

Extracted from: <www.stopbullying.gov/cyberbullying/what-is-it>. Accessed on: May 21, 2016.

3. Read the text on page 146 again and write **T** (true), **F** (false), or **NM** (not mentioned).

a. ☐ Cyberbullying is the use of electronic technology to embarrass another person.

b. ☐ Cell phones are the most used devices to spread cyberbullying.

c. ☐ Rumors aren't harmful, so they can't be considered an example of cyberbullying.

d. ☐ A person that is cyberbullied can be bullied in person too.

e. ☐ It's very easy to find the source of messages and pictures after they have been posted.

The word **bullying** comes from the word **bully**, which defines a person who frightens or hurts someone that is weaker than they are.

4. Make the sentences meaningful by completing them with their corresponding parts from the box.

be alone when bullied happen any time send mean messages by email or text them usually done anonymously

a. A cyberbullying victim can ____________________.

b. Cyberbullying is ____________________.

c. Bullies can ____________________.

d. Cyberbullying can ____________________.

5. Check what a person can do to avoid spreading cyberbullying.

a. ☐ If you see embarrassing pictures or posts on social networks, don't like or share them.

b. ☐ If you notice that your friend is a bully, talk to him or her about how wrong his or her attitude is.

c. ☐ Ignore what you see or read.

d. ☐ Delete fake profiles and inform the social network provider.

e. ☐ Ask your parents or teacher for advice.

6. Write one more item to be included with the ones you checked in activity 5.

____

AFTER READING

- Who can you turn to, in case you want to report or talk about someone's bullying behavior?
- How can family members help avoid problems caused by the inadequate use of technology among students?

TEXT 2

BEFORE READING

1. Look at the poster and underline the correct answer to the following question: Who is the target audience?

   a. Teens and parents.

   b. Teachers and parents.

2. Read the title of the poster and answer: What is its topic?

> • ***Cyberbully***
> Direction: Charles Binamé. Canada: Discovery – Gaiam, 2011. 87 min.
> This movie tells the story of struggle and resilience of a girl who suffers cyberbullying when using a social network website.

READING

3. Read the poster below and check if your answer in activity 1 is correct.

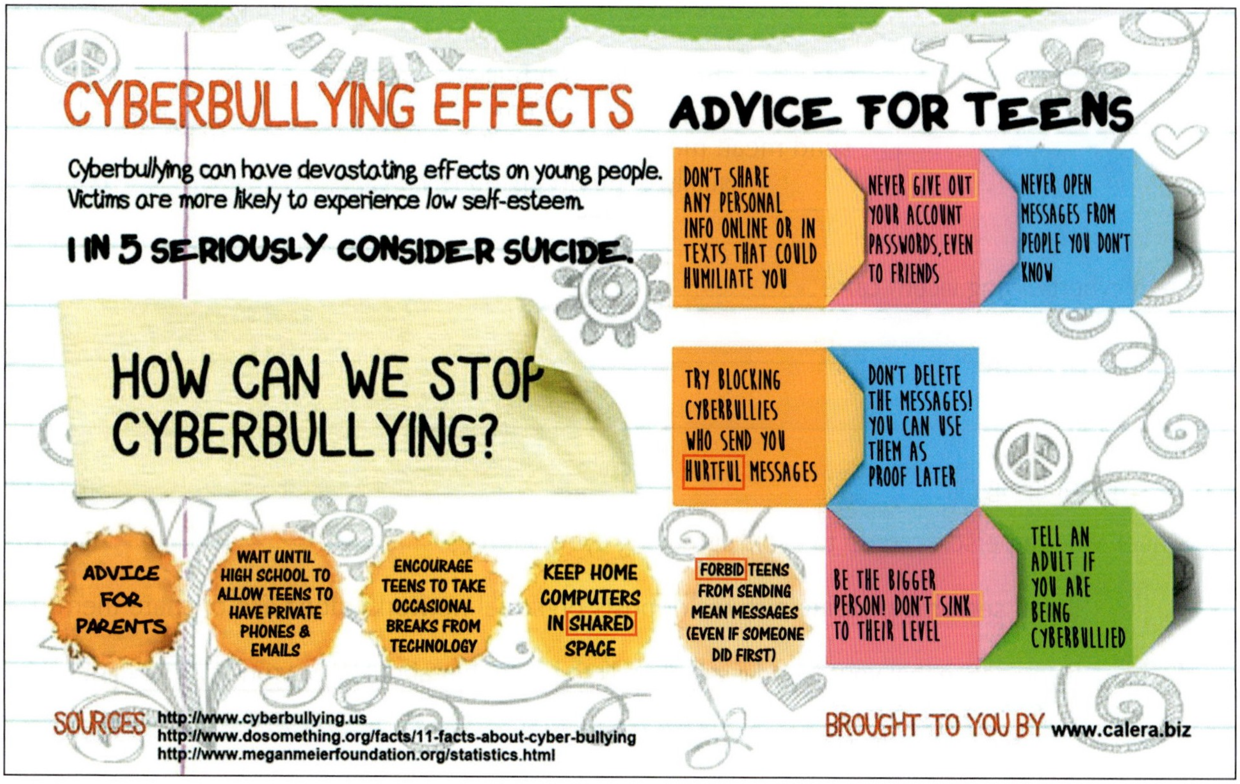

Extracted from: <terkinn.wordpress.com/category/cyber-bulling/page/2/>. Accessed on: Apr. 17, 2015.

give out: entregue
hurtful: ofensivas
shared: compartilhado
forbid: proibir
sink: caia

> Before you start reading a text, research about the topic and talk to people about the issue. Having background knowledge makes the reading more satisfying.

> • **https://esafety.gov.au/?from=cybersmart**
> Australian government's official website about cyberbullying. There are sections aimed at teenagers, with videos and games about the topic to help them prevent cyberbullying.
> • **http://www.stopbullying.gov/**
> Anti-bullying website from different American governmental agencies. There is information about how to prevent and deal with bullying and cyberbullying.

4. Check the pieces of advice related to cyberbullying prevention. Then answer the question that follows.

- NEVER GIVE OUT YOUR ACCOUNT PASSWORDS, EVEN TO FRIENDS. ☐
- DON'T DELETE THE MESSAGES! YOU CAN USE THEM AS PROOF LATER. ☐
- DON'T SHARE ANY PERSONAL INFO ONLINE OR IN TEXTS THAT COULD HUMILIATE YOU. ☐
- TELL AN ADULT IF YOU ARE BEING CYBERBULLIED. ☐

What are the other pieces of advice related to?

____

____

____

5. Read the pieces of advice given to parents. Do you agree with all of them? Why?

____

____

____

6. Write a piece of advice similar to the ones in the poster against bullying and cyberbullying. Then share it with a classmate.

____

____

____

7. Read the poster again and check some of its characteristics.

a. ☐ It presents a title.

b. ☐ It is colorful, so it calls people's attention to the message.

c. ☐ The text is long and detailed.

d. ☐ The text is short, so the information is quick and efficient.

AFTER READING

- Do you agree that both the bully and the bullied need help? Justify.
- Why are antibullying campaigns important?

FOCUS ON VOCABULARY

1. Match the pictures to the sentences.

THINKSTOCK/GETTY IMAGES

THINKSTOCK/GETTY IMAGES

O DRISCOLL IMAGING/SHUTTERSTOCK

☐ The girls from 8C are spreading terrible rumors about Betty. They are making her feel uncomfortable and sad.

☐ Carmen is very mean to her friend Tess. Carmen likes to intimidate her just because Carmen is older than Tess.

☐ Ryan is embarrassed to tell his teacher that kids at school are sending him insulting text messages.

2. Find the words from the box on the poster on page 148 and circle them. Use the words to complete the sentences.

advice	mean	self-esteem	share

a. It is good to ______________ – but sometimes sharing online can be dangerous.

b. Sending ______________ messages or threats to a person's email account or cell phone is considered cyberbullying.

c. ______________ is made up of the thoughts, feelings and opinions we have about ourselves.

d. Celia gave me some wise ______________: "Tell your parents or go to the school principal".

3. Check the appropriate alternatives and complete the sentences.

a. Kathleen is getting many cruel messages in her email account. She needs to ____________ this user ID as soon as possible.

☐ block ☐ post

b. Gunther is rude to Samantha. He is ____________, such as chubby and four eyes. I really don't like this.

☐ being nice calling her ☐ calling her names

c. Emily sometimes posts some ____________ messages on the school website about me and my family. We are no longer friends.

☐ embarrassing ☐ happy

d. Building self-esteem is important for bullying ____________.

☐ prevention ☐ motivation

- ***Next Door***

  Robert Campbell. Helbling Readers. Starter. 1 ed. São Paulo: Disal, 2010.

  Strange things happen when a family with twins moves to a house next to Eoin's. The twins are bullied by their other students at school, who say the twins are from a different planet. Eoin decides to investigate the twins' origin.

- ***"Mean"***

  Taylor Swift. CD *Speak Now*. Big Machine, 2010. Track 6.

  The song claims that bullying hurts, but people can overcome and defeat it.

4. Read the quote from the Chinese actor Jackie Chan and write **T** (true) or **F** (false).

"I was bullied quite a lot when I was growing up in my Peking Opera School. I allowed myself to be bullied because I was scared and didn't know how to defend myself. I was bullied until I prevented a new student from being bullied. By standing up for him, I learned to stand up for myself."
(Jackie Chan)

GLOBE PHOTOS/ZUMA PRESS/GLOW IMAGES

Extracted from: <nobullying.com/cyber-bullying-quotes>. Accessed on: May 21, 2016.

a. ☐ Jackie Chan was strong and confident when he was a child.

b. ☐ He was scared and had no idea how to defend himself.

c. ☐ By helping a new student, he learned to defend himself.

d. ☐ He was bullied on movie sets.

- **www.chegadebullying.com.br**

  This Brazilian website is about bullying and its consequences and how to prevent it.

IT'S YOUR TURN!

Walk around the classroom and ask two classmates if they have a sidekick friend or family member in their lives. You can ask: *Do you have a sidekick friend in your life? Who is he/she?* Share this information with your classmates. You can say: *Melinda's sidekick is her best friend Susanne.*

LANGUAGE IN USE

Simple past (regular verbs)

1. Read the comic strip and check the correct alternatives to complete the statements.

on purpose: de propósito

a. The first panel of the comic strip is about a situation

☐ in the present.

☐ in the past.

b. Jon burned Garfield's toast

☐ every morning.

☐ that Monday morning.

c. Jon burned Garfield's toast because he

☐ wanted to do that.

☐ was on the phone with Liz.

d. In the last panel, Garfield's thoughts indicates that

☐ Jon is never hostile on Mondays.

☐ this wasn't Jon's first hostile Monday morning.

e. Initially, Jon

☐ seems sad. But then he says he did that on purpose.

☐ is hostile because Garfield doesn't want to eat the burned toast.

2. Match the parts to form sentences about the simple past.

a. We use the simple past to talk about completed actions...

b. Regular verbs such as **to burn** in the comic strip above...

☐ end in **-ed**.

☐ that started and finished at a specific time in the past.

3. Check the alternative that best completes the dialogue. Then write the verbs in the spaces provided.

Connor: Hi, Mrs. Andrews. Can I talk to you for a moment?
Mrs. Andrews: Sure, Connor. How can I help you?
Connor: It turns out that I was with Michelle yesterday and a strange thing ________. She ________ at her cell phone and ________ to cry. I ________ her what was wrong, and she ________ that it was nothing. Later, I found out that the girls from 8B were bullying her. I think Michelle is scared and she won't tell her friends or parents about what is going on.
Mrs. Andrews: This is a serious matter. I'll talk to the principal right now. Thank you, Connor.
Connor: Thanks for your help, Mrs. Andrews.

a. ☐ asked, looked, answered, wanted, started

b. ☐ happened, looked, started, asked, answered

c. ☐ happened, looked, answered, wanted, started

PRONUNCIATION PRACTICE

27 Listen to the verbs below and pay attention to the pronunciation of the -**ed** endings.

a. lov**ed** /d/, play**ed** /d/
b. watch**ed** /t/, look**ed** /t/
c. start**ed** /id/, want**ed** /id/

28 Now listen to the verbs from the box. Write them in the correct column. Then listen again, check, and repeat.

called kissed rested saved stopped studied

/d/	/t/	/id/
________	________	________
________	________	________
________	________	________

4. Circle the verb with a different -**ed** sound.

a. started – helped – visited
b. opened – learned – invited
c. missed – lived – called
d. worked – liked – cleaned
e. laughed – brushed – raised
f. ended – cleared – edited
g. wanted – played – allowed
h. helped – closed – lived

5. Read the cartoon. Then answer the question the cartoon presents.

STEVE DELMONTE VIA CARTOONSTOCK

"Who **WAS** this bully who poured Superglue on your report card and then folded it?"

Superglue is a trade name for a very strong and fast-acting adhesive.

6. Join the parts using a verb from the box in the simple past, and then write meaningful sentences.

attend collect create

In order to prevent bullying, students	an anti-bullying lecture last week.
Students from 7C	donations to raise funds for the local orphanage.
All the neighbors	a campaign against all kinds of prejudice.

a. ______________________________

b. ______________________________

c. ______________________________

HANDS ON!

Write three affirmative sentences about what you did at school last week. You can use the verbs from this unit or look up new verbs in a dictionary. Give the sentences to your teacher. As he/she reads everybody's sentences aloud, you and your classmates have to guess whom the sentences refer to.

Simple past (affirmative)

We use subject + regular verb + -**ed** + complement to form affirmative sentences in simple past.

HERO IMAGES/GETTY IMAGES

I **called** you last night.

TODD WARNOCK/THINKSTOCK/GETTY IMAGES

We **changed** a lot in the past three years.

ZOONAR GMBH/ALAMY STOCK PHOTO/FOTOARENA

You **worked** as a driver.

CAIAIMAGECLOSED/GETTY IMAGES

She **played** soccer with us.

If the verb ends in -**e**, just add -**d**.

HILL STREET STUDIOS/GETTY IMAGES

I **danced** all night long.

If the verb ends in -**y** preceded by a consonant, substitute -**y** by -**ied**.

ROB LEWINE/GETTY IMAGES

I **copied** the answers from the board.

If the verb ends in a single vowel and a single consonant (e.g. cl**ap**), double the consonant before adding -**ed**.

CHRIS RYAN/GETTY IMAGES

All the students **clapped** their hands in the end.

1. Complete the text with the past form of the verbs.

a. My fiancé ______________________ (dress) very quickly for the wedding.

b. We ______________________ (help) our mother make cookies last Saturday.

c. I ______________________ (walk) in the park this morning.

d. They ______________________ (wash) their clothes in the new washing machine.

e. Mary ______________________ (watch) a very interesting documentary.

f. My father ______________________ (work) in his vintage car in the garage.

g. My sister ______________________ (play) basketball in high school.

h. My cat ______________________ (skip) a meal. Do I have to take him to the veterinarian?

i. It ______________________ (rain) a lot on my vacations.

j. She ______________________ (kiss) her daughter and ______________________ (close) the door.

2. Complete the text with the past tense form of the verbs in the box.

arrive	borrow	call	cook	decide	help	plan	play
start	stop	study	talk	want	wash		

Yesterday was a busy day for me. First, I ________________ my brother with his homework during breakfast. Then I ________________ my school presentation and ________________ the students in my group to organize it. I ________________ for the Math test and ________________ my clothes. Then I ________________ my lunch, because my mother was busy. I ________________ at school at 1 pm and ________________ to my friends before the class ________________. After school, I ________________ by Sheila's house. I ________________ her notebook the day before and I ________________ to give it back. I ________________ some video games at home and ________________ to go to bed early.

MIKE HARRINGTON/GETTY IMAGES

LISTENING COMPREHENSION

BEFORE LISTENING

1. Match the pictures to the actions. Then check the ones related to bullying.

ILUSTRAÇÕES: VICENTE MENDONÇA

A

B

C

D

E

F

- [ ] Be nice and help classmates.
- [ ] Leave friends alone.
- [ ] Be kind to everyone.
- [ ] Show violent attitudes.
- [ ] Get rude and mean messages.
- [ ] Use negative words to refer to someone.

LISTENING

2. Listen to part of the song "Dare To Be Different" and number the stanzas in the sequence you hear them.

Dare To Be Different

By Rachael Lynn

☐

His mom don't ask
And he won't tell
All his friends
Don't know him oh so well

☐

He walks to school
Nobody notices
He hides the bruises
Underneath his clothes

☐

Nobody knows that he's breaking?
Nobody knows where he's been
Everybody says that he's broken
But I think, he's just bent
Dare to be different

Extracted from: <www.lyricsreg.com/lyrics/rachael+lynn/Dare+To+Be+Different>. Accessed on: May 21, 2016.

Rachael Lynn by herself

"I am sixteen years old, I live in California, USA. I've been singing since I was very young! I wrote this song because I was bullied at a younger age, and was witnessing extreme amounts of bullying around me, I wanted everyone to know how the victim of bullying felt, and to show how bad bullying really is and spread awareness."

Jan. 28, 2015.

3. What do you think the title of the song "Dare To Be Different" means? Check the sentence that best defines it.

a. ☐ You have to do what other people do.

b. ☐ You need to have the courage to be yourself.

c. ☐ Words do not hurt anyone.

AFTER LISTENING

4. Go back to the song, choose the verse you like the most, and write it down here. Explain your choice to a classmate. Change roles.

____

____

____

____

SPEAKING

1. Here are some kinds of bullying. Rate them from 1 to 7, 1 is the worst. Then talk to your classmates about it.

a. ☐ verbal
b. ☐ physical
c. ☐ social
d. ☐ written
e. ☐ emotional
f. ☐ intimidation
g. ☐ discrimination

2. Here is a list of situations you may have to deal with in your daily life. What would you do in each situation? Make notes and be prepared to talk about them later.

a. You see someone sad and alone.

____

____

b. An old man has difficulty in going up the stairs.

____

____

c. You see some boys from your class throwing a student's school supplies all over the floor.

____

____

d. A new student in your class has difficulty in reading and writing. You notice he/she is always alone.

____

____

e. A tourist is lost in your city. He/She doesn't have any idea where he/she is.

____

____

f. You see someone holding a pile of books and trying to catch another one that is on the top shelf.

____

____

3. Talk to a classmate about what you would do in the situations presented in activity 2. Would your classmate do the same thing?

Reflecting on the theme

How do you usually respond to injustices or situations that harm people? Exemplify.

WRITING

BEFORE WRITING

1. Read the poster and check the correct alternatives.

a. What does this poster present?

- [ ] The meaning of cyberbullying.
- [ ] Tips to stop cyberbullying.

b. What does the poster recommend you do if you get a message from a bully?

- [ ] Save the message and show it to an adult.
- [ ] Respond to the message immediately.

c. What should you do with emails from a bully?

- [ ] Block emails and do not respond to them.
- [ ] Respond to them.

WITS PROGRAM

2. Compare this poster to the one on page 148. Then join the parts to form true statements about the characteristics of posters.

a. Posters have to be placed where

b. Posters have

c. The text is simple so the reader

- [ ] a catchy phrase. They are colorful and attractive too.
- [ ] can read it easily when passing by.
- [ ] a well-defined purpose and a title.
- [ ] the target audience can see them.

WRITING

3. In pairs, follow the steps to create a poster for a campaign against bullying and cyberbullying at your school.
   - Discuss with your classmates and teachers about what can be done to prevent bullying and cyberbullying.
   - Take notes of all the important points discussed.
   - Organize your notes and write a draft of the poster text.
   - If necessary, use a dictionary.
   - Show your draft to your teacher.
   - Ask him/her for suggestions on how to improve your text and adjust it accordingly.
   - Rewrite the text on a cardboard.
   - Include images to illustrate the poster and cause visual impact.

AFTER WRITING

- Hang the posters around the school.
- If possible, photograph the posters and post them on the school website.
- Invite students from other classes to read the posters and find out more about how to prevent bullying and cyberbullying.

SELF-EVALUATION

Check the true sentences about your learning in Unit 8.
In this unit you have learned to:

- [ ] reflect and express your opinion about bullying and cyberbullying;
- [ ] talk about events that happened in the past;
- [ ] read and write posters.

Reflecting...

- **What did I learn about the use of verbs in the past?**
- **What did I learn about writing posters?**
- **What questions do I still have about cyberbullying?**

1. Read the infographic published by the organization Making Health Easier and check the correct answers.

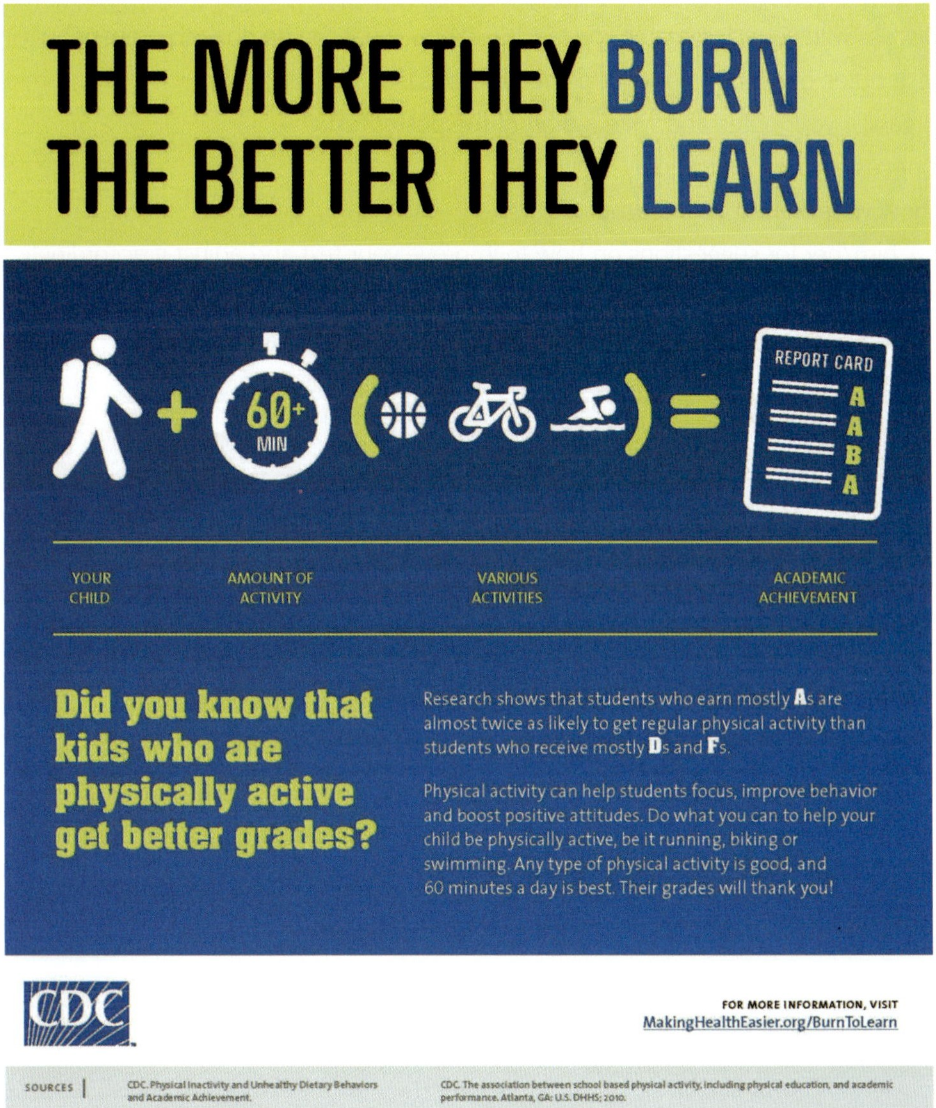

CENTERS FOR DISEASE CONTROL AND PREVENTION

Extracted from: <http://makinghealtheasier.org/profiles/blogs/the-more-they-burn-the-better-they-learn>. Accessed on: Jan. 20, 2016.

a. In the sentence "The more they burn the better they learn", the pronoun **they** refers to

☐ parents. ☐ students.

b. Which kids get better grades?

☐ Kids that do not practice any sport. ☐ Kids who are physically active.

2. Read the infographic once again and answer the questions.

a. How can physical activities help students?

____

b. Which physical activities are mentioned in the infographic?

____

3. Read the poster below and check the best answers to the questions.

a. What is the objective of the poster?

I. ☐ To help people, especially teenagers who do not eat and exercise regularly.

II. ☐ To help people, especially teenagers who do not get enough sleep.

b. How many hours should you sleep, according to the poster?

I. ☐ At least 9 hours.

II. ☐ Less than 9 hours.

c. Is it possible to catch up on missed sleep?

I. ☐ Yes, you can do it on the weekends.

II. ☐ No, you should not sleep more than 9 hours on the weekends.

UNITYPOINT HEALTH

Extracted from: <www.unitypoint.org/blankchildrens/filesimages/Education%20Center/Posters/Adolescent/Sleep%20Poster.pdf>. Accessed on: May 21, 2016.

4. Complete the sentences using the words from the box.

sleep	sleeping	tips	uncommon

a. The boy in the poster is ____________________ during class.

b. A classroom is one of the ____________________ places to fall asleep.

c. The poster presents some ____________________ to help you get enough sleep.

d. According to Blank Children's Hospital, we have to ____________________ 9 hours a day.

5. Is there any tip mentioned in the poster you already do? Which one? If not, which one do you intend to do?

____

____

____

6. Unscramble the letters and find some words you will hear about the young fashion designer Elena Velez.

CATWALKING/GETTY IMAGES

I F R G N E

F__________________

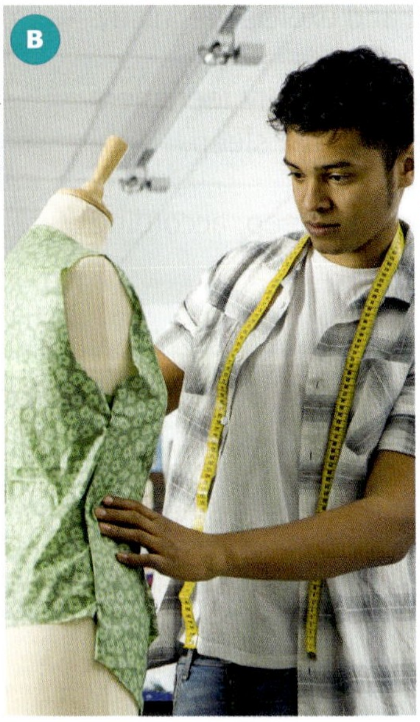

IAN LISHMAN/JUICEIMAGES/DIOMEDIA

S R E N D I G E

D__________________

THINKSTOCK/GETTY IMAGES

T E P T A N R

P__________________

7. Listen and check the true sentences about Elena Velez. (30)

a. ☐ Elena is young and very talented.

b. ☐ She is famous all over the world.

c. ☐ She can draw.

d. ☐ She sells the clothes she designs.

8. Complete the paragraph about Elena Velez using the verbs from the box. Then listen and check. (31)

BIS

be	can't	has	making

[...] She __________________ even drive yet, but she's already __________________ an impression in the local fashion design world. Remember her name. This young lady __________________ the talent and drive to __________________ a world-class designer someday.

[...]

Transcripted from: <www.youtube.com/watch?v=Sp-XDVexVhQ>. Accessed on: May 21, 2016.

9. Now answer these questions.

a. Where is Elena from?

____

b. How old is she?

____

10. Use the verbs from the box in the present continuous to complete the lyrics of the song "Tom's Diner", by Suzanne Vega. Then listen to the song and check your answers.

32

come in	kiss	look	pretend
shake	sit	wait	

Tom's Diner

Suzanne Vega

I ____________________
In the morning
At the diner
On the corner

I ____________________
At the counter
For the man
To pour the coffee

And he fills it
Only halfway
And before
I even argue

He ____________________
Out the window
At somebody
____

"It is always
Nice to see you"
Says the man
Behind the counter

To the woman
Who has come in
She ____________________
Her umbrella

And I look
The other way
As they ____________________
Their hellos

And I ____________________
Not to see them
And instead
I pour the milk

[...]

Extracted from: <www.suzannevega.com/toms-diner/>. Accessed on: May 21, 2016.

1. Discuss the following questions with your classmates.

a. Do you know your neighbors?

b. Do you help each other when any of you needs something?

c. Are you friends?

2. Look at the information in activity 3 and answer the questions.

a. What is the name of the event of the poster?

____

____

____

b. What is the relationship between the people illustrated on the poster?

____

____

____

WWW.EUROPEAN-NEIGHBOURS-DAY.EU

3. Read the text about Neighbours' Day and choose the correct options.

Neighbours' Day

Concept

Neighbours' Day is above all a state of mind, a different way of experiencing your city.

Neighbours' Day means feeling concerned about your environment, being attentive and open to others, becoming a participant in your neighbourhood.

It's also an opportunity to smile at your neighbours, strengthen community ties and develop a feeling of belonging to the same neighbourhood. It also creates closeness among neighbours and helps counteract isolation and exclusion.

History

In 1999, Atanase Périfan and the "Paris d'amis" Association launched the "Immeubles en Fête" activity in France. [...] "Immeubles en Fête", renamed "Neighbours' Day", was transformed into the major event we know today, with [...] over 20 million [participants] in 36 countries around the world in 2014. [...]

How to host a party

1 Order your communication material (posters, invitations, door hangers, balloons)! [...]

2 Invite your neighbours using the communication material. [...]

3 Have a party!

[...]

Extracted from: <lafetedesvoisins.be/en/>. Accessed on: May 21, 2016.

neighbors (Am.E.), neighbours (Br.E.): vizinhos
concerned: preocupado
strengthen: fortalecer
closeness: proximidade

a. Neighbours' Day **discourages/encourages** people's participation in their communities, neighborhoods and cities.

b. On Neighbours' Day you can **become closer to/discuss problems with** your neighbors.

c. Thanks to this initiative, communities become **stronger/weaker**.

d. People feel **more/less** isolated and excluded after the party.

e. The party was first created in **France/2014**.

f. You **have to create/can order** invitations, posters, and balloons.

g. This party takes place **in many countries around the world/in Europe only**.

4. Discuss the questions.

a. Is there a party like Neighbours' Day on your street, in your building, or in you neighborhood?

b. If so, are they similar or different than the one described on page 166? Why? Does it improve the neighbors' relationships? Why?

c. If not, would you like your community to organize this kind of party? How would everyone benefit from it?

5. Do you know the Hindu festival called Raksha Bandhan? Read about it and do the activitiy.

www.factmonster.com.ipka/A0932495.html

Every August, brothers and sisters in northern India show their love for each other by celebrating Raksha Bandhan. This tradition dates back more than 500 years. The girls tie a bracelet of **silk threads**, called a *rakhi*, around their brothers' **wrists**. The boys then promise to protect their sisters. The siblings also give each other a piece of Indian candy, called *laddu*. At the end of the ceremony, the children exchange gifts.

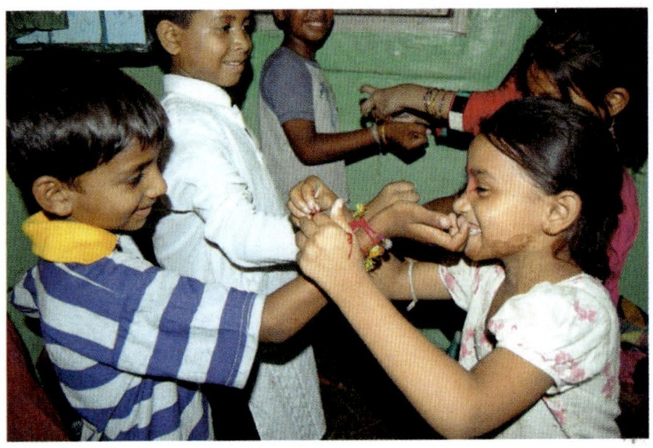

NANCY KASZERMAN/ZUMA PRESS/GLOW IMAGES

Extracted from: <www.factmonster.com/ipka/A0932495.html>. Accessed on: May 21, 2016.

silk threads: fios de seda
wrists: pulsos

According to the text, are the sentences **T** (true) or **F** (false)?

☐ Raksha Bandhan is celebrated once a year.

☐ Raksha Bandhan is an old festivity.

☐ Indian girls promise to protect their brothers.

☐ *Rakhi* is a piece of Indian candy.

☐ Brothers and sisters exchange presents at the end of the celebration.

6. Do you know who Anne Frank was? Let's see what you know about her. Choose the correct options in the text.

Anne Frank is a **Jewish/Catholic** girl who has to go into hiding during World War Two to avoid the **Nazis/French**. Together with seven others she hides in the Secret Annex on the Prinsengracht 263 in **Warsaw/Amsterdam**. After almost 2 years in hiding they are discovered and deported to concentration camps. Anne's father, Otto Frank, is the only one of the eight people to survive. After her death Anne becomes world famous because of the **diary/book** she wrote while in hiding.

Extracted from: <www.annefrank.org/en/Anne-Frank/Anne-Franks-history-in-brief/>. Accessed on: May 21, 2016.

7. Read part of Anne's diary with the description of the Secret Annex and write the correct forms of the verbs in parentheses. Then listen to the text and complete the gaps with parts and equipments of the house.

33

A few days after going into hiding, Anne provides a detailed description of her new surroundings. [...]

"The door to the right of the landing ____________________ (lead) to the Secret Annex at the back of the ____________________. [...] Straight ahead of you is a steep flight of stairs. To the left is a narrow hallway opening onto a room which ____________________ (serve) as the Frank family's ____________________ and ____________________. Next door is a smaller room, the ____________________ and ____________________ of the two young ladies of the family. [...] To the right of the stairs is a windowless washroom with a ____________________. The door in the corner leads to the ____________________, and another one to Margot's and my room. If you ____________________ (go) up the stairs and open the door at the top, you're surprised to see such a large, light and spacious ____________________ in an old canal, side house like this. It ____________________ (contain) a ____________________, thanks to the fact that it used to be Mr. Kugler's laboratory, and a sink. This will be the ____________________ and also Mr. and Mrs. Van Pels's ____________________, as well as the general ____________________, ____________________ and ____________________ for us all."

Transcripted from: <www.annefrank.org/en/Subsites/Home/Enter-the-3D-house/#/house/0/hotspot/5205/video/>. Accessed on: May 21, 2016.

stairs: escada
windowless: sem janelas
corner: canto
sink: pia

8. Read the jokes and complete them with days of the week and months. Can you guess the answers? Which is your favorite?

a. What are the strongest days of the week?

____. All the rest are weak days!

b. What two days start with the letter 'T'?

____

c. What day of the week do fish hate?

____

d. Months with 30 days: ________________, September, __________________.

Months with 31 days: ____.

_________________ has only 28 days in it. How many months have 28 days?

____

9. (34) You are going to listen about CAFOD (Catholic Agency For Overseas Development), an organization that supports social projects around the world. Some of the projects are in Recife and in the Amazon, Brazil. Check the information you think you will hear. Then listen and check.

a. ☐ Brazilian people love music and dance.

b. ☐ Some traditional dances are performed on special occasions.

c. ☐ The Brazilian government does not accept any help from foreign organizations.

d. ☐ Music and dance can keep teenagers away from violence.

e. ☐ Some projects raise funds for politicians.

10. (35) Listen to the audio again and match the questions to their corresponding answers.

a. Where is Miratu located?	☐ Berry juice.
b. What do young people use to paint their faces?	☐ In the Amazon.
c. Where is Recife?	☐ Because they are celebrating their culture.
d. What do people use to decorate carnivals?	☐ Recycled rubbish.
e. Why do they feel happy?	☐ On the coast of Brazil.

1. Read the movie review and check the correct answer to the question.

www.commonsensemedia.org/movie-reviews/night-at-the-museum-secret-of-the-tomb

Night at the Museum: Secret of the Tomb

Review Date: December 19, 2014 | Rated: PG | Genre: Action/Adventure | Release Year: 2014 | Running Time: 97 minutes

AGE — 2 | 4 | 6 | 7 | 8 | 10 | 12 | 14 | 16 | 17

QUALITY ★★☆☆☆

20TH CENTURY FOX

[...]

Parents need to know that *Night at the Museum: Secret of the Tomb* follows the same formula as the first two movies (*Night at the Museum* and *Night at the Museum: Battle of the Smithsonian*), this time taking Larry and his gang of historical friends on the road to London. Expect more of the same slapstick (and sometimes crude) humor fans will already be familiar with. Some kids might find a few scenes scary – ancient statues come to life, a giant snake attacks the group, characters are trapped by a volcano's fiery output, and at one point it appears as if significant characters have died – and there's talk that the "end will come." There's also some flirting and kissing between a Neanderthal and a security guard, as well as mild language ("hell," etc.) and a little drinking. While this installment isn't as lively as the first two, it does have positive messages about friendship and loyalty.

Extracted from: <www.commonsensemedia.org/movie-reviews/night-at-the-museum-secret-of-the-tomb>. Accessed on: May 21, 2016.

How can we compare this movie to the first two movies of the franchise?

a. ☐ This one, as well as the other ones, was shot in London.

b. ☐ The first two movies are livelier than this one.

2. Match the questions to their corresponding answers.

a. What does the star rating mean?

b. What is the positive message in the movie about?

☐ Friendship and loyalty.

☐ It represents the audience's opinion about the movie.

3. List your top three movie genres and give some examples of movies. Then answer the question.

movie genres	examples of movies
1	
2	
3	

Why are these your favorite movie genres?

____

____

4. Complete the book review of *The Night at the Museum* with the verbs from the box in the correct form.

become	feature	rush	think	wake

www.amazon.com/The-Night-Museum-Milan-Trenc/dp/0764136313

MILAN TRENC

Here is the original inspiration for the blockbuster *Night At The Museum* movies – starring Ben Stiller – from 20th Century Fox.

In this charming, funny picture book that started it all, Larry ____________________ a night guard at New York's Museum of Natural History. He ____________________ it's going to be an easy job, but he is in for a surprise. After dozing off, he ____________________ up to find the most amazing vanishing act in the museum's history. The museum's entire collection of dinosaur skeletons has disappeared! In a panic, Larry ____________________ from one room to the next – then dashes outside into Central Park, and then next door into the planetarium. Where did the skeletons go? Who is the dinosaur thief? How in the world will Larry ever get those dinosaur bones back? Originally published by Barron's in 1993, this mystery-comedy picture book ____________________ the author's original captivating, hilarious, full-color illustrations on every page.

Extracted from: <www.amazon.com/The-Night-Museum-Milan-Trenc/dp/0764136313>. Accessed on: May 21, 2016.

5. Read the cartoon and write **T** (true) or **F** (false).

a. ☐ People are at home.

b. ☐ Only the couple is talking.

c. ☐ The woman seems annoyed.

d. ☐ She can't pass him the remote control because they aren't at home.

"What do you mean, 'pass the remote control'? We're at the cinema!"

CARTOONSTOCK

6. Based on the cartoon below, answer the question.

Are the couple in the cinema for the same reason? Explain.

____

____

____

" She wants to see the movie. I'm just here for the popcorn. "

CARTOONSTOCK

7. You are going to listen to some teenagers talking about their favorite free time activities. Check some of the activities they mention.

36

a. ☐ go on the internet
b. ☐ go swimming
c. ☐ play rugby
d. ☐ see a concert
e. ☐ sing
f. ☐ skateboard

8. Listen again and underline the correct options.

37

Australian/British people spend their free time in a lot of **different/particular** ways. They **play/do** sports, they watch sports, they visit **interesting/touristic** places, and they **have/enjoy** hobbies.

9. Write **T** (true) or **F** (false). Correct the false sentences. Then listen and check.

38

a. ☐ The interviewer asks the teenagers, "What do you do in your free time?".

____

b. ☐ One of the girls says she likes to watch television and play music a lot.

____

c. ☐ There is a boy who likes skateboarding and rollerblading.

____

d. ☐ The boy who plays rugby for Oxford Rugby Club also plays tennis.

____

e. ☐ One of the girls plays sport and goes to the beach to see her friends.

____

10. Do Brazilians do the same kind of activities as the British in their free time? Discuss with your classmates.

11. You want to buy a ticket for the play *Romeo and Juliet* at the Globe Theatre, where you can watch Shakespeare's plays, in London. Look at its ticketing website and answer the questions.

tickets.shakespearesglobe.com/eventlist.asp?ShoCboEvent=True

TICKETS

Romeo and Juliet

Venue: Shakespeare's Globe

SHAKESPEARE'S GLOBE

Available Dates and Times

Any date or time not listed may be sold out. Only currently available dates that match your search criteria are displayed.

PLEASE NOTE:

Please contact the Box Office on 020 7401 9919 if you want to book for a Group; if your require access bookings; if you have children U18 or would like to use Theatre Tokens. N.B. Concessions do not apply to Senior citizens for theatre performances. Discounts cannot be applied retrospectively.

There is a £2.50 transaction fee per booking.

1. Select a Performance.

	14:00	19:30
Mon 27 Apr		●
Tue 28 Apr	🔵	
Wed 29 Apr		●
Thu 30 Apr	○	
Fri 01 May		●
Sat 02 May	●	
Mon 04 May		●
Tue 05 May	○	
Wed 06 May		●
Thu 07 May	🔵	
Fri 08 May		●

KEY ○ AVAILABLE 🔵 LIMITED AVAILABILITY ● SOLD OUT

SHAKESPEARE'S GLOBE

Extracted from: <tickets.shakespearesglobe.com/eventlist.asp?ShoCboEvent=True>. Accessed on: Mar. 23, 2015.

a. What does £2.50 refer to?

☐ The price of the ticket. ☐ The fee you pay to get a ticket online.

b. If you are going to watch the play with a group of friends, you should

☐ phone the box office. ☐ go to the box office. ☐ buy online.

c. What time is the performance on April 29th? Are there tickets for this performance?

___

d. Which performances have seats available? Write the dates using ordinal numbers.

___

1. Scan the poster. Check what it is about and who can be interested in it.

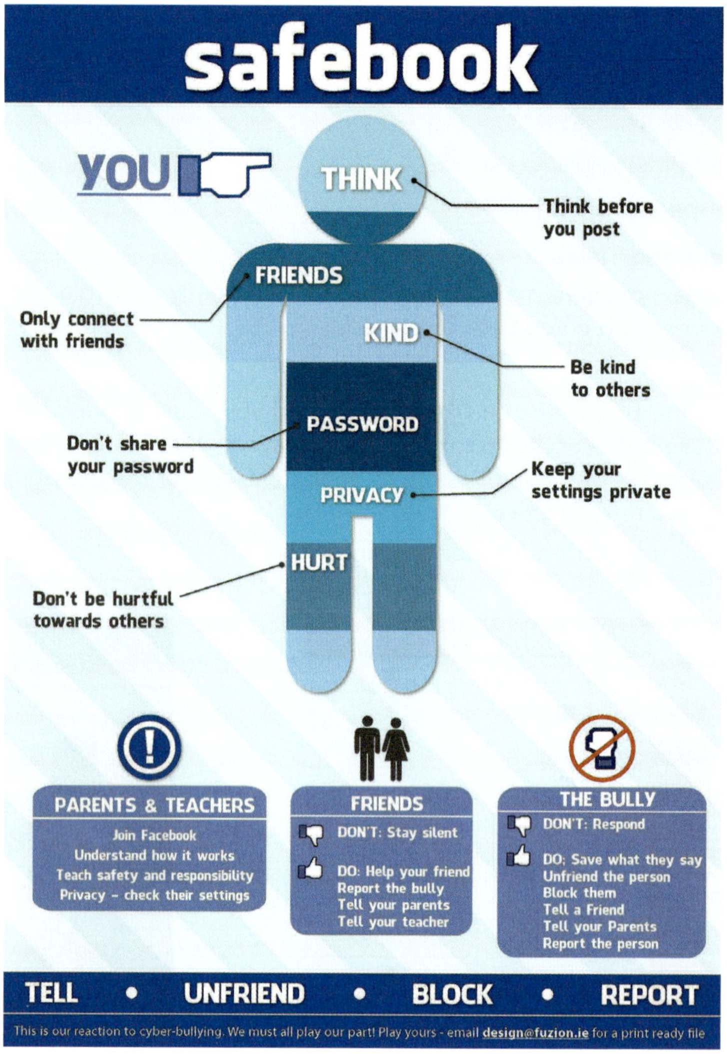

FUZION MARKETING PR DESIGN

Extracted from: <www.fuzion.ie/safebook>. Accessed on: May 21, 2016.

☐ It is about safety on social networks. Everyone who accesses social networks or knows someone who does can be interested in this kind of information.

☐ It is about internet safety. Only people who access social networks can be interested in this infographic.

2. Based on the information on the poster, use the words from the box to complete these sentences.

help	save	share

a. It's not a good idea to _________________ your password.

b. If your friend is bullied, _________________ him or her.

c. If you are bullied, _________________ what the bully says.

3. What are the synonyms for the words in bold? Check.

a. Vancouver, BC – As the province of B.C. marks Pink Shirt Day on Feb. 25, one health authority has taken steps to ensure that the anti-bullying message is heard every day of the year. Vancouver Coastal Health (VCH) is the first employer in Canada to offer a confidential 1-800 line to report bullying and **disrespectful** behaviour.
[...]

Extracted from: <www.vch.ca/about_us/news/news_releases/vch-stamping-out-bullying-in-the-workplace>. Accessed on: Mar. 17, 2015.

☐ hurtful ☐ kind

b. Family Lives offers a **confidential** and free helpline service (previously known as Parentline). Please call us on 0808 800 2222 for information, advice, guidance and support on any aspect of parenting and family life, including bullying. [...]

Extracted from: <www.familylives.org.uk/how-we-can-help/confidential-helpline/>. Accessed on: May 23, 2016.

☐ silent ☐ private

4. Read the text and check the true information about Steve Jobs.

Steve Jobs: How He Changed our World

This week in the News: October 14, 2011

On Wednesday, October 5, 2011, Steve Jobs died of complications from a long battle with pancreatic cancer. CEO and co-founder of Apple Computers, Jobs revolutionized our lives. He introduced products that changed how we communicate, interact, and are entertained. His influence altered the face of computers, the music industry, phones, and movies. The personal desktop and laptop computer, iPhone, iPad, iPod, iTunes, apps, and Pixar exist because of Steve Jobs. It is not hyperbole to say: Steve Jobs changed how we interact with technology and how we communicate with each other. In that sense, he changed the world.

SEAN GALLUP/GETTY IMAGES

[...]

Extracted from: <www2.cincinnati.com/niecincy/archive/2011/10/10/>. Accessed on: Jan. 20, 2016.

CEO: Chief Executive Officer

a. ☐ Steve Jobs died from a sudden and fast disease.

b. ☐ The company he founded has changed everyone's life.

c. ☐ Jobs revolutionized the communication and entertainment industries.

d. ☐ He founded Apple Computers by himself.

5. Go back to the text in activity 4 and copy the parts that justify why some sentences were not checked.

___

___

6. According to the text, which adjectives best describe Steve Jobs? Check them. Use a dictionary if necessary.

a. ☐ talented

b. ☐ generous

c. ☐ influential

d. ☐ innovative

e. ☐ adventurous

7. Use the adjectives you checked in activity 6 to complete these texts.

a. Who is the most ____________________ person in technology: Mark Zuckerberg or the late Steve Jobs? It's a question that has divided some of the country's most powerful tech executives.
[...]

Extracted from: <www.afr.com/p/futureforums/steve_jobs_or_mark_zuckerberg_who_pulACJ7rLf53OYIWeXikGJ>. Accessed on: May 21, 2016.

b. Enroll your gifted child in computer-based multimedia courses in Mathematics, Physics, English, Computer Programming, and other subjects. Guided by ongoing research at Stanford University, we provide ____________________ educational tools, unmatched expertise and a supportive community to help advanced students and those seeking academic excellence achieve their greatest potential. Visit the new home of EPGY at GiftedandTalented.com.

Extracted from: <epgy.stanford.edu/>. Accessed on: May 21, 2016.

c. Cardiff University's School of Computer Science and Informatics is looking for ____________________ Brazilian students to work alongside leading researchers in the following areas:

- Distributed & Scientific Computing
- Informatics

[...]

Extracted from: <www.cardiff.ac.uk/for/prospective/international/countries/brazil/universia.html>. Accessed on: May 21, 2016.

8. Listen to Emma talking about cyberbullying and join the parts to make meaningful sentences.

39

a. Emma probably heard the term cyberbullying

b. She understood cyberbullying was

c. She never thought that cyberbullying

☐ could really happen to her.

☐ when she was in the end of 6th grade.

☐ people being mean to each other online over the phone, or text messaging.

9. Listen to the rest of Emma's story and check **YES** or **NO**.

40

	YES	NO
a. Emma was involved in a cyberbullying situation.		
b. Her friend offended her on the phone and over text messages.		
c. Emma was also mean to the friend that was bullying her.		

10. Read about a famous person who has been bullied and complete the text using the verbs from the box.

started	used

Christian Bale ____________________ acting at 13. His fellow classmates ____________________ this as a reason to bully and beat up the actor who went on to play Batman.

Extracted from: <www.ranker.com/list/famous-people-who-were-bullied/celebrity-lists>. Accessed on: May 21, 2016.

CINDY ORD/GETTY IMAGES NORTH AMERICA/AFP

11. Read the cartoon below. Then choose the correct alternatives.

a. The mother tells her daughter something about

☐ the past.

☐ the future.

b. The girl

☐ knows what a store is.

☐ doesn't know what a store is.

c. The cartoon shows the

☐ generation gap between the parent and the child.

☐ similarities between the parent and the child.

In the year 2030.

JOHN MCPHERSON VIA CARTOONSTOCK

hon (honey): querida
instead of: em vez de

PROJECT 1

Conscious consumption of clothes

In this project you will:

- understand and reflect about the importance of conscious consumption;
- form an opinion and take action about consumerism;
- prepare a workshop to raise awareness about the creative reuse and recycling of clothes.

1. Read the text and check **YES** or **NO**.

coatallysustainable.wordpress.com/2011/12/01/fast-fashion-and-overconsumption/

Fast Fashion and Overconsumption

DECEMBER 1, 2011

THINKSTOCK/GETTY IMAGES

Fast fashion describes the trend of buying new clothes frequently to keep up with the latest trends. Clothing manufacturers make huge profits from pumping out new styles at relatively inexpensive prices. Many shoppers revel in the opportunity to buy new, on-trend fashions that don't break the bank. Fast fashion is great for business and great for keeping an up-to-date wardrobe, but what is this trend doing to the environment? The answer is obvious, fast fashion results in more clothing waste and more harmful emissions from clothing production.

According to an article in the *New York Times*, fast-fashion clothing, like all forms of clothing, results in increased carbon emissions during clothing production that wreak havoc on the atmosphere because they are known to contribute to global warming. While it is tempting to buy cheap, on-trend clothes, it is important to consider what went into making them. To reduce your impact, buy clothes that are high-quality and will have a long life. Look for items that are easy to clean and don't require a lot of energy to do so. Fast fashion is tempting, but by purchasing these clothes we are perpetuating a trend that jeopardizes the health of the environment.

Extracted from: <coatallysustainable.wordpress.com/2011/12/01/fast-fashion-and-overconsumption/>. Accessed on: May 21, 2016.

trends: tendências
revel: deleitam-se
break the bank: ultrapassem o orçamento
wreak havoc: fazem estragos

	YES	NO
a. Fast fashion is designed to make you feel "out of trend" in a very short time.		
b. One of the negative aspects of fast fashion is that the clothes are overpriced.		
c. Fast fashion production is harmful to the planet.		
d. Consumers should buy long-life clothes in order to reduce the impact of their production.		

Group discussion

- We know all our actions have consequences. Even ordinary actions, like buying something, involves many issues, such as the social and environmental impact of the product we have just bought. In groups, discuss what actions a conscious consumer should take before making a purchase. Do you consider yourself a conscious consumer? Justify.

Project

- In groups, talk to your Science teacher about the impact of the fashion industry on the environment; with your Geography teacher, talk about the areas where the fashion industry is present and the consequence of this presence for the community and also about the issue of slave labor in this type of industry; with your History teacher discuss how the fashion industry can identify and be related to a certain historical and social period.
- Take notes of the information discussed with the teachers and make a list of actions to be taken for a more conscious clothing consumption.
- Also, discuss with classmates about organizing a workshop for recycling, reusing and creating clothes and accessories.
- In groups, research about different ways of reusing clothes and accessories like jeans, T-shirts, belts, etc.
- Name your workshop creatively.
- Make posters inviting students and school staff for the event. Write them in English and in Portuguese. Don't forget to mention the date, place and time of the event. Use sentences that can impact the reader.
- Make tags to present the name of the pieces of clothes in English during the workshop.
- Arrange the necessary material for you to make a demonstration to the workshop audience (classmates, teachers and school staff).
- Make a poster listing the actions for conscious consumption of clothes and accessories and plan how to justify each item during your workshop presentation.
- During the workshop, talk to the audience about what you found out during your research with the teachers.
- If possible, film or photograph the event and post it on the school website or school's pages on social networks.

Research suggestions

- make-do-and-mend.org/overconsumption_of_clothes__2.html
- www.mma.gov.br/responsabilidade-socioambiental/producao-e-consumo-sustentavel/conceitos/consumo-sustentavel
- www.huffingtonpost.com/beth-greer/fashion-environment_b_3527049.html
- dgi.unifesp.br/ecounifesp/index.php?option=com_content&view=article&id=11:consumo-consciente&catid=2:ecodicas&Itemid=15
- www.dosomething.org/facts/11-facts-about-sweatshops
- www.treehugger.com/style/are-these-unethical-fashion-brands-hiding-in-your-closet/page2.html>
- www.youtube.com/watch?v=I2CrkTE8NSI

Accessed on: May 21, 2016.

PROJECT 2

Let's act in a play!

In this project you will:

- reflect about the benefits of theater for both actors and audience;
- recognize some professionals that work in a play production;
- perform a play.

1. Read the text about the history of the theater and match the parts to make true sentences.

www.knowitall.org/kidswork/theater/history/index.html

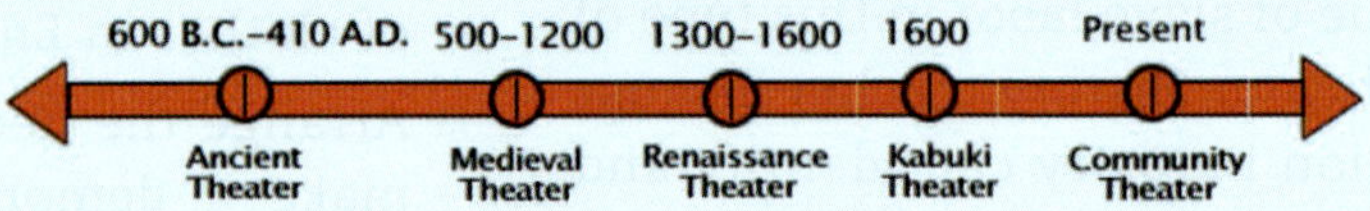

History of the Theater

The word theater means a "place for seeing," but theater is more than just a building where plays are performed. It's the whole idea behind what happens there. Theater is where playwrights write scripts, directors supervise rehearsals, set designers and technical crew work behind-the-scenes, and the actors perform on stage. All of these people have an important role in the theater, but it is not true theater until an audience is there to experience it.

Exactly when theater began is a mystery. Prehistoric hunters acted out stories about their hunting expeditions. Ancient Egyptians performed sacred songs and danced for their gods in religious ceremonies, but the idea of theater as dramatic entertainment came later.

THINKSTOCK/GETTY IMAGES

Extracted from: <www.knowitall.org/kidswork/theater/history/index.html>. Accessed on: May 21, 2016.

a. A theater is

b. A theater needs an

c. There are many

☐ much more than a building.

☐ professionals involved in a play.

☐ audience to experience it.

Group discussion

Dramaturgy is the craft of dramatic composition and the representation of the main elements of drama on the stage. The expert in this art is called dramaturge.

- What benefits do you think that theater can bring to those who act and to those who watch a play?

Project

- Form groups of five or six students and talk about the books that you have read, the stories that you have heard, the movies that you like or plays that you have seen. Choose a passage from one of these stories to act out. You can also create your own story and transform it into a play.
- In case you choose a historical text, ask your History teacher for help, so you do not leave any important historical reference out of the play. Likewise, make sure you talk to other teachers in case your selection is related to any other academic discipline.
- Organize your play: check how many characters it will have, how many scenes will be necessary, who is going to play which character, what kind of theatrical scenery needs to be arranged for each scene, etc.
- Write the first draft of the text, including the dialogues. Remember that you are writing an adaptation, so your text should not be a copy of the original. Ask your teacher and classmates for suggestions on how to improve your text and adjust it accordingly to write a final version.
- Make copies of the text, assign the character roles to each member of the group and ask everyone to rehearse their lines.
- Ask your Art teacher to help you with ideas for the theatrical scenery and costumes and give you some assistance during the rehearsals.
- Have a pre-opening of the play for your classmates and teacher. A pre-opening is a good opportunity to adjust your play and make final modifications in the organization and performance, before the official opening. Ask for everyone's feedback.
- Set up a date for the opening and invite students, teachers and school staff to attend it.

Research suggestions

- www.youtube.com/watch?v=nAvjVFNTpt0
- cultura.culturamix.com/curiosidades/pecas-de-teatro-para-apresentar-na-escola
- www.bbc.co.uk/schools/primaryhistory/famouspeople/william_shakespeare/
- www.theatrefolk.com
- www.npr.org/sections/ed/2015/07/30/427138970/the-most-popular-high-school-plays-and-musicals
- www.pioneerdrama.com/plays-full.asp

Accessed on: May 21, 2016.

Present continuous

Usamos o *present continuous* para descrever ações que estão acontecendo no momento da fala. O *present continuous* é formado pelo verbo *to be* no presente (*am*, *is*, *are*) + verbo principal no gerúndio (*-ing*).

Na forma negativa, inserimos *not* entre o verbo *to be* e o verbo principal.

Para formar a interrogativa, invertemos a posição do verbo *to be* e do sujeito. Observe os exemplos no quadro abaixo.

Affirmative	Negative	Interrogative
I **am**/I**'m wearing** the new school uniform.	I **am not**/I**'m not wearing** the new school uniform.	**Am** I **wearing** the new school uniform?
You **are**/You**'re studying** the wrong lesson.	You **are not**/You**'re not**/ You **aren't studying** the wrong lesson.	**Are** you **studying** the wrong lesson?
He **is**/He**'s listening** to music.	He **is not**/He**'s not**/He **isn't listening** to music.	**Is** he **listening** to music?
She **is**/She**'s reading** a novel.	She **is not**/She**'s not**/She **isn't reading** a novel.	**Is** she **reading** a novel?
It **is**/It**'s raining** cats and dogs here.	It **is not**/It**'s not**/It **isn't raining** cats and dogs here.	**Is** it **raining** cats and dogs here?
We **are**/We**'re taking** an umbrella with us.	We **are not**/We**'re not**/We **aren't taking** an umbrella with us.	**Are** we **taking** an umbrella with us?
You **are**/You**'re trying** our new dish.	You **are not**/You**'re not**/You **aren't trying** our new dish.	**Are** you **trying** our new dish?
They **are**/They**'re walking** home.	They **are not**/They**'re not**/They **aren't walking** home.	**Are** they **walking** home?

Short answers – affirmative and negative

Interrogative	Affirmative short answer	Negative short answer
Is he surfing the internet?	Yes, he is.	No, he is not / he's not / he isn't.
Are they playing video games?	Yes, they are.	No, they are not / they're not / they aren't.

Geralmente usamos expressões de tempo, como *now*, *today* e *at the moment*, no final das frases. Podem também aparecer no início das frases, mas não é tão comum.

Today we are learning about dinosaurs.

Are you working **at the moment**?

It isn't raining **now**.

Spelling rules

Em geral, para formar o *present continuous*, acrescentamos *-ing* ao final dos verbos. Observe:

eat → eat**ing**

look → look**ing**

stand → stand**ing**

try → try**ing**

Existem, contudo, algumas exceções. Observe:

1. Para verbos terminados em consoante + *e*, eliminamos o *e* e, em seguida, acrescentamos *-ing*:

   live → liv**ing**

   write → writ**ing**

2. Para verbos terminados em *ie*, trocamos *ie* por y e, em seguida, acrescentamos *-ing*:

   die → d**ying**

   lie → l**ying**

3. Para verbos monossilábicos terminados em vogal + consoante, dobramos a última consoante e, em seguida, acrescentamos *-ing*:

   stop → stop**ping**

   swim → swim**ming**

4. Para verbos com duas ou mais sílabas, que tenham como sílaba tônica a última, dobramos a última consoante e, em seguida, acrescentamos *-ing*:

   begin → begin**ning**

   occur → occur**ring**

How many...?

Usamos *how many* quando queremos informação sobre a quantidade de um substantivo contável. Por exemplo:

A: **How many** students are there in your classroom?

B: There are **twenty-six** students.

A: **How many** bathrooms are there in your house?

B: There are **two** bathrooms in my house.

Demonstrative pronouns

Os *demonstrative pronouns* são usados para indicar a posição de alguém ou de alguma coisa em relação a quem fala. No plural, usamos *these* quando nos referimos a pessoas ou objetos próximos de quem fala e *those* quando nos referimos a pessoas ou objetos distantes de quem fala.

DMITRY KALINOVSKY/SHUTTERSTOCK

Mom: Are **these** the shoes you want, Clara?

Clara: Yes, they are, Mom.

THINKSTOCK/GETTY IMAGES

Sarah: Are **those** the snacks you like, Mel?

Mel: No, **those** are too salty.

Why? Because...

Usamos *why* em uma pergunta quando queremos saber a razão de alguma coisa. Usamos *because* no início ou no meio de uma frase para responder a uma pergunta feita com *why*.

Observe:

A: **Why** are the students in the school gym?

B: **Because** they are training for the big soccer game tonight.

A: **Why** can't you read this note?

B: **Because** I forgot my glasses.

Prepositions of time: in and on

Usamos as preposições de tempo *in* e *on* para indicar quando alguma coisa acontece.

1. *In* é usado antes de períodos do dia, meses e estações do ano, anos, décadas e séculos.

   I play volleyball **in** the morning.

   My big wedding party is **in** September.

   I love going to the beach **in** the summer.

   In 2022 I'll be attending high school.

   She wrote this book **in** the 19th century.

2. *On* é usado antes de dias da semana e datas.

   Do you have Math class **on** Monday?

   My birthday is **on** April 3rd.

Simple present

Usamos o *simple present* para falar de hábitos, *hobbies* e atividades rotineiras.

Na forma afirmativa, o *simple present* é formado pelo verbo no infinitivo sem o *to* para as pessoas do singular *I* e *you* e para as pessoas do plural *you*, *we* e *they*.

Para a terceira pessoa do singular, *he*, *she* e *it*, acrescentamos *-s*, *-es* ou *-ies* ao final do verbo.

It rains a lot here in the winter.

She goes to the gym three times a week.

He cries every time **he watches** that movie.

Spelling rules

1. Quando utilizamos verbos com os pronomes *he*, *she* e *it*, acrescentamos -s ao final da maioria deles:

   live → live**s**

   work → work**s**

2. Para verbos terminados em *-o*, *-s*, *-ss*, *-sh*, *-ch* ou *-x*, acrescentamos *-es* ao final deles:

   go → go**es**

   teach → teach**es**

3. Para verbos terminados em -y precedido por uma vogal, acrescentamos -s ao final deles:

   enjoy → enjoy**s**

   play → play**s**

4. Para verbos terminados em -y precedido por uma consoante, substituímos o y por i e acrescentamos *-es* ao final:

   fly → fl**ies**

   study → stud**ies**

5. *Have* é um verbo irregular. Usamos *has* para *he*, *she* e *it*.

   Jane has an electric bike.

Negative and interrogative

Para a forma negativa, acrescentamos o *not* depois do auxiliar *do* e de sua variação na terceira pessoa do singular, *does*, antes do verbo principal.

Para formar a interrogativa, invertemos a posição do verbo auxiliar e do sujeito. Observe os exemplos a seguir.

Affirmative	Negative	Interrogative
I **teach** at a school near my house.	I **do not/don't teach** at a school near my house.	**Do** I **teach** at a school near my house?
You **clean** your room.	You **do not/don't clean** your room.	**Do** you **clean** your room?
He **studies** in Colombia.	He **does not/doesn't study** in Colombia.	**Does** he **study** in Colombia?
She **has** a sister.	She **does not/doesn't have** a sister.	**Does** she **have** a sister?
It **rains** a lot in the summer.	It **does not/doesn't rain** a lot in the summer.	**Does** it **rain** a lot in the summer?
We **live** in Campo Grande.	We **do not/don't live** in Campo Grande.	**Do** we **live** in Campo Grande?
You **like** country music.	You **do not/don't like** country music.	**Do** you **like** country music?
They **walk** to work.	They **do not/don't walk** to work.	**Do** they **walk** to work?

Short answers – affirmative and negative

No quadro a seguir, observe que, para formarmos as respostas curtas (*short answers*) com o *simple present*, não usamos os verbos principais, mas sim o verbo auxiliar *do*.

Affirmative	Negative
Yes, I/you/we/they **do**.	No, I/you/we/they **do not/don't**.
Yes, he/she/it **does**.	No, he/she/it **does not/doesn't**.

Which...?

Usamos *which* quando queremos fazer uma pergunta que requer a escolha entre algumas opções. Veja:

A: **Which** color does your sister prefer: black or white?
B: I guess she prefers black.

A: **Which** is your favorite day of the week?
B: It's Saturday.

How much...?

How much, dentre outros usos, pode ser utilizado para perguntar sobre o preço de alguma coisa. Observe os exemplos a seguir.

A: **How much** is this bag?
B: It's twenty dollars.

A: **How much** are these shoes?
B: They're thirty-five pesos.

Would... like to...?

Para fazer um convite ou oferecer algo a alguém usamos a expressão *Would* + sujeito + *like to* seguida do verbo principal. Observe:

A: **Would you like to go** to the movies with me tonight?
B: I'm sorry, I can't. I have to study.

A: **Would she like to learn** French?
B: Sure. She'd love to!

Adverbs of frequency

Usamos os *adverbs of frequency* para indicar a frequência com que realizamos uma ação ou que alguma coisa acontece. A seguir, veja os advérbios de frequência que são normalmente usados no *simple present*.

100% of the time ↑	always
	usually/generally
	often/frequently
	sometimes/occasionally
	rarely/seldom
0% of the time ↓	never

Em geral, colocamos os advérbios de frequência:

- antes do verbo principal;
- depois do verbo *to be* e dos verbos auxiliares.

Leia os exemplos a seguir com atenção.

Mike **never plays** soccer on weekends.

Julia **is often** late for school.

I **don't usually** do my homework in the evening.

Assim como os advérbios mencionados, algumas expressões que indicam frequência são posicionadas no final das frases, mas podem ser usadas também no início delas. Observe os exemplos:

My mother calls me **twice a day**.

Once a week, they have P.E. classes.

I don't go to the movies **on Fridays**.

How often...?

Usamos *How often...?* quando queremos saber com que frequência alguém faz alguma coisa. A resposta a essa pergunta sempre contará com um advérbio ou expressão de frequência, como *every day/night*, *once a day/week/month/year*, *twice a week* etc. Veja os exemplos a seguir.

A: **How often** do you use the internet?
B: I **rarely** use the internet.

A: **How often** do you practice yoga?
B: **Twice a week**.

A: **How often** does your grandma visit you?
B: My grandma usually visits us **on Sundays**.

Let's

A expressão *let's* é a forma contraída de "*let us*". Quando queremos sugerir alguma coisa ou fazer um convite a alguém, usamos *let's* seguido do verbo principal no infinitivo sem o *to*.

A: **Let's** order some food.

B: Excellent idea! I'm hungry.

A: **Let's** go, Daniel. We're late for school.

B: OK. I'm ready!

Simple past (verb to be)

Usamos o *simple past* do verbo *to be* para falar de pessoas, ações e situações que aconteceram no passado. Observe os exemplos no quadro abaixo:

Affirmative	Negative	Interrogative	Short answers
I **was** at home at 2 yesterday.	I **was not/wasn't** at home at 2 yesterday.	**Was** I at home at 2 yesterday?	Yes, you **were**. / No, you **were not/weren't**.
You **were** late for today's class.	You **were not/weren't** late for today's class.	**Were** you late for today's class?	Yes, I **was**. / No, I **was not/wasn't**.
He **was** at the gym in the morning.	He **was not/wasn't** at the gym in the morning.	**Was** he at the gym in the morning?	Yes, he **was**. / No, he **was not/wasn't**.
She **was** sick last week.	She **was not/wasn't** sick last week.	**Was** she sick last week?	Yes, she **was**. / No, she **was not/wasn't**.
It **was** hot this morning.	It **was not/wasn't** hot this morning.	**Was** it hot this morning?	Yes, it **was**. / No, it **was not/wasn't**.
We **were** good friends at school.	We **were not/weren't** good friends at school.	**Were** we good friends at school?	Yes, you **were**. / No, you **were not/weren't**.
You **were** there with me.	You **were not/weren't** there with me.	**Were** you there with me?	Yes, we **were**. / No, we **were not/weren't**.
They **were** nice cousins.	They **were not/weren't** nice cousins.	**Were** they nice cousins?	Yes, they **were**. / No, they **were not/weren't**.

Veja que, assim como no *simple present* e no *present continuous*, também no *simple past* há algumas expressões temporais que são empregadas para marcar um tempo definido e preciso no passado. Algumas delas são: *yesterday*, *last night*, *last week*, *last month*, *last year*, *three hours ago*, *two months ago*, *four years ago*, *in 2014* etc.

Veja os exemplos a seguir.

Where were you **last night**?

Bertha wasn't at school **yesterday**.

We were in Amazonas **two weeks ago**.

Were you at the party **last weekend**?

Was Tina at home **two hours ago**?

We were in Canada **in 2015**.

Simple past (regular verbs)

Usamos o *simple past* para falar de ações e situações passadas que ocorreram em um tempo definido.

Os verbos regulares são aqueles aos quais acrescentamos *-ed*, *-d* ou *-ied* ao final. Os verbos irregulares têm sua forma própria.

They **played** in the park last Sunday.

We **decided** to travel in July.

I **studied** Spanish yesterday.

Spelling rules

1. Em geral acrescentamos *-ed*.

   listen → listen**ed**

   open → open**ed**

2. Se o verbo terminar em *-e*, acrescentamos somente *-d*.

   decide → decide**d**

   live → live**d**

3. Para verbos terminados em *-y* precedido por uma consoante, substituímos o y por i e acrescentamos *-ed*.

   carry → carr**ied**

   cry → cr**ied**

4. Para verbos monossilábicos formados por consoante + vogal + consoante no final, dobramos a última consoante e, em seguida, acrescentamos *-ed*.

   hug → hug**ged**

   stop → stop**ped**

Observe mais alguns exemplos:

I **changed** my computer password last night.

You **behaved** really well at the party yesterday, Maggie.

Pamela **helped** her little brother with his homework.

Kevin Danton **lied** to me about his birthday party last Saturday.

The meeting room we **occupied** two weeks ago was clean and neat.

Mike and Susan **traveled** to Europe in May.

I **asked** a lot of questions during class.

We **worked** a lot last weekend.

She **planned** the event all by herself.

I **visited** my grandmother last Sunday.

UNIT 1

TRACK 2
Page 17, activity 4

Now listen to the words and say them.

a. head
b. eyes
c. nose
d. ear
e. mouth
f. neck
g. shoulder
h. arm
i. hand
j. fingers
k. leg
l. knee
m. foot
n. toes

TRACK 3
Page 24, activity 3

Listen to the verbal description of a sculpture and answer the questions.

Hello, I'm Beth C. Palmer, and I want to describe for you one of my favorite things in Central Park: the bronze sculpture of a Danish writer of the 1800s called Hans Christian Andersen. He's best known for his wonderful children stories, such as The Emperor's New Clothes, The Little Mermaid, and The Ugly Duckling. The sculpture was created by George Lober (L-O-B-E-R) and installed in the park in 1956.

Transcripted from: <www.artbeyondsight.org/mei/verbal-description-training/samples-of-verbal-description>. (00:00-00:32). Accessed on: May 21, 2016.

TRACK 4
Page 24, activity 4

Listen again and check the correct answers.

Hello, I'm Beth C. Palmer, and I want to describe for you one of my favorite things in Central Park: the bronze sculpture of a Danish writer of the 1800s called Hans Christian Andersen. He's best known for his wonderful children stories, such as The Emperor's New Clothes, The Little Mermaid, and The Ugly Duckling. The sculpture was created by George Lober (L-O-B-E-R) and installed in the park in 1956.

Transcripted from: <www.artbeyondsight.org/mei/verbal-description-training/samples-of-verbal-description>. (00:00-00:32). Accessed on: May 21, 2016.

TRACK 5
Page 24, activity 5

Listen to the next part of the verbal description. Draw the sculpture as it is described.

To understand the pose of the sculpture, I'd like you to try and imitate it, if you will. Sit on the edge of a bench, or couch. Lean to the right, placing your right hand down about a foot away from your right knee and letting it support the weight of your body. This pose makes your whole body lean slightly to the right, and your legs are slightly apart. On your left thigh rests a large open book, showing two pages of the Ugly Duckling story. You and Hans Christian Andersen are not looking down at the book. Instead, it's as if he's paused in his reading, looking up to his right and gazing into the distance, deep in thought.

Transcripted from: <www.artbeyondsight.org/mei/verbal-description-training/samples-of-verbal-description>. (03:21-04:07). Accessed on: May 21, 2016.

UNIT 2

TRACK 6
Page 38, Pronunciation practice

Listen and practice the *-ing* endings in the following verbs. Then choose the correct option to complete the pronunciation rule.

smile: smil**ing**

talk: talk**ing**

run: runn**ing**

listen: listen**ing**

TRACK 7
Page 42, activity 4

Listen to Anshu Gupta talking about his organization. Check the sentences you hear.

[...]

The moment you open your *armoire*, first thing which you see is a T-shirt which you don't need. Am I right? First thing that you see is that one T-shirt which you don't need. You're sick and tired of it. You want to get rid of it. You don't know what to do with it.

[...]

My name is Anshu Gupta, and I initiated this organization called GOONJ in 1998. We work on a very basic issue of clothing. It's something like, out of three basic needs, where you say food, clothes, and shelter. We target the clothing part.

[...]

Anything which is not usable, if it is repairable, we will repair it, and then it will be utilized, but even if there is a cloth which is, which is like we cannot use for anything, we can work it into two different products.

Transcripted from: <www.globalonenessproject.org/library/films/not-just-piece-cloth> (00:16-00:29; 00:58-01:16; 01:39-01:53). Accessed on: May 21, 2016.

TRACK 8

Page 42, activity 5

Complete this extract with the expressions from the box. Then listen and check your answers.

Anything which is not usable, if it is repairable, we will repair it, and then it will be utilized, but even if there is a cloth which is, which is like we cannot use for anything, we can work it into two different products.

Transcripted from: <www.globalonenessproject.org/library/films/not-just-piece-cloth> (01:39-01:53). Accessed on: May 21, 2016.

UNIT 3

TRACK 9

Page 54, activity 3

Listen and check. Which house is being described?

You may be wondering how you make a large steel sphere into a home. Well, here's the answer: you split it over three levels, add two bedrooms, a bathroom, a kitchen, and a living room. And there you have it.

Transcripted from: <www.youtube.com/watch?v=yKcQhTX9XFM> (01:17-01:31). Accessed on: May 21, 2016.

TRACK 10

Page 55, activity 4

Listen again and complete the floor plan with the rooms that are mentioned.

You may be wondering how you make a large steel sphere into a home. Well, here's the answer: you split it over three levels, add two bedrooms, a bathroom, a kitchen, and a living room. And there you have it.

Transcripted from: <www.youtube.com/watch?v=yKcQhTX9XFM> (01:17-01:31). Accessed on: May 21, 2016.

TRACK 11

Page 62, activity 2

Listen to the description of another rental apartment. Check the floor plan that corresponds to the description.

[...]

All right, let's take a look inside this unit. So, this is a great one bedroom unit with a ton of amenities. When you first walk in you get a nice peek at the living room/family room space and the kitchen is here on your right.

[...]

The bedroom is located here and they softened it up a little bit by adding some carpet. Nice and comfy. Nice big window facing the front. Ceiling fan. You also get a walking closet, here. And naturally, your own personal restroom.

Transcripted from: <www.youtube.com/watch?v=k27RThud9SI> (00:21-00:38; 01:25-01:49). Accessed on: May 21, 2016.

UNIT 4

TRACK 12

Page 73, activity 2

Listen to part of *The Lego Movie* (2014) and check what event they talk about.

And don't forget Taco Tuesday's coming next week! That's the day every rule-following citizen gets a free taco and my love!

Transcripted from: <www.youtube.com/watch?v= tEnQnei6dk8> (00:07-00:13). Accessed on: Jan. 22, 2016.

TRACK 13

Page 75, Pronunciation practice

Listen to the months of the year and pay attention to the stress.

January	July
February	August
March	September
April	October
May	November
June	December

TRACK 14

Page 82, activity 2

Listen about the Chinese New Year celebration. Number the facts in the sequence they are mentioned.

Every winter, 1/6 of the world's population, including more than 1 billion Chinese citizens, celebrate Chinese New Year. The 15-day festival, also known as Lunar New Year or the Spring Festival, keeps up on the second new moon after the winter solstice.

[...]

Chinese New Year remains the country's most important social and economic holiday.

[...]

Transcripted from: <www.history.com/topics/holidays/chinese-new-year-traditions> (00:00-00:16; 00:42-00:47). Accessed on: May 21, 2016.

TRACK 15

Page 82, activity 3

In pairs, check the correct alternatives to complete the sentences. Then listen again and check your answers.

[...]

Over the centuries, holiday festivities have spread far beyond China and now take place all over the world. In

fact, the biggest celebration outside of China takes place in the United States, San Francisco to be exact. Ever since the gold rush in 1840s and 50s brought an influx of Chinese immigrant workers to Northern California, the cities held a massive pray for Chinese New Year. According to Chinese tradition, each year is named for one of the 12 animals associated with the Chinese zodiac. Two of those animals, the dragon and the rabbit, are particularly important to Chinese New Year. You'll see dragons everywhere.
[...]

Transcripted from: <www.history.com/topics/holidays/chinese-new-year-traditions> (00:47-01:25). Accessed on: May 21, 2016.

UNIT 5

TRACK 16

Page 100, activity 2

Listen to an extract of the movie *Back to the Future* and underline the correct options.

Marty: Doc?

Doc: Don't say a word.

Marty: Doc.

Doc: I don't wanna know your name. I don't wanna know anything about you.

Marty: Listen, Doc.

Doc: Quiet!

Marty: Doc, Doc, it's me, Marty.

Doc: Don't tell me anything.

Marty: Doc, you gotta help...

Doc: Quiet. Quiet. I'm gonna read your thoughts. Let's see now, you've come here from a great distance?

Marty: Yeah, exactly.

Doc: Uh, don't tell me. Uh, you want me to buy a subscription to the *Saturday Evening Post*?

Marty: No.

Doc: Not a word, not a word, not a word now. Quiet, uh, donations. You want me to make a donation to the Coast Guard Youth Auxiliary.

Marty: Doc, I'm from the future. I came here in a time machine that you invented. Now, I need your help to get back to the year 1985.

Doc: My God!

Transcripted from: <www.youtube.com/watch?v=SR5BfQ4rEqQ> (00:05-01:17). Accessed on: May 21, 2016.

TRACK 17

Page 100, activity 3

Listen to the dialogue between Marty and Doc Brown again. Write **T** (true) or **F** (false).

Marty: Doc?

Doc: Don't say a word.

Marty: Doc.

Doc: I don't wanna know your name. I don't wanna know anything about you.

Marty: Listen, Doc.

Doc: Quiet!

Marty: Doc, Doc, it's me, Marty.

Doc: Don't tell me anything.

Marty: Doc, you gotta help...

Doc: Quiet. Quiet. I'm gonna read your thoughts. Let's see now, you've come here from a great distance?

Marty: Yeah, exactly.

Doc: Uh, don't tell me. Uh, you want me to buy a subscription to the *Saturday Evening Post*?

Marty: No.

Doc: Not a word, not a word, not a word now. Quiet, uh, donations. You want me to make a donation to the Coast Guard Youth Auxiliary.

Marty: Doc, I'm from the future. I came here in a time machine that you invented. Now, I need your help to get back to the year 1985.

Doc: My God!

Transcripted from: <www.youtube.com/watch?v= SR5BfQ4rEqQ> (00:05-01:17). Accessed on: May 21, 2016.

UNIT 6

TRACK 18

Page 112, activity 2

Match the times to their corresponding clocks. Then listen and repeat.

What time is it?

a. It's eight-oh-five.
b. It's eleven o'clock.
c. It's three thirty.
d. It's four fifteen.
e. It's midday.
f. It's midnight.

TRACK 19

Page 113, activity 3

Look at the number chart below and write the missing ordinal numbers. Then listen and repeat.

first	fourteenth
second	fifteenth
third	sixteenth
fourth	seventeenth
fifth	eighteenth
sixth	nineteenth
seventh	twentieth
eighth	twenty-first
ninth	twenty-second
tenth	twenty-third
eleventh	thirtieth
twelfth	thirty-first
thirteenth	

TRACK 20

Page 113, Pronunciation practice

Underline the correct numbers according to what you hear.

a. 13th
b. 21
c. 10
d. 4th
e. 15
f. 17th
g. 30th

TRACK 21

Page 116, activity 4

Use the verbs in parentheses in the simple present or present continuous to complete what the tour guide says during a tour. Then listen and check.

We are in front of the City Museum. This museum exhibits the works of man from prehistoric to modern times. Today they are displaying three different exhibitions. See that artist over there? He is painting a canvas to show his technique to the visitors. In some museums, that's a routine: an artist demonstrates his abilities to visitors. Most exhibitions here don't require tickets, but some do. Let's go and enjoy your visit.

TRACK 22

Page 120, activity 3

Listen to a reporter talking about the Football Museum and answer the questions.

Over one hundred years of football history in one of the most emblematic stadiums in the world. After visiting this museum you'll understand why Brazilians live and breathe this sport. As you enter the stadium, Brazilian football legend and three-time World Cup champion, Pelé welcomes you personally in three languages. In fact, he greets about 1,000 visitors per day on average.

Transcripted from: <www.youtube.com/watch?v=fm1vxlcszTw> (00:00-00:25). Accessed on: Jan. 18, 2015.

TRACK 23

Page 120, activity 4

Read the first part of the reporter's speech and complete it using the words from the box. Then listen and check.

Over one hundred years of football history in one of the most emblematic stadiums in the world. After visiting this museum you'll understand why Brazilians live and breathe this sport.

Transcripted from: <www.youtube.com/watch?v=fm1vxlcszTw> (00:00-00:11). Accessed on: May 21, 2016.

UNIT 7

TRACK 24

Page 138, activity 4

Listen to a reporter talking about Mr. Singh and check if your predictions in activity 3 are correct.

In Education News, an Indian boarding school in Bihar State uses Skype to help enhance students' learning.
At the Chaitanya Gurukul Public School in the village of Chamanpura, pupils get extra courses in the evenings and on weekends via the free computer online communication program, Skype.
A projector allows the class to easily view the lesson.
Founder of the school, Mr. Chandrakant Singh, age 36, is committed to providing top-rate schooling to youngsters living in remote areas. One of the students, 12-year-old Pragya Parashar said, "I like these lessons, it helps me understand things better."
Our sincere appreciation, Mr. Chandrakant Singh and dedicated instructors involved in this wonderful endeavor. May all young people be blessed with loving families and bright opportunities.

Transcripted from: <www.youtube.com/watch?v=DFl0ZgM2LVo> (00:00-00:42). Accessed on: May 21, 2016.

TRACK 25

Page 138, activity 5

Listen to the reporter again and match the following questions to their appropriate answers.

In Education News, an Indian boarding school in Bihar State uses Skype to help enhance students' learning.
At the Chaitanya Gurukul Public School in the village of Chamanpura, pupils get extra courses in the evenings and on weekends via the free computer online communication program, Skype.
A projector allows the class to easily view the lesson.
Founder of the school, Mr. Chandrakant Singh, age 36, is committed to providing top-rate schooling to youngsters living in remote areas. One of the students, 12-year-old Pragya Parashar said, "I like these lessons, it helps me understand things better."
Our sincere appreciation, Mr. Chandrakant Singh and dedicated instructors involved in this wonderful endeavor. May all young people be blessed with loving families and bright opportunities.

Transcripted from: <www.youtube.com/watch?v=DFIOZgM2LVo> (00:00-00:42). Accessed on: May 21, 2016.

TRACK 26

Page 138, activity 6

Write **T** (true) or **F** (false). Then listen to the reporter once again and check your answers.

In Education News, an Indian boarding school in Bihar State uses Skype to help enhance students' learning.
At the Chaitanya Gurukul Public School in the village of Chamanpura, pupils get extra courses in the evenings and on weekends via the free computer online communication program, Skype.
A projector allows the class to easily view the lesson.
Founder of the school, Mr. Chandrakant Singh, age 36, is committed to providing top-rate schooling to youngsters living in remote areas. One of the students, 12-year-old Pragya Parashar said, "I like these lessons, it helps me understand things better."
Our sincere appreciation, Mr. Chandrakant Singh and dedicated instructors involved in this wonderful endeavor. May all young people be blessed with loving families and bright opportunities.

Transcripted from: <www.youtube.com/watch?v=DFIOZgM2LVo> (00:00-00:42). Accessed on: May 21, 2016.

UNIT 8

TRACK 27

Page 153, Pronunciation practice

Listen to the verbs below and pay attention to the pronunciation of the **-ed** endings.

a. lov**ed** /d/, play**ed** /d/
b. watch**ed** /t/, look**ed** /t/
c. start**ed** /id/, want**ed** /id/

TRACK 28

Page 153, Pronunciation practice

Now listen to the verbs from the box. Write them in the correct column. Then listen again, check and repeat.

called
kissed
rested
saved
stopped
studied

TRACK 29

Page 158, activity 2

Listen to part of the song "Dare to be Different" and number the stanzas in the sequence you hear them.

He walks to school
Nobody notices
He hides the bruises underneath his clothes

His mom don't ask, he won't tell
All his friends don't know him oh so well

Nobody knows that he's breaking
Nobody knows where he's been
Everybody says that he's broken
But I think he's just bent
Dare to be different

Transcripted from: <www.youtube.com/watch?v=j17axG1s1fo> (00:24-01:22). Accessed on: May 21, 2016.

FURTHER PRACTICE 1
(UNITS 1 & 2)

TRACK 30

Page 164, activity 7

Listen and check the true sentences about Elena Velez.

[...]
She can't even drive yet, but she's already making an impression in the local fashion design world. Remember her name. This young lady has the talent and drive to be a world-class designer some day.
[...]
Elena Velez of New Berlin is only 15 years old.
"And then I got some fringe and decided to start a pattern with the fringe."

But already she has an impressive collection of couture. "I do it because I just like how I can make whatever I want and anything I draw I can put a life."
Elena brings her designs to life by selling them herself. "I like the patterns, different patterns. Clothes you normally wouldn't put together and sort of eclectic feel with different shapes."

Transcripted from: <www.youtube.com/watch?v=Sp-XDVexVhQ> (00:17-00:29; 00:40-01:15). Accessed on: May 21, 2016.

TRACK 31

Page 164, activity 8

Complete the paragraph about Elena Velez using the verbs from the box. Then listen and check.
She can't even drive yet, but she's already making an impression in the local fashion design world. Remember her name. This young lady has the talent and drive to be a world-class designer someday.

Transcripted from: <www.youtube.com/watch?v=Sp-XDVexVhQ> (00:17-00:29). Accessed on: May 21, 2016.

TRACK 32

Page 165, activity 10

Use the verbs from the box in the present continuous to complete the lyrics of the song "Tom's Diner", by Suzanne Vega. Then listen to the song and check your answers.

I am sitting
In the morning
At the diner
On the corner

I am waiting
At the counter
For the man
To pour the coffee

And he fills it
Only halfway
And before
I even argue

He is looking
Out the window
At somebody
Coming in

"It is always
Nice to see you"
Says the man
Behind the counter

To the woman
Who has come in
She is shaking
Her umbrella

And I look
The other way
As they are kissing
Their hellos

And I'm pretending
Not to see them
And instead
I pour the milk

[...]

Extracted from: <www.suzannevega.com/toms-diner/> (00:00-01:31). Accessed on: May 21, 2016.

FURTHER PRACTICE 2
(UNITS 3 & 4)

TRACK 33

Page 168, activity 7

Read part of Anne's diary with the description of the Secret Annex and write the correct forms of the verbs in parentheses. Then listen to the text and complete the gaps with parts and equipment of the house.

A few days after going into hiding, Anne provides a detailed description of her new surroundings. [...]
"The door to the right of the landing leads to the Secret Annex at the back of the house. [...] Straight ahead of you is a steep flight of stairs. To the left is a narrow hallway opening onto a room which serves as the Frank family's living room and bedroom. Next door is a smaller room, the bedroom and study of the two young ladies of the family. [...] To the right of the stairs is a windowless washroom with a sink. The door in the corner leads to the toilet, and another one to Margot's and my room. If you go up the stairs and open the door at the top, you're surprised to see such a large, light and spacious room in an old canal side house like this. It contains a stove, thanks to the fact that it used to be Mr. Kugler's laboratory, and a sink. This will be the kitchen and also Mr. and Mrs. van Pels's bedroom, as well as the general living room, dining room and study for us all."

Transcripted from: <www.annefrank.org/en/Subsites/Home/Enter-the-3D-house/#/house/0/hotspot/5205/video/>. (00:09-00:16; 03:04-03:09; 03:29-03:49; 04:05-04:33). Accessed on: May 21, 2016.

TRACK 34

Page 169, activity 9

You are going to listen about CAFOD (Catholic Agency For Overseas Development), an organization that supports social projects around the world. Some of the projects are in Recife and in the Amazon, Brazil. Check the information you think you will hear. Then listen and check.

Music and dance play a special part in the lives of people in Brazil. In Miratu, in the Amazon, young people learn traditional dances and perform them on special occasions. They use plants from the rainforest and paint their faces with berry juice. Celebrating their culture makes them feel happy and proud. CAFOD supports these communities.
In Recife, a city on the coast of Brazil, CAFOD helps people but use music and dance to keep kids away from violence on the streets. Young people take part in special carnivals where they wear costumes and decorations that they've made out of recycled rubbish. It's a good way to clean up their neighborhood and bring people together.

Transcripted from: <www.youtube.com/watch?v=02vrmWGoJRk> (00:00-01:06). Accessed on: May 21, 2016.

TRACK 35

Page 169, activity 10

Listen to the audio again and match the questions to their corresponding answers.

Music and dance play a special part in the lives of people in Brazil. In Miratu, in the Amazon, young people learn traditional dances and perform them on special occasions. They use plants from the rainforest and paint their faces with berry juice. Celebrating their culture makes them feel happy and proud. CAFOD supports these communities.

In Recife, a city on the coast of Brazil, CAFOD helps people but use music and dance to keep kids away from violence on the streets. Young people take part in special carnivals where they wear costumes and decorations that they've made out of recycled rubbish. It's a good way to clean up their neighborhood and bring people together.

Transcripted from: <www.youtube.com/watch?v=02vrmWGoJRk> (00:00-01:06). Accessed on: May 21, 2016.

FURTHER PRACTICE 3
(UNITS 5 & 6)

TRACK 36

Page 172, activity 7

You are going to listen to some teenagers talking about their favorite free time activities. Check some of the activities they mention.

British people spend their free time in a lot of different ways. They do sports, they watch sports, they visit interesting places, and they have hobbies.

[...]

"What do you do in your free time?"

"I like to watch television and listen to music a lot, but I do go on the internet as well."

"I like to skateboard and rollerblade in my free time."

"I play rugby in my free time for Oxford Rugby Club and I also play tennis."

"In my free time I usually play sports which is usually tennis if the weather's nice or swimming."

"I like playing rugby. I'm a member of a rugby team. I like swimming, playing tennis and football."

"Play football for a football team. Play a lot of tennis as well."

"I play rugby or cricket or go sailing."

"I play sport and go to town to see my friends."

"In my free time I go to a drama group and a dance group."

Transcripted from: <www.youtube.com/watch?v=pYCr9cl-YQY> (00:00-00:13; 00:35-01:23). Accessed on: May 21, 2016.

TRACK 37

Page 172, activity 8

Listen again and underline the correct options.

British people spend their free time in a lot of different ways. They do sports, they watch sports, they visit interesting places, and they have hobbies.

Transcripted from: <www.youtube.com/watch?v=pYCr9cl-YQY> (00:00-00:13). Accessed on: May 21, 2016.

TRACK 38

Page 172, activity 9

Write T (true) or F (false). Correct the false sentences. Then listen and check.

British people spend their free time in a lot of different ways. They do sports, they watch sports, they visit interesting places, and they have hobbies.

[...]

"What do you do in your free time?"

"I like to watch television and listen to music a lot, but I do go on the internet as well."

"I like to skateboard and rollerblade in my free time."

"I play rugby in my free time for Oxford Rugby Club and I also play tennis."

"In my free time I usually play sports which is usually tennis if the weather's nice or swimming."

"I like playing rugby. I'm a member of a rugby team. I like swimming, playing tennis and football."

"Play football for a football team. Play a lot of tennis as well."

"I play rugby or cricket or go sailing."

"I play sport and go to town to see my friends."

"In my free time I go to a drama group and a dance group."

Transcripted from: <www.youtube.com/watch?v=pYCr9cl-YQY> (00:00-00:13; 00:35-01:23). Accessed on: May 21, 2016.

FURTHER PRACTICE 4
(UNITS 7 & 8)

TRACK 39

Page 176, activity 8

Listen to Emma talking about cyberbullying and join the parts to make meaningful sentences.

The first time I probably heard the term cyberbullying I was in probably the end of 6th grade. I understood that it was just people being really mean to each other online or over the phone or text messaging. I don't think I thought that it could happen really. It was kinda like in another world, kind of a thing.

Transcripted from: <d1pmarobgdhgjx.cloudfront.net/digitalcitizenship/DC_EmmasStory.mp4> (00:00-00:26). Accessed on: May 21, 2016.

TRACK 40

Page 177, activity 9

Listen to the rest of Emma's story and check YES or NO.

I had a best friend and she, uh, we got into this really big fight and then she was saying really mean things to me over text messages and on the phone. The main thing that I remember that she said was that I was a horrible person and that she didn't understand why anyone else would ever wanna be my friend. That like really hurt me and like... I like will never forget that. She would write something public and it was just something really mean like "Oh, I hate her." Everyone knew that we're best friends, but then we were in a fight. So everyone knew it was about me and it was really embarrassing. There's nothing that I could do and I didn't wanna write something like that about her cause I knew it wasn't right. I wouldn't wanna tell my mom but then it got really bad and I just knew that I needed my mom to help me so I told my mom and then she helped me. I think dealing with the cyberbullying situation is really hard to just deal with it by yourself, talk to your parents and your close friends and try and get them to help you because the longer that you don't send out for yourself, the longer the cyberbullying will go on.

Transcripted from: <d1pmarobgdhgjx.cloudfront.net/digitalcitizenship/DC_EmmasStory.mp4> (00:29-01:53). Accessed on: May 21, 2016.

GLOSSARY

A

ability habilidade
above acima
accept aceitar
acclaim elogio
achieve atingir
achievement realização
across em todo
actually na verdade
ad anúncio
addressed direcionado
admission entrada
adventure aventura
advertisement anúncio
advice conselho
advisory boletim
afraid of ter medo
after depois
afternoon tarde (período)
again novamente
age idade
agree concordar
aim almejar, visar
allow permitir
alone sozinho
aloud em voz alta
already já
always sempre
amazing fantástico
amount quantidade
anger raiva
ankle tornozelo
annoyed irritado
anonymously anonimamente
any longer não mais
appear aparecer
appearance aparência
appliance aparelho
apply aplicar
approach abordagem
argue discutir
arm braço
around ao redor
arrange marcar (hora)
arrive chegar
ashamed envergonhado
asleep adormecido
attached anexo
attend comparecer
attendee participante
attentive atento
attic sótão
audience plateia
available disponível
average média
avoid evitar
awarded premiado
awareness consciência

B

back fundo
baker padeiro
battle batalha
beach praia
bear urso
beat up espancar
beauty beleza
because porque
become tornar-se
before antes
begin começar
beginning início
behavior comportamento
behind atrás
believe acreditar
beloved querido, amado
below abaixo
belt cinto
benefit beneficiar-se
bent amassado
berry fruto silvestre
better melhor

big screen cinema
bleachers arquibancadas
blend mescla
blockbuster sucesso de bilheteria
blond loiro
blueprint planta (de imóvel)
boarding school internato
bone osso
boost aumentar
both ambos
bother incomodar-se
bountiful abundante
box office bilheteria
break quebrar
breathe respirar
bright claro
broken quebrado
brown marrom
bruise hematoma
budget reservar
build construir; constituição (corpo)
bullet marcador (de tópicos)
bullied assediado
bully pessoa que comete *bullying*
burn queimar
busy cheio, agitado, ocupado

C

campaign campanha
campsite área de acampamento
canvas tela (pintura)
caption legenda
care importar-se
career carreira
caste casta
catch up tirar o atraso
catchy contagiante, que fica no ouvido
cause causar; causa
cease parar
certain certos
change mudança
channelize canalizar
character personagem
characteristic característica
chart tabela
cheek bochecha
chick pea grão-de-bico
child criança
choice escolha
choose escolher
cider cidra
clear claro
clearly claramente
clutch bolsa *clutch*
coach treinador
coconut coco
come in entrar
compliment elogiar
comprise constituir-se
concern preocupação
concert *show*, concerto
confidence confiança
confident confiante
confidential confidencial
consumed consumido
cool fresco; legal, descontraído
cool off relaxar
cordless kettle chaleira elétrica sem fio
corner esquina
cost custar
costume fantasia
counselor psicoterapeuta
counter balcão
counteract combater
country rube caipira
countryside campo, interior
cover capa (de livro)
covered coberto
creek riacho
crop safra
crude tosco
cry chorar

cue pista
curly cacheado
cusp prestes, extremidade

D

damage dano
dare ousar
dark escuro
darkish moreno
dash correr
dead morto
death morte
deeper mais grave (som)
defeat derrota
degree grau
depict retratar
detailed detalhado
develop desenvolver
development desenvolvimento
device aparelho
die morrer
diner lanchonete
dining room sala de jantar
disappear desaparecer
discover descobrir
disease doença
disrespectful desrespeitoso
diverse diverso
donation doação
doom destino
double bed cama de casal
doze off cochilar

E

each cada
ear orelha
earn ganhar
easier mais fácil
employer empregador
empty vazio
endeavor empenho
engage chamar (atenção), envolver-se
enhance melhorar
enjoy gostar, aproveitar
enough suficiente
enroll matricular
ensure garantir
entrepreneur empresário
environment meio ambiente
establish fundar
even mesmo
every todo
everyone todas as pessoas
everywhere todos os lugares
excerpt trecho
exchange trocar
exchange student estudante de intercâmbio
exhibit expor; exposição
expensive caro
expertise competência
extensive extenso
extract excerto

F

fair feira
fairy tale conto de fadas
fake falso
fall outono
fall asleep cair no sono
feature apresentar
feel sentir(-se)
fellow colega
few poucos
fiery output erupção intensa
fill encher, preencher
find encontrar
find out descobrir
fit servir
fit in ajustar-se
flat apartamento
flight of stairs lance de escadas

GLOSSARY

flirting paquera
flooding inundação
floor chão, piso
floor plan planta (de imóvel)
follow seguir
foreign estrangeiro
formerly antigamente
freedom liberdade
fridge geladeira
fringe franja
fry fritar
full cheio
full-color colorido
funny engraçado
furnished mobiliado
furniture móveis
further information mais informações

G

gap lacuna
gift presente
gifted talentoso
give dar
glasses óculos
go back voltar
go out sair
go shopping fazer compras
good manners boas maneiras
grade ano escolar, nota (escolar)
grain grão
graph gráfico
grass grama
grow crescer
grow up crescer, tornar-se adulto
guess adivinhar

H

hail from ser originário de
halfway pela metade
hallway *hall*
hang out passear, andar
happen acontecer
hard difícil
harmful nocivo
harvest colheita
heartfelt sincero
height altura
hide esconder(-se)
hitchhiker viajante que pede carona
hold ter, segurar
home-made caseiro
hoodie blusão, capuz
houseboat barco-casa
housed alojado
how about que tal
how many quantos
how much quanto
how often com que frequência
Human Rights Direitos Humanos
hungry com fome
hurt somebody's feelings magoar
hurtful cruel

I

if se
imply implicar
improve melhorar
improvement melhoramento
inch polegada
infer deduzir
inland no interior
innovative inovador
insecure inseguro
inside dentro
inspection visita
installment episódio
insulting ofensivo
intently fixamente
interested interessado
invitation convite

J

Jewish judeu
join juntar(-se)
journey viagem
judge julgar
juice suco
jungle selva

K

keep manter
keyboard teclado
kid criança
kind tipo
kindly amável
kindness gentileza
kiss beijar
knee joelho
know saber, conhecer
known conhecido

L

label etiqueta; nomear
landing patamar
landscape paisagem
lap colo
last durar
laugh risada
laundry room lavanderia
lawyer advogado
lead levar
leading role papel principal
learn aprender
learning aprendizado
lease contrato de aluguel
lease of life sopro de vida
leave sair, deixar
lecture palestra
left esquerda
leisure lazer
lesser-known menos conhecido
let deixar
letter letra, carta
light claro
lip lábio
listen ouvir
lively animado
locate localizar
located localizado
look olhar, aparentar; olhada
look down on fazer pouco de
look for procurar
look up consultar
lost perdido
lots muitos
low cost baixo custo
loyalty lealdade
luck sorte

M

magazine revista
main principal
major importante
make fazer
make sure assegurar
make-up maquiagem
marital status estado civil
match relacionar; partida, jogo
Math matemática
matter questão, problema
maybe talvez
meal refeição
mean significar; maldoso
meaning significado
meaningful significativo
medium sized de tamanho médio
meet conhecer, encontrar
microwave oven forno de micro-ondas
midday meio-dia
Middle Ages Idade Média
middle-class classe média

midnight meia-noite
mild leve, suave
mime fazer mímica
mime game jogo de mímica
mine meu(s), minha(s)
mirror espelho
misadventure desventura
miss perder, faltar
missing que falta
mistake erro
mix up confundir
motion picture filme cinematográfico
movie theater cinema (sala)
mow cortar (grama)
mud lama
musicality musicalidade
must-see imperdível

N

name call insultar
named nomeado
narration narração
narrow estreito
national team seleção (futebol)
nationwide em todo o país
nearby nas proximidades
neck pescoço
need necessidade
neighborhood bairro
net worth patrimônio líquido
never nunca
new novo
newer mais novo
newspaper jornal
NGO (Non-Governmental Organization) ONG (Organização Não Governamental)
nickname apelido
night guard guarda noturno
no matter não importa
North Norte
Northeast Nordeste
northern do norte
notice notar, perceber
noun substantivo
now and then de vez em quando
noxious nocivo

O

odd estranho
of course é claro
office escritório
often frequentemente
oil heat aquecimento a óleo
oily oleoso
olden antigo
once uma vez
ongoing em curso
online ad anúncio virtual
only somente
open aberto
opening abertura
opinion opinião
orphanage orfanato
outfit roupa
outside do lado de fora
over and over várias vezes
overcome resolver, superar
overcritical supercrítico
overseas estrangeiro
own próprio

P

pain dor
paint pintar; tinta
painter pintor
pair par
pants calças
parents pais
party festa
pass by passar (por lugar)
paste colar

patched clothes roupas remendadas
patience paciência
pattern estampa
perhaps talvez
person pessoa
persuasive persuasivo
phantom fantasma
Physics física
picture foto, pintura
picture book livro de ilustrações
piece peça
pimple espinha (na pele)
pioneer pioneiro
place lugar
play peça (de teatro)
player jogador
plot enredo
plug conectar
point of view ponto de vista
politician político
popcorn pipoca
post postar, publicar
pour despejar
powder paint tinta em pó
powerful poderoso
practice sports praticar esportes
prediction previsão
prejudice preconceito
pretend fingir
prevent impedir
principal diretor (de escola)
printed impresso
printer impressora
privacy privacidade
private privado
production produção
profile perfil
projected projetado
projector projetor
promise prometer
properly bem, direito
protect proteger
prove provar
provide fornecer, prover
puberty puberdade
publish publicar
pulp polpa
purpose propósito
puzzle quebra-cabeça

Q

quality qualidade
question questão, pergunta
quick rápido
quiet quieto
quit desistir, deixar
quite a few bastante

R

rabbit coelho
radio show programa de rádio
rain chover
raincoat capa de chuva
raise levantar
raise funds levantar fundos
rarely raramente
rating classificação
raw bruto
reach atingir
read ler
reader leitor
ready pronto
real real
realize perceber
reason razão
receive receber
record-breaking que quebra recordes
refer referir-se
regularly regularmente
relationship relação, relacionamento
release date data de lançamento

remain permanecer
remarkable notável
remember lembrar-se
remind lembrar
reminiscent que faz lembrar
renamed renomeado
rental aluguel
repair consertar
report relatório
require requerer
research pesquisar; pesquisa
reside residir
resolution resolução
rest descansar
review rever; crítica
revolutionize revolucionar
rhyme rimar; rima
rice cooker panela de arroz
ride a bike andar de bicicleta
right correto
rise subir
road estrada
road trip viagem de carro
roast torrar
role papel, função
rollerblading andar de patins
romantic comedy comédia romântica
room sala, cômodo
root raiz
rubbish lixo
rude grosseiro
rugby rúgbi
run correr
running corrida
runtime duração
rush correr com pressa

S

sad triste
safety segurança
same mesmo
sample amostra
save poupar, salvar, guardar
say dizer
scarcely quase não, mal
scared assustado
scary assustador
scene cena
schedule horário
school supplies material escolar
school work trabalho escolar
science ciência
sci-fi (science fiction) ficção científica
score pontuação; placar
screen tela
screen name nome de usuário
screening type tipo de projeção
sculpture escultura
search procurar; busca
season estação do ano; temporada
seat assento
seat number número de assento
second hand segunda mão
security entrance entrada de segurança
security guard guarda, segurança
see ver
seek procurar
self-evaluation autoavaliação
self-steem autoestima
sell vender
send enviar
sensitive sensível
sentence frase, sentença
set conjunto
several vários
shake chacoalhar
shamed envergonhado
shape forma
share compartilhar
shelter abrigo (construção)
shine brilhar
shirt camisa

shop fazer compras; loja
shopping precinct zona comercial
short curto
shorter mais baixo
shot filmado
shoulder ombro
show mostrar
show up aparecer
shower chuveiro
showtimes horários das sessões de filmes
side lado
sing cantar
singer cantor
sink pia
sit sentar-se
size tamanho
skateboard andar de *skate*
skim ler por alto
skin pele
skinny muito magro
skirt saia
sky céu
slapstick humor palhaçada
slew grande quantidade
slim magro
slow down ir mais devagar
smart inteligente
smile sorrir
smoke fumar
snack bar lanchonete
snake cobra
snow neve
soccer team time de futebol
social network rede social
social project projeto social
soil solo
sold out esgotado
soldier soldado
sometimes às vezes
song canção
soon enough em breve
sound som
source of wealth fonte de riqueza
South American sul-americano
Southeast Sudeste
southern do sul
spend passar, gastar
sponsor patrocinador
spread espalhar
spring primavera
square dance quadrilha (dança)
stairs escada
stand up for defender
standard padrão
stanza estrofe
star estrela
stare olhar fixamente
starring estrelando
start começar
state estado
statue estátua
stay ficar
steep íngreme
step passo
stick with manter
still ainda
stop parar
story história; pavimento, andar
stove fogão
straight ahead bem em frente
straw palha
straw hat chapéu de palha
strong forte
strongest mais forte
study estudar; escritório (em casa)
subject assunto
subscription assinatura (de revista, jornal)
successful bem-sucedido
sudden repentino
suddenly de repente
suit combinar

GLOSSARY

summary resumo
summer verão
support apoiar; apoio
supporter torcedor
surroundings ambiente
survey questionário
survival kit *kit* de sobrevivência
survive sobreviver
swim nadar
swimming natação
swimming pool piscina

T

take advantage aproveitar
take place acontecer, ocorrer
take turns revezar
talented talentoso
talk conversar
tall alto
target audience público-alvo
target alvo
taste gosto
teenager adolescente
tell dizer
tennis court quadra de tênis
textile produto têxtil
theater teatro
theme tema
thicker mais grosso
thief ladrão
thin fino, magro
thing coisa
think pensar, achar
thought pensamento
thrift store brechó
throughout por todo
throw atirar, arremessar
tiger tigre
time hora, tempo
tip dica
tired cansado
title título
toast torrada
toaster torradeira
today hoje
toe dedo (do pé)
together juntos
tomb tumba
tomorrow amanhã
tones toneladas
tonight hoje à noite
tool ferramenta
top rate schooling ensino da melhor qualidade
touch tocar
towards com respeito a
town clerk escrivão
trace localizar
trapped encurralado
travel viajar
treat presente
trip viagem
trouble dificuldade
troupe grupo, trupe
true verdadeiro
trust confiar
trusted de confiança
try tentar
T-shirt camiseta
tune música
twin brother irmão gêmeo
twist toque
type digitar; tipo

U

umbrella guarda-chuva
uncomfortable incômodo
uncommom incomum
under abaixo
underline sublinhar
underneath embaixo
understand entender

undone inacabado
unless a não ser que
unlimited ilimitado
unmatched único, melhor
unquestionably sem dúvida
unscramble desembaralhar
until até
upset transtornar
usable utilizável
user usuário

V

value valor
vanishing desaparecimento
variety variedade
varying variado
venue local
view ver; vista
viewer espectador
village cidade pequena
voice voz
voiced dublado

W

wait esperar
wake up acordar
walk andar
war guerra
waste desperdício
watch assistir
water água
water usage consumo de água
wave onda
way modo
weak fraco
wear vestir
weather tempo (meteorologia)
weekday dia de semana
weigh pesar
welcome dar as boas-vindas; bem-vindo
well-defined bem definido
well-known bem conhecido
what o que, qual
when quando
whenever toda vez
where onde
which qual, quais
whistle apito
who quem
whole inteiro
why por que (pergunta)
wide grande
wildlife fauna e flora
window janela
winter inverno
wish desejo
witch bruxa
within dentro
without sem
witness testemunhar
wonderful maravilhoso
wood madeira
word palavra
work funcionar
worker trabalhador
world mundo
world-class de nível internacional
World War Guerra Mundial
worldwide no mundo todo
worn acabado
worry preocupar-se
worth digno, merecedor
write escrever
writer escritor
written escrito
wrong errado

Y

year ano
young jovem
youngster o mais jovem

Z

zodiac zodíaco

BIBLIOGRAPHY

ABREU-TARDELLI, L. S.; CRISTOVÃO, V. L. L. (Orgs.). *Linguagem e educação*: o ensino e aprendizagem de gêneros textuais. Campinas: Mercado de Letras, 2009.

BRASIL. MINISTÉRIO DA EDUCAÇÃO. *Lei de Diretrizes e Bases da Educação Nacional*. Brasília: Ministério da Educação, 1996.

______. *Parâmetros Curriculares Nacionais* – Língua estrangeira. Brasília: Ministério da Educação, 1998.

______. *Ensino Fundamental de nove anos* – Orientações gerais. Brasília: Ministério da Educação, Secretaria de Educação Básica, Departamento de Políticas de Educação Infantil e Ensino Fundamental, Coordenação Geral do Ensino Fundamental, 2004. Disponível em: <portal.mec.gov.br/seb/arquivos/pdf/Ensfund/noveanorienger.pdf>. Acessado em: 23 maio 2016.

COPE, B.; KALANTZIS, M. Multiliteracies: The Beginning of an Idea. In: COPE, B.; KALANTZIS, M. (Eds.). *Multiliteracies*: Literacy Learning and The Design of Social Futures. London: Routledge, 2000. p. 3-8.

CROSS, D. *Large Classes in Action.* Hertfordshire: Prentice Hall International, 1995.

DIONÍSIO, A. P.; MACHADO, A. R.; BEZERRA, M. A. (Orgs.). *Gêneros textuais & ensino*. São Paulo: Parábola Editorial, 2010.

FREIRE, P. *Pedagogia da autonomia*: saberes necessários à prática educativa. São Paulo: Paz e Terra, 1996.

GRELLET, F. *Developing Reading Skills.* Cambridge: Cambridge University Press, 1981.

HEIDE, A.; STILBORNE, L. *Guia do professor para a internet*: completo e fácil. Trad. Edson Furmankiewz. 2. ed. Porto Alegre: Artmed, 2000.

HOFFMANN, J. *Avaliar para promover*: as setas do caminho. Porto Alegre: Mediação, 2001.

LAPKOSKI, G. A. O. *Do texto ao sentido*: teoria e prática de leitura em língua inglesa. Curitiba: Ibpex, 2011.

MARCUSCHI, L. A. Gêneros textuais: definição e funcionalidade. In: MARTINEZ, P. *Didática de línguas estrangeiras.* São Paulo: Parábola Editorial, 2009.

MOITA-LOPES, L. P. Ensino de inglês como espaço de embates culturais e de políticas da diferença. In: GIMENEZ, T. *et al.* (Orgs.). *Perspectivas educacionais e o ensino de inglês na escola pública.* Pelotas: Educat, 2005.

______. *Oficina de linguística aplicada.* Campinas: Mercado de Letras, 2000.

RAIMES, A. *Techniques in Teaching Writing.* New York, Oxford: Oxford University Press, 1983.

RICHARDS, J. C.; RENANDYA, W. A. (Eds.). *Methodology in Language Teaching*: an Anthology of Current Practice. New York: Cambridge University Press, 2002.

RODRIGUES, D. (Org.). *Inclusão e educação*: doze olhares sobre a educação inclusiva. São Paulo: Summus, 2006.

SOUZA, A. G. F. *et al. Leitura em língua inglesa*: uma abordagem instrumental. São Paulo: Disal, 2005.

TOMLINSON, B. *Developing Materials for Language Teaching.* London: Continuum, 2003.

VYGOTSKY, L. S. *Pensamento e linguagem.* São Paulo: Martins Fontes, 1993.

WALESKO, A. M. H. *Compreensão oral em língua inglesa.* Curitiba: Ibpex, 2010.

TIME TO SHARE Jornadas

Workbook 7

Organizadora:

Editora Saraiva

Obra coletiva organizada e produzida pela Editora Saraiva

Editor responsável:

Vicente Martínez

Licenciado em Tradução/Interpretação pela Universidad Pontificia de Comillas (Madrid)

Editor de conteúdos didáticos

Coordenadora:

Gisele Aga

Licenciada em Letras pela FMU – Faculdades Metropolitanas Unidas

Professora de Inglês na rede particular de ensino e em cursos de idiomas

Coordenadora pedagógica em cursos de idiomas

Editora de conteúdos didáticos

Editora Saraiva

PRESENTATION

Caro estudante,

Este caderno foi elaborado com a finalidade de ajudá-lo a organizar seu conhecimento. Ao resolver as atividades propostas, você terá a oportunidade de buscar informações, utilizar a própria experiência e conhecimento prévio sobre os assuntos tratados, desenvolver habilidades, elaborar opiniões sobre assuntos da atualidade, refletir sobre atitudes e comportamentos e ampliar a sua visão do mundo.

As atividades estão distribuídas em oito unidades, correspondendo às unidades do livro para que possa retomar e ampliar os tópicos estudados. A cada unidade, você encontrará as seguintes seções: *Review the journey*, *Another look* e *Reading the world*.

- Em *Review the journey*, você irá aplicar os conceitos gramaticais apresentados na unidade.
- A seção *Another look* propõe uma leitura complementar (verbal ou não verbal) ligada a algum tema ou gênero trabalhado na unidade do livro. As atividades visam trabalhar aspectos que não foram abordados no livro ou que são tratados sob outro aspecto. Além disso, nas últimas atividades você será incentivado a refletir e se posicionar em relação ao assunto tratado na seção.
- Em *Reading the world*, você lerá textos com temáticas instigantes, como aspectos culturais de diversos países, novas tecnologias, entre outras. Ao final das atividades, você poderá contar com uma produção (oral ou escrita).

Esperamos que sua jornada por este caderno seja bastante produtiva e o auxilie a desenvolver a autonomia nos estudos.

Os editores

CONTENTS

UNIT 1

Changes

Review the journey

1. Look at the pictures and write what the people are doing.

a.

SHUTTERSTOCK

wait for the bus

____

c.

THINKSTOCK/GETTY IMAGES

play soccer

____

b.

GETTY IMAGES/ISTOCKPHOTO

wear a blue dress

____

d.

SHUTTERSTOCK

swim

____

2. Unscramble the words to write names of the body parts.

a. ARE

b. SEYE

c. GISNEFR

d. HEDA

e. KEEN

f. KENC

g. SONE

h. HUSDORLE

Another look

1. Look at the text and image below and choose the correct alternative to complete the sentences.

a. The text is from an art ____________________.

☐ catalog ☐ book

b. This text was published by ____________________.

☐ a school ☐ a museum

2. Check the elements of this text genre.

a. ☐ organization in bullets

b. ☐ informal language

c. ☐ long descriptive section

d. ☐ short sentences

www.britishmuseum.org/research/collection_online/collection_object_details.aspx?objectId=466190&partId=1

THE PORTLAND VASE

- **OBJECT TYPE** Amphora
- **TITLE (object)** The Portland Vase
- **DESCRIPTION** Amphora in translucent dark cobalt blue and opaque white cameo glass. Figured design carved in the white glass, divided into two portions by a bearded head. One group of four persons shows a young man emerging from a sanctuary. His right arm clasps his cloak; his left arm stretched before him clasps the right arm of a lady seated on the ground turning back towards him and caressing a serpent-like creature. Eros flies to the right, above the lady, holding a bow in the left hand, a torch in his right. To the right stands a bearded man resting his chin on his right arm that rests on his right knee, the foot supported by a tree that spreads out its branches; behind him is another tree. On the other side, there is a young man seated to the left on a rock with his head turned back towards a girl reclining to the right with her right arm raised up to her head; from her left hand hangs a burning torch. To her right, seated to the right and looking back towards the scene, sits another girl holding a sceptre in her left hand.
- **CULTURE/PERIOD** Roman
- **DATE** 1-25 (circa)
- **MATERIAL** glass
- **ACQUISITION DATE** 1945

Adapted from: <www.britishmuseum.org/research/collection_online/collection_object_details.aspx?objectId=466190&partId=1>. Accessed on: Apr. 9, 2016.

3. Answer **T** (true) or **F** (false) according to the text.

a. ☐ The Portland vase is made of glass.

b. ☐ Eros is flying.

c. ☐ There are only four people depicted on the vase.

d. ☐ The serpent-like creature is next to a man.

e. ☐ The woman is sitting in front of a tree.

4. Label the picture with the correct part of the text from the box.

His left arm stretched before him clasps the right arm of a lady seated on the ground.

A bearded man resting his chin on his right arm.

Eros holding a bow in the left hand, a torch in his right.

A girl reclining to the right with her right arm raised up to her head.

____

5. Answer these questions.

a. What period is the vase from? ______________________

b. How old is the vase approximately? ______________________

c. What colors are present on the vase? ______________________

1. In your opinion, why is it important to keep information about a work of art in a catalog?

____

____

2. The Portland Vase was intentionally broken in 1845 and then restored to the form you saw in the picture on page 5. How important is it to preserve works of art? Justify your answer.

____

____

Reading the world

1. Read the title of the text. What is its main purpose?

a. ☐ To advertise free museums. b. ☐ To sell museum tickets.

www.timeout.com/london/museums/free-museums-in-london

FREE MUSEUMS IN LONDON

Culture needn't cost the earth. Here's our guide to free museums in London

SCIENCE MUSEUM

The Science Museum features seven floors of educational and entertaining exhibits, including the Apollo 10 command module and a flight simulator. The Medical History Gallery contains a substantial collection of medical history treasures. Launch Pad is a popular hands-on gallery where children can explore basic scientific principles.

NATURAL HISTORY MUSEUM

It houses a collection that contains some 70 million plant, animal, fossil, rock and mineral specimens. The Natural History Museum's Life Galleries are devoted to displays on animal life, from creepy crawlies to the plaster cast of a Diplodocus that lords it over the Central Hall.

V&A MUSEUM OF CHILDHOOD

Home to one of the world's finest collections of children's toys, dolls' houses, games, costumes, puppets and Barbie Dolls, the V&A Museum of Childhood shines after refurbishment. It has been collecting childhood-related objects since 1872.

Adapted from: <www.timeout.com/london/museums/free-museums-in-london>.
Accessed on: Apr. 9, 2016.

2. Read the text. Write **S** for Science Museum, **NH** for Natural History Museum and **C** for V&A Museum of Childhood.

a. ☐ It has dinosaurs.
b. ☐ It has spaceships.
c. ☐ It has Barbie dolls.
d. ☐ It has medical instruments.
e. ☐ It has games.
f. ☐ It has spiders and scorpions.

3. Number the museums in the order of your preference.

☐ Science Museum
☐ Natural History Museum
☐ V&A Museum of Childhood

UNIT 2

What are you wearing?

Review the journey

1. Look at the pictures and write sentences.

a.

THINKSTOCK/GETTY IMAGES

She isn't holding a clutch.

She's holding a bag.

b.

THINKSTOCK/GETTY IMAGES

____

____

2. Complete the descriptions with the words from the box. Then match to the corresponding images.

blond	eyes	green	hair	height	slim	tall

a. Sarah has brown __________ and __________ hair. She's medium __________ and she's __________ .

b. Sophia has __________ eyes and brown __________ . She's very __________ .

☐ 

GETTY IMAGES

☐ 

HERO IMAGES/GETTY IMAGES

Another look

1. Look at the text below and check the correct alternative to complete the sentences.

a. It is ______________________.

☐ an ad ☐ a leaflet

b. It was probably published ______________________.

☐ on TV ☐ in a magazine

2. Check the characteristics of this text genre.

a. ☐ important use of images

b. ☐ formal language

c. ☐ short text

d. ☐ persuasive language

e. ☐ descriptive text

f. ☐ irrelevant images

CAMPANHA DA ONG SAFERNET BRASIL/HELPLINE.BR – CRIAÇÃO: AGÊNCIA PROPEG

3. Read the text and complete the sentence: The main purpose of this text is to

a. ☐ convince people to buy a product.

b. ☐ encourage people to do something.

4. Study the visual elements of the text and circle the correct alternative to complete the sentences.

a. The person in the photo is **a child/an adult**.

b. The photo is strange because **the proportions are wrong/the girl is wearing adult makeup and hair style**.

c. Her face expresses **confusion/happiness**.

d. Her clothes **don't look natural on a young girl/are typical of young girls**.

e. She is **curvy/slim**.

5. Read the text again and write **T** (true) or **F** (false).

a. ☐ The first sentence in the text is what the ad is defending.

b. ☐ The imperative is used to ask for help.

c. ☐ This ad promotes internet safety for children.

d. ☐ SaferNet is an American only organization.

6. Answer these questions.

a. What's the girl wearing? ______________________________

b. Describe her eyes. ______________________________

1. Why is the ad in English if the organization is called SaferNet Brasil? Who is the intended audience for this ad?

____

____

2. How do you feel when you look at the girl? Justify your answer.

____

____

Reading the world

1. Scan the text and check its main topic.

a. ☐ Clothes in different parts of the USA. **b.** ☐ Clothes from India and Africa.

BIS

CLOTHES FROM DIFFERENT CULTURES

1 The traditional dress for an Indian woman is a **sari** – a large piece of cloth that can be wrapped around the body in various styles. The most common style of wearing a sari is wrapped around the waist, with one end draped over the shoulder. Most women wear a short-sleeved blouse underneath.

2 Traditional clothing for Indian men includes a knee-length (or longer) shirt (note women may also wear these). It's usually worn over loose trousers.

3 Traditional African costume varies widely across the continent, although there are some similarities. Tunics or kaftans (long shirts, usually to the floor) are popular clothing for men, worn with loose trousers.

4 Women may wear toga-inspired garments, wrapped around their bodies. Bright coloured fabrics and beaded jewellery are popular.

fabric: tecido, estrutura

Adapted from: <www.bbc.co.uk/schools/gcsebitesize/drama/drama_wjec/galleries/costumes16.shtml>. Accessed on: Apr. 10, 2016.

2. Read the text and number the pictures according to the paragraph in which these clothes are described.

TIM GRAHAM/ROBERT HARDING/AFP

☐

SHUTTERSTOCK

☐

ALAMY/FOTOARENA

☐

ALAMY/FOTOARENA

☐

UNIT 3 Houses around the world

Review the journey

1. Look at the image on the right to ask and answer questions.

a. a TV / living room

Is there a TV in the living room?

No, there isn't.

b. two beds / bedroom

____

____

c. a stove / kitchen

____

____

d. three bedrooms / apartment

____

____

e. sink / bathroom

____

____

2. Look at the pictures to complete the crossword. What is the mystery word?

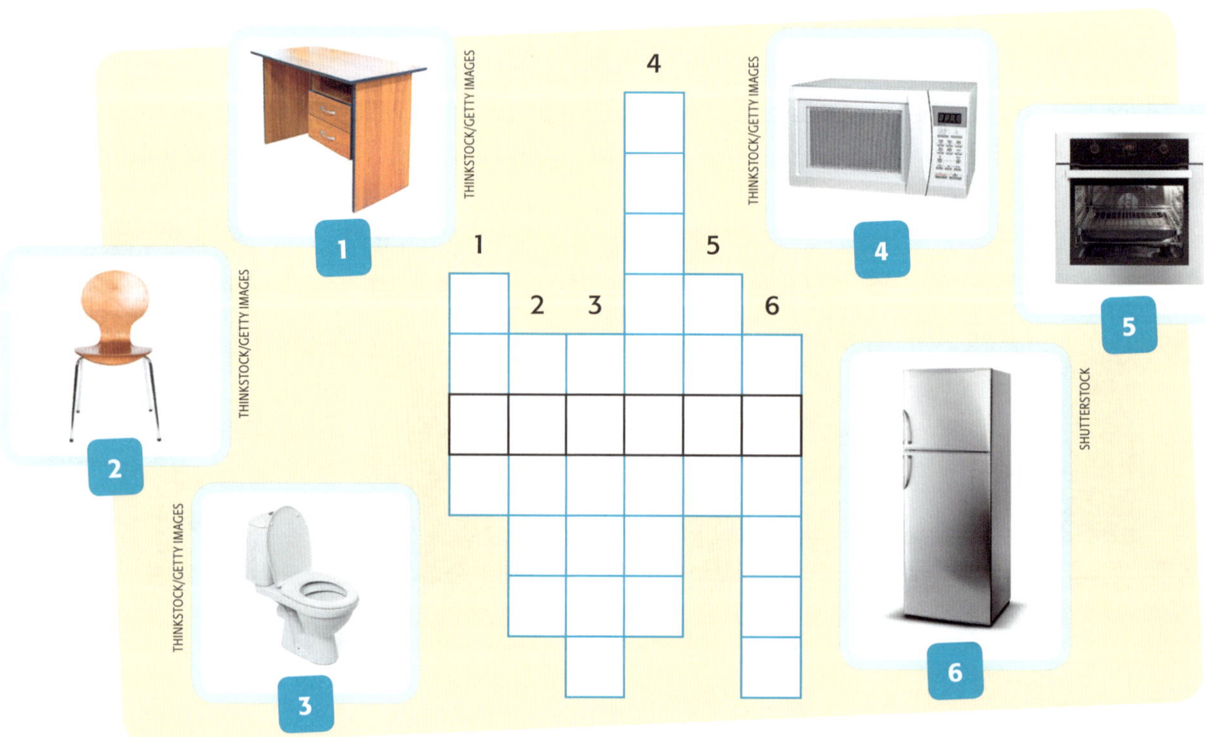

3. Look at the pictures. Complete the sentences with **this**, **that**, **these**, **those** and the correct form of **to be**.

a.

__________ my sisters, Louisa and Paula.

c.

__________ my friends. __________ Bob and __________ Jake.

b.

__________ my mother when she was younger.

Her name __________ Savannah.

d.

ILUSTRAÇÕES: ZUBARTEZ

__________ my bedroom.

It __________ small.

4. Answer these questions about yourself.

a. How many students are there in your class?

____

b. How many beds are there in your bedroom?

____

c. How many books are there in your backpack right now?

____

d. How many people are there in your family?

____

Another look

1. Look at the text. Then circle the correct option to complete the sentence.

The text is an **ad for a house/article about American houses.**

2. Read the text. What is its main objective?

a. ☐ To show how Americans live.

b. ☐ To convince people to buy the house.

www.realtor.com/realestateandhomes-detail/920-SW-19th-St_Fort-Lauderdale_FL_33315_M53896-20510

SHUTTERSTOCK

1

____

Adorable renovated (2007) POOL and separate jacuzzi with private garden, mature landscaping, two living rooms, three bedrooms, two full bathrooms and attached garage. Kitchen bar area, kitchen pantry and laundry unit. Generous closet space in each bedroom, ceiling fans, security alarm. This is the property which should not be overlooked!

2

____

- Style: Ranch House
- Single family home
- Year built: 1953
- Price/Sq Ft: $233

3

____

- Croissant Park Elementary School
- Seagull School
- Whiddon Rodgers Education Center
- New River Middle School
- Stranahan High School

Adapted from: <www.realtor.com/realestateandhomes-detail/920-SW-19th-St_Fort-Lauderdale_FL_33315_M53896-20510>. Accessed on: Apr. 10, 2016.

3. Go back to the text and write the headings in the corresponding sections.

KEY FACTS | PROPERTY DETAILS | SCHOOLS

4. Write **T** (true) or **F** (false) according to the text.

a. ☐ There are two pools.

b. ☐ The garage is connected to the house.

c. ☐ There are closets in all the bedrooms.

d. ☐ This is a stilt house.

5. Answer these questions.

a. How many bedrooms are there?

____

b. How many bathrooms are there?

____

c. Is there a dining room?

____

d. Is there an alarm?

____

e. How many schools are there in the neighborhood?

____

f. Is there a garden?

____

1. Why was information about schools in the area included in the ad?

____

____

2. Which piece of information did you find the most interesting and what would make you want to visit the house? Justify your answer.

____

____

Reading the world

1. Look at the text below and check the correct alternative.

a. The text is an

- [ ] informative article.
- [ ] advertisement.

b. The readers of the text are probably

- [ ] looking for a house to live.
- [ ] interested in different house types.

2. Scan the text and find:

a. the name of the tribe: ______________________________

b. the country where they live: ______________________________

c. the maximum height of the tree houses: ______________________________

BIS

www.amusingplanet.com/2012/10/the-tree-houses-of-korowai-tribe-of-new.html

THE TREE HOUSES OF THE KOROWAI TRIBE OF NEW GUINEA

SHUTTERSTOCK

1 Deep within the jungle lives the Korowai tribe – a clan totally isolated from the rest of the world. They are hunter-gatherers living in a small society of traditional family ties who need to share all they have in order to survive. Until their discovery in 1974, the Korowai had no contact with the outside world.

2 The Korowai people live in tree houses ranging in height from 6 to 12 meters, but some are as high as 35 meters above the ground. Usually the houses are built on a single tree but frequently the base of the house consists of several living trees. These tree houses protect families not only against mosquitoes, but also against ward off annoying neighbours and evil spirits.

3 Several documentaries have been made about the Korowai people and countless articles written. In 1993, a film crew documented the Korowai tree house construction and the practice of cannibalism as a form of criminal justice. In 2011, the Korowai tribe was shown in the BBC documentary *Human Planet*.

hunter-gatherers: pessoas que caçam animais e colhem frutos para seu próprio sustento

Adapted from: <www.amusingplanet.com/2012/10/the-tree-houses-of-korowai-tribe-of-new.html>. Accessed on: Apr. 10, 2016.

3. Read the text and number the items below according to the theme of each paragraph.

a. ☐ appearances in the media

b. ☐ description of the Korowai people

c. ☐ description of the houses

4. Match the numbers to what they represent.

a. 1974	☐ average height of the tree houses in meters
b. 6-12	☐ BBC documentary *Human Planet*
c. 35	☐ discovery of the tribe
d. 1993	☐ documentary about house construction and cannibalism
e. 2011	☐ maximum height of the tree houses in meters

5. Write **T** (true), **F** (false) or **NM** (not mentioned) according to the text.

a. ☐ The Korowai live in the jungle.

b. ☐ They never had contact with other cultures.

c. ☐ They were discovered by a Dutch explorer.

d. ☐ The Korowai believe in evil spirits.

e. ☐ The Korowai practice cannibalism.

f. ☐ The film crew was attacked by cannibals.

6. Answer these questions.

a. Are the Korowai farmers?

____

b. Usually, how many trees are there under the house?

____

c. How many articles about the Korowai are there?

____

d. How old is the BBC documentary?

____

UNIT 4

What's your favorite festivity?

Review the journey

1. Find the 7 days of the week. Write them in order.

Sunday, ______________________________

K	Z	Y	D	Q	V	C	Y	Y	U	S	U	B	S	T
L	W	A	R	T	C	E	A	V	M	K	B	U	U	T
X	M	V	H	P	D	K	D	W	W	P	E	B	N	X
U	V	O	U	S	R	P	S	H	W	D	B	C	D	S
W	B	N	N	U	S	L	R	K	A	G	U	N	A	O
U	J	D	T	D	U	I	U	E	R	J	U	G	Y	A
F	J	A	S	D	A	U	H	T	U	E	S	D	A	Y
R	T	O	B	E	M	Y	T	W	H	F	F	J	B	R
I	X	K	W	Q	W	A	L	Z	U	L	O	W	U	L
D	S	A	T	S	V	D	H	G	O	Q	C	K	Q	Y
A	N	H	U	G	T	Q	W	Z	I	V	P	S	M	P
Y	Z	Q	O	W	Q	I	Y	A	D	R	U	T	A	S
S	I	H	A	F	B	X	C	L	D	R	C	V	B	R
C	A	W	I	C	I	J	T	C	Q	S	D	Z	M	D
I	W	E	D	N	E	S	D	A	Y	V	A	U	H	S

2. Complete the conversation with **in** or **on**.

Joe: Hey, Serena. Are you studying?

Serena: Yes, I am. I have a test ____________ Monday about American holidays.

Joe: Oh! Well, I can help you. Christmas is ____________ December!

Serena: Yeah, duh, ____________ December 25! But when is Veteran's Day?

Joe: Hmmm... Is it ____________ January?

Serena: No, it's ______________ November 11.

Joe: Oh, OK. Thanksgiving is ______________ November too, right?

Serena: Yes, it's ______________ the fourth Thursday ______________ November.

Joe: That one I know! I always go shopping ______________ Black Friday!

Serena: Oh, Joe, you're terrible!

3. Look at Elena's schedule and write sentences.

BIS

MONDAY	TUESDAY	WEDNESDAY	THURSDAY	FRIDAY
7:30 - 12:00 PM SCHOOL	7:30 - 12:00 PM SCHOOL	7:30 - 12:00 PM SCHOOL	7:30 - 12:00 PM SCHOOL	7:30 - 12:00 PM SCHOOL
12:30 - 1:30 PM LUNCH WITH DAD			12:30 - 1:30 PM LUNCH WITH GRANDMA	
	2:00 - 3:00 PM TENNIS		2:00 - 3:00 PM TENNIS	
3:00 - 4:00 PM FRENCH		3:00 - 4:00 PM FRENCH		2:30 - 3:30 PM PIANO

a. lunch with her dad

Elena has lunch with her dad on Mondays.

____

b. tennis

____

____

c. French

____

____

d. piano

____

____

e. lunch with her grandma

____

____

f. school

____

____

Another look

1. Look at the following travel guide and check the characteristics of this text genre.

a. ☐ information about dates and location

b. ☐ fictional narrative

c. ☐ description of the event

d. ☐ use of adjectives

e. ☐ use of images

f. ☐ use of imperatives

BIS

INDIA

WHEN IS HOLI?

SHUTTERSTOCK

The date of Holi is different every year in India! In most of India, Holi is celebrated at the end of winter, on the day after the full moon in March each year. On the eve of Holi, large bonfires are lit to mark occasion and to burn evil spirits. This is known as Holika Dahan.

However, in the states of West Bengal and Odisha, the Holi festival is celebrated a day earlier as Dol Jatra or Dol Purnima.

Holi Dates Detailed Information

- **The Timing of Holika Dahan** – The *muhurta* for Holika Dahan in India has been calculated by most astrologers to be from sunset until around 9 pm (depending on location).
- In the afternoon, before the bonfire is lit, a special *puja* is performed to keep children healthy and safe from evil influences.
- **Holi** is a day simply for enjoyment, particularly for children. There are no rituals that need to be performed.

Dol Purnima (Dol Jatra) celebrations in West Bengal and Odisha, which take place on the full moon day before Holi, are dedicated to Lord Krishna. Colors are thrown at people on the streets! Festivities actually begin six days before, on Phagu Dashami.

Adapted from: <http://goindia.about.com/od/indiafestivaldates/f/When-Is-Holi.htm>. Accessed on: Apr. 11, 2016.

2. Read the text. What is its main purpose?

a. ☐ To give information about a festival.

b. ☐ To convince people to buy tickets.

3. Write the captions under the corresponding pictures.

Kids have fun on Holi. | People light bonfires. | People throw colors at others.

a. 

ALAMY/FOTOARENA

____

b. 

ALAMY/FOTOARENA

____

c. 

ALAMY/FOTOARENA

____

4. Write **T** (true) or **F** (false) according to the text.

a. ☐ The date of Holi depends on the moon.

b. ☐ People light bonfires on the day of Holi.

c. ☐ They light bonfires because they want to destroy bad spirits.

d. ☐ Astrologers calculate the exact time of Holika Dahan for all India.

e. ☐ The objective of the *puja* is to make kids happy.

5. Answer the questions.

a. In what month is Holi usually celebrated?

____

b. Where is Holi celebrated on a different day?

____

c. When do festivities begin in West Bengal?

____

1. Would you like to participate in a Holi festival? Why?

____

____

2. How do moon phases influence the festival? Why do you think this happens?

____

____

Reading the world

1. Look at the text and check the correct alternative.

a. The text is from

☐ a magazine. ☐ an Internet slideshow.

b. The paragraph is the

☐ introduction. ☐ invitation to the event.

BIS

www.theatlantic.com/photo/2016/01/the-2016-harbin-ice-and-snow-festival/422655/

The 2016 Harbin Ice and Snow Festival

ALAN TAYLOR | JAN 5, 2016 | 23 PHOTOS | IN FOCUS

Every year, in northeast China's Heilongjiang province, the city of Harbin hosts the Harbin International Ice and Snow Sculpture Festival, featuring massive ice and snow sculptures – more than a million visitors are anticipated this year. At night, the sculptures are colorfully illuminated and visitors can climb and play on some of the structures. The festival officially opened on January 5, and will run through the end of February.

Skip to the next and previous photo by typing j/k or ← / → .

SHUTTERSTOCK

2. Visitors walk through the China Ice and Snow World during the Harbin International Ice and Snow Festival on January 11, 2016

Adapted from: <www.theatlantic.com/photo/2016/01/the-2016-harbin-ice-and-snow-festival/422655/>. Accessed on: Apr. 11, 2016.

2. Scan the text and find

a. the name of the city: ______________________________

b. the complete name of the festival: ______________________________

c. the dates of the 2016 edition of the event: ______________________________

3. Complete the sentences with the verbs in the simple present tense. Then match them to the corresponding pictures.

a. A man ______________ (stand) with his horse in front of ice sculptures in Harbin on January 4, 2016.

b. Two policewomen ______________ (chat) in front of ice sculptures at the China Ice and Snow World during the Harbin Ice and Snow Festival on January 5, 2016.

c. A swimmer ______________ (compete) in a pool carved into ice-covered Songhua River in Harbin on January 5, 2016.

d. A worker ______________ (polish) an ice sculpture ahead of the festival in Harbin on January 4, 2016.

e. People ______________ (work) on a snow sculpture at the Snow Sculpture Art Expo in Harbin on December 22, 2015.

ALY SONG/REUTERS/LATINSTOCK

KIM KYUNG-HOON/REUTERS/LATINSTOCK

ALY SONG/REUTERS/LATINSTOCK

DAVID GRAY/REUTERS/LATINSTOCK

WANG ZHAO/AFP

UNIT 5 Let's have fun!

Review the journey

1. Look at the images and answer the questions.

a.

THINKSTOCK/GETTY IMAGES

Do they play volleyball on the weekend?

No, they don't play volleyball on the weekend. They play soccer.

c.

ALAMY/FOTOARENA

Does she study French?

____

____

b.

THINKSTOCK/GETTY IMAGES

Does he hang out with his friends in the morning?

____

____

d.

THINKSTOCK/GETTY IMAGES

Do they wear shorts to school?

____

____

2. Ask questions for the underlined parts of the sentences.

a. ______________________________

My brother lives <u>in Mexico City</u>.

b. ______________________________

The ticket costs <u>$12.00</u>.

c. ______________________________

I'd like to watch <u>*Inside Out*</u>.

d. ______________________________

My friends <u>hang out</u> on the weekend.

3. Look at the table and write sentences about Toby and Mary. Use **loves**, **likes**, **doesn't like** or **hates**.

	action movies	dramas	war movies
Toby			
Mary			

a. Mary / dramas

Mary loves dramas.

b. Toby / war movies

____

c. Toby / dramas

____

d. Mary / action movies

____

e. Mary / war movies

____

f. Toby / action movies

____

4. Solve the riddles.

a. This kind of movie is serious, but interesting. It shows true facts and we learn a lot when we watch it. What movie genre is it?

It is a documentary.

b. This kind of movie is funny. Some situations are confusing, but the end is usually happy. People like this kind of movie because it makes them laugh. What movie genre is it?

____

c. This kind of movie is scary. Sometimes there are monsters or other supernatural creatures. What movie genre is it?

____

d. This kind of movie has situations in the future. Sometimes there are flying cars, space travel and aliens. What movie genre is it?

____

e. In this kind of movie, people sing and dance. Sometimes, the conversations are in the form of music! What movie genre is it?

____

5. Write a similar riddle for a romantic comedy.

____

Another look

1. Look at the text and circle the correct alternative to complete the sentences.

a. The text is a **DVD cover/movie synopsis**.

b. It was extracted from a **DVD cover/website**.

2. Check the elements of this text genre.

a. ☐ rating
b. ☐ price
c. ☐ summary of the plot
d. ☐ cast list (actors)
e. ☐ location of theaters
f. ☐ duration
g. ☐ genre
h. ☐ days and times

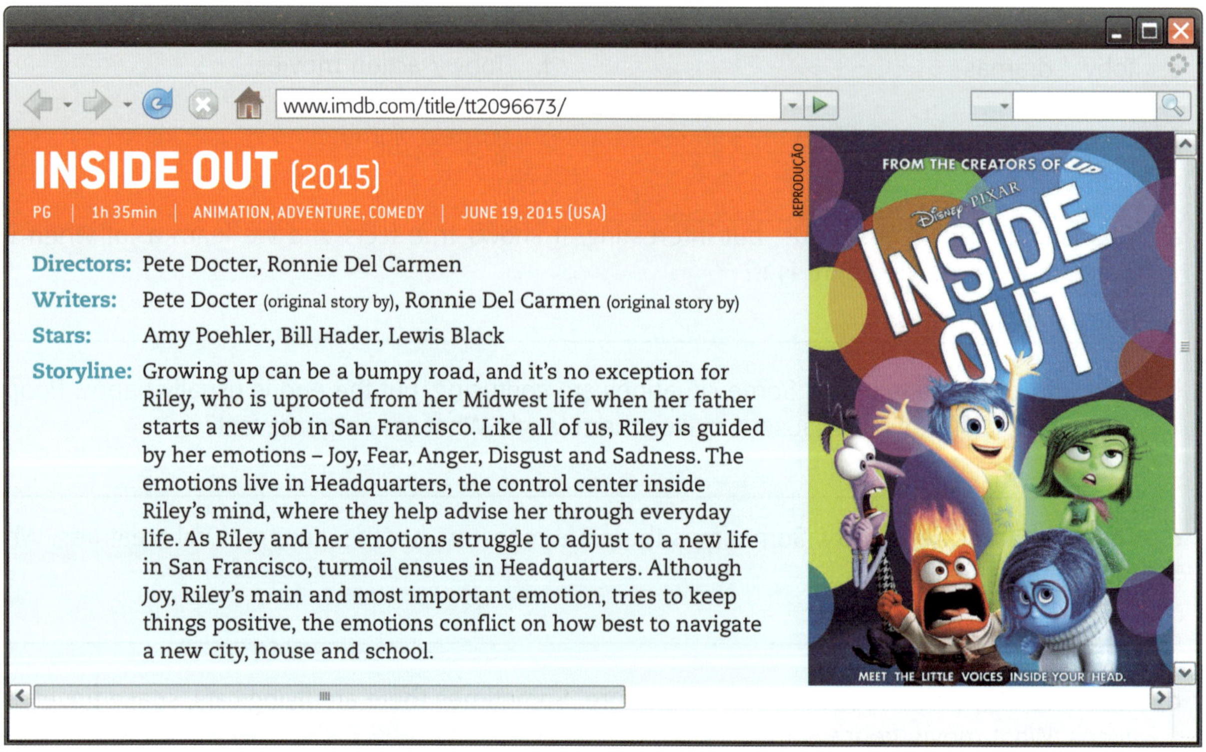

www.imdb.com/title/tt2096673/

INSIDE OUT (2015)

PG | 1h 35min | ANIMATION, ADVENTURE, COMEDY | JUNE 19, 2015 (USA)

Directors: Pete Docter, Ronnie Del Carmen

Writers: Pete Docter (original story by), Ronnie Del Carmen (original story by)

Stars: Amy Poehler, Bill Hader, Lewis Black

Storyline: Growing up can be a bumpy road, and it's no exception for Riley, who is uprooted from her Midwest life when her father starts a new job in San Francisco. Like all of us, Riley is guided by her emotions – Joy, Fear, Anger, Disgust and Sadness. The emotions live in Headquarters, the control center inside Riley's mind, where they help advise her through everyday life. As Riley and her emotions struggle to adjust to a new life in San Francisco, turmoil ensues in Headquarters. Although Joy, Riley's main and most important emotion, tries to keep things positive, the emotions conflict on how best to navigate a new city, house and school.

Adapted from: <www.imdb.com/title/tt2096673/>. Accessed on: Apr. 13, 2016.

3. Read the text. Its main objective is to

a. ☐ entertain people who like movies.

b. ☐ provide general information about a movie.

4. Match the five emotions described in the text to the corresponding images.

Anger	Disgust	Fear	Joy	Sadness

a. 

____

b. 

____

c. 

____

FOTOGRAFIAS: PHOTOS 12 CINEMA/DIOMEDIA

d. 

____

e. 

____

5. Read the text again to complete the sentences with the correct numbers.

a. There are **two** directors and ______________ writers.

b. There are ______________ emotions.

c. The movie lasts ______________ hour and ______________ minutes.

d. The first showing was on June ______________.

6. Read the text again and write **T** (true), **F** (false) or **NM** (not mentioned).

a. ☐ Riley's having trouble adjusting to a new city.

b. ☐ She sometimes ignores what her emotions say.

c. ☐ Her father doesn't live in San Francisco.

d. ☐ Her parents don't understand her.

e. ☐ Joy is a strong emotion in Riley's mind.

1. Do you usually read movie synopses? Justify your answer.

____

____

Reading the world

1. Answer the following questions.

a. Do you know any movies from India?

____

b. Would you like to see a movie from India? Why or why not?

____

2. Read the text and underline the transparent words.

BIS

www.timeout.com/london/film/a-beginners-guide-to-bollywood-and-hindi-movies

A BEGINNER'S GUIDE TO BOLLYWOOD AND HINDI MOVIES

by Rahul Verma
Posted: Thursday March 5 2015

EVERETT COLLECTION/AGB PHOTO

What exactly is Bollywood? Why is it wrong to think that "Bollywood" simply means "Indian cinema"? Here, you'll find answers to all those questions and much more.

WHAT IS BOLLYWOOD?

Bollywood is the popular name for the mainstream Hindi film industry based in Mumbai/Bombay, which each year produces around 800 films and sells 4 billion tickets. Historically Bollywood's appeal has been based around family-friendly entertainment, with songs, elaborate dance sequences and heroic action scenes in 180 minutes of escapist melodrama.

WHICH RECENT FILMS HAVE BEEN BOLLYWOOD HITS?

Recent hits include *Kahaani* (2012), a crime thriller with a pregnant woman (and no male hero) as the central character, and *English Vinglish* (2012), an Indian *Shirley Valentine* that sees a middle-aged mum rediscover herself through learning English.

HOW IS BOLLYWOOD CHANGING?

Sixty-five percent of India's 1.3 billion population is under 25 and much of it has grown up with satellite TV, and so with Rachel and Ross, Tony Soprano and Homer Simpson. As a result, the song-and-dance film is on the down and films reflecting urban anxieties are on the up.

Adapted from: <www.timeout.com/london/film/a-beginners-guide-to-bollywood-and-hindi-movies>. Accessed on: Apr. 13, 2016.

Bollywood: junção dos nomes Bombay (cidade na Índia) e Hollywood (distrito de Los Angeles)
Mumbai: nome moderno da cidade de Bombay

3. The main topic of the text is

a. ☐ Indian movie genres.

b. ☐ Indian movie industry.

4. Match the numbers to what they represent.

a. 1.3 billion	☐ number of tickets sold
b. 4 billion	☐ year of release of two hits
c. 25	☐ 65% of the population in India is under this age
d. 180	☐ number of films produced annually
e. 800	☐ total population of India
f. 2012	☐ duration of the movies in minutes

5. Answer these questions.

a. Who is the author of the text? ______________________________

b. What city is Bollywood from? ______________________________

c. What type of movie is *Kahaani*? ______________________________

6. Read the text again and write **T** (true), **F** (false) or **NM** (not mentioned).

a. ☐ The term Bollywood describes typical movies from a region in India.

b. ☐ Most Bollywood movies are musicals.

c. ☐ In one of the recent successes, a man is the most important person in the story.

d. ☐ Young people in India prefer action movies.

e. ☐ Old people don't have satellite TV.

7. Bollywood movies are usually musical and melodramatic. Create a good title for a Bollywood movie. Use your imagination!

____

UNIT 6

Let's go to the theater

Review the journey

1. Write the words in the correct order to form sentences.

a. usually hangs Peter friends with out his

b. shopping mall never to Maria goes the

c. is Kate school late sometimes for

d. part rarely James plays in school takes

2. Look at the clocks. What time is it?

a.

SHUTTERSTOCK

c.

SHUTTERSTOCK

e.

SHUTTERSTOCK

b.

SHUTTERSTOCK

d.

SHUTTERSTOCK

f.

SHUTTERSTOCK

3. Circle the correct alternative.

SHUTTERSTOCK

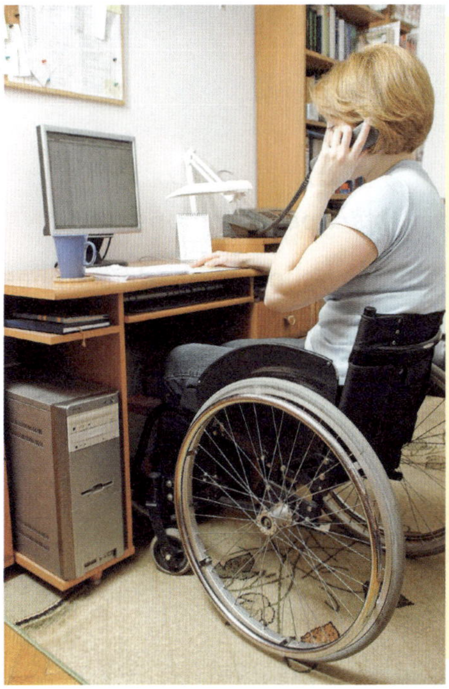

Amy: Hey, Hannah, what **are you doing/do you do**?

Hannah: Oh, hi, Amy. I **am studying/study** math at the moment.

Amy: Why **are you studying/do you study** math? We **aren't having/don't have** any tests this week.

Hannah: I know, but I always **studying/study** math on Friday afternoon. I **am loving/love** math!

Amy: Well, Cheryl is here and we **are watching/watch** some romantic comedies now. **Are you wanting/Do you want** to come over later?

Hannah: Sorry, I can't. I usually **going/go** out with my parents on Friday evening.

Amy: So let's get together tomorrow!

Hannah: OK!

4. Write the dates with ordinal numbers.

a.

BLEND RF/ARIEL SKEL/DIOMEDI

Christmas Day

____

c.

SHUTTERSTOCK

Discovery of Brazil

____

b.

SHUTTERSTOCK

New Year's Day

____

d.

FAIRFAX MEDIA VIA GETTY IMAGES

International Women's Day

____

Another look

1. Scan the text and underline the correct alternative to complete the sentences.

a. The text is **a DVD cover/a flyer**.

b. The publisher of the text is **British Academy of International Arts/Open Auditions**.

c. The images have the objective of **showing the children in the play/showing readers scenes of the story**.

2. Check the characteristics of this text genre.

a. ☐ It publishes information about an event.

b. ☐ It is transmitted on radio or TV.

c. ☐ Different font sizes are used.

d. ☐ There are long sentences with many adjectives.

3. Read the text and complete the sentence:

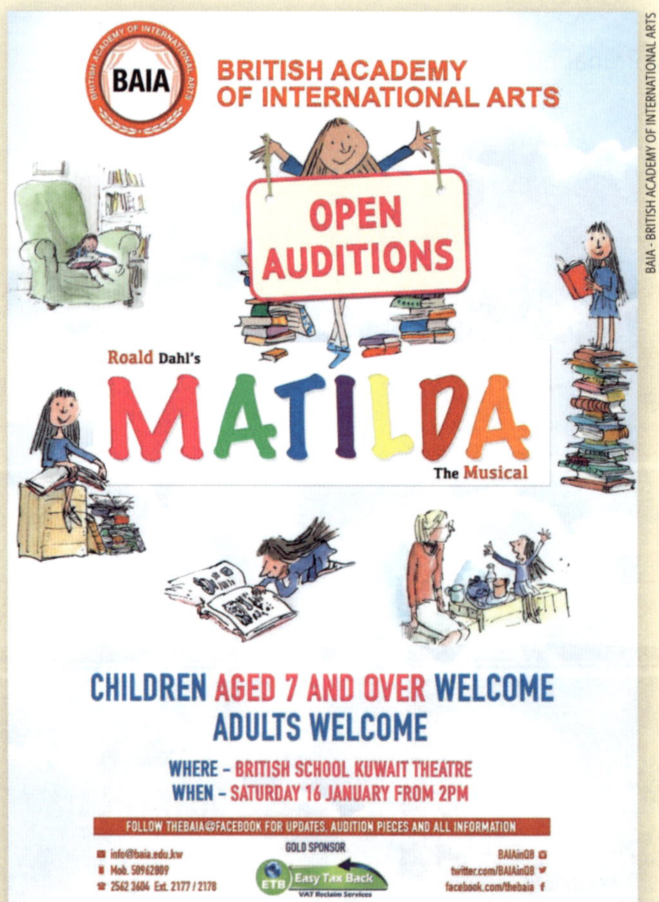

The main objective of the text is to

a. ☐ sell tickets to the show.

b. ☐ invite actors to try out for the show.

4. What's Matilda doing in the pictures?

a. in a big armchair: *She is reading in a big armchair.*

b. on top of a chest of drawers: __________

c. on the floor: __________

d. to her teacher: __________

e. on top of a pile of books: __________

5. Read the text again and write **T** (true), **F** (false), or **NM** (not mentioned).

a. ☐ *Matilda* is based on a book by Roald Dahl.

b. ☐ In the story, Matilda probably hates books.

c. ☐ Anyone who is over 7 can participate in the audition.

d. ☐ The director is British.

6. Answer the following questions.

a. Where are the auditions?

____

b. When are the auditions?

____

c. What time do the auditions start?

____

1. How often do you usually read?

____

2. What kinds of books do you usually read? What about other media, like magazines, newspapers, websites, comics? What do you like to read?

____

____

____

Reading the world

1. Scan the text and check the correct alternative.

a. This text is a

☐ flyer. ☐ travel guide.

b. It is about

☐ attractions in a part of London. ☐ English theater and museums.

2. Read the text and answer the questions that follow.

BIS

www.visitlondon.com/discover-london/london-areas/central/west-end

LONDON'S WEST END

London's West End is famous for its fantastic range of theatres, tourist attractions, hotels and shopping. There's always something happening on these central London streets.

No visit to London would be complete without the West End. It is one of London's most vibrant areas for shopping, shows, culture and history.

When people refer to London's West End, they are talking about:

- London's entertainment district around Leicester Square and Covent Garden
- Shopping along Oxford Street, Regent Street, and Bond Street
- The city centre area to the west of the historic City of London, within the City of Westminster.

THINKSTOCK/GETTY IMAGES

TRAVEL TO AND AROUND THE WEST END

London's West End is a large area. You'll need to travel around by bus, tube or taxi. Or, if you're feeling fit, on two wheels under the London Cycle Hire Scheme.

There are many underground stations around the West End. The major ones include Oxford Circus, Covent Garden, Piccadilly Circus and Leicester Square. If you're going to be in London for more than a day, it's worth buying a Visitor Oyster Card. It is one of the easiest ways to get around London.

SHUTTERSTOCK

THINGS TO DO IN THE WEST END: MUSEUMS AND GALLERIES

London's top attractions include sites within the West End. The most popular museums and galleries in the area are The National Gallery, The National Portrait Gallery, The Royal Academy of Arts and the London Transport Museum.

SHUTTERSTOCK

Adapted from: <www.visitlondon.com/discover-london/london-areas/central/west-end>. Accessed on: Apr. 14, 2016.

3. Match the beginning and the end of the sentences.

a. It's possible to do

b. There are subway or underground stations

c. There are shops

d. There are at least four

☐ museums in the area.

☐ near the attractions.

☐ on Regent, Bond and Oxford Streets.

☐ a lot of different things in the West End.

4. Answer these questions.

a. Is the West End in the extreme west or in central London?

____

b. Is it a quiet area?

____

c. When is it a good idea to buy a Visitor Oyster Card?

____

5. Find the names of these London attractions.

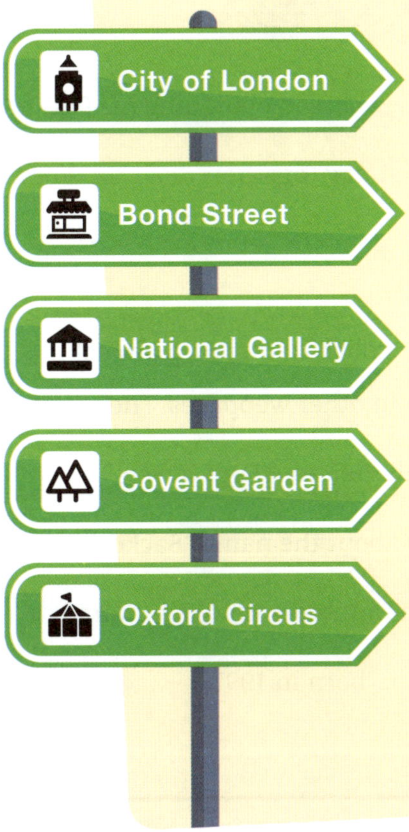

L	C	M	C	K	Y	L	O	C	X	F	P	R	F	Q
G	B	C	H	P	H	N	P	O	D	H	R	F	L	C
N	P	B	C	W	E	I	M	V	L	W	L	E	N	I
E	C	L	O	L	L	C	E	E	N	E	O	U	E	T
V	H	Q	B	N	L	E	J	N	W	O	X	Y	D	Y
C	Q	Q	E	E	D	P	O	T	Y	K	F	S	R	O
T	D	K	I	K	G	S	Z	G	N	M	O	A	A	F
V	L	S	S	F	L	A	T	A	T	T	R	B	G	L
O	X	F	O	R	D	C	I	R	C	U	S	X	T	O
R	N	Y	Z	I	N	E	L	D	E	M	C	E	N	N
T	Q	Q	S	U	O	Q	P	E	R	E	I	B	E	D
U	S	J	U	B	I	I	K	N	I	I	T	U	V	O
N	B	L	D	K	T	G	C	Y	E	Z	C	P	O	N
N	A	T	I	O	N	A	L	G	A	L	L	E	R	Y
M	C	R	W	Q	J	E	R	R	G	W	S	U	G	A

UNIT 7

What internet activities do you do?

Review the journey

1. Complete the text with **was** or **were**.

www.biography.com/news/google-founders-history-facts

THE GOOGLE CHRONICLES: FACTS ON FOUNDERS LARRY PAGE & SERGEY BRIN

SARA KETTLER

CORBIS VIA GETTY IMAGES

In 1995, Larry Page, then 22, visited Stanford University as prospective PhD student in computer science. His tour guide ______ Sergey Brin, a 21-year-old mathematical whiz who ______ already pursuing his PhD in that department. Despite their common interests, their first day together ______ spent arguing. Fortunately for them, their relationship ______ going to get much better.

By 1996 he and Brin ______ good friends who ______ collaborating on a project called "Backrub", which investigated how sites linked back to other webpages. They ______ busy with their PhD research, so they tried to sell their idea! But buyers ______ not interested... Also, they ______ not happy about the name "Backrub". They ______ inspired by the word googol (the term for a number with one hundred zeros), and with a small change in spelling, Google ______ born in 1997.

BIS

Adapted from: <www.biography.com/news/google-founders-history-facts>. Accessed on: Apr. 15, 2016.

2. Answer the questions about the text with short answers.

a. Was Larry Page 25 years old in 1995?

____

b. Were Larry and Sergey friends in 1996?

____

c. Was Google the project's first name?

____

d. Were Larry and Sergey busy at university?

____

3. Ask questions about the text.

a. ______________________________? He was 21 years old.

b. ______________________________? No, they were not happy about that name.

c. ______________________________? Google was born in 1997.

4. Look at the pictures and write the words. What's the mystery sentence?

a.

THINKSTOCK/GETTY IMAGES

1 2 3 4 5 2 6

b.

THINKSTOCK/GETTY IMAGES

7 8 9 10 11 | 12 6 4 13 14

c.

THINKSTOCK/GETTY IMAGES

15 14 16 17 2 9 6 12

d.

THINKSTOCK/GETTY IMAGES

11 14 9 12 18 11 2 3 14 10

5 11 14 | 7 4 6 10 5 | 1 14 C 11 9 3 4 C 9 8

C 2 1 P U 5 14 6 | W 9 10

4 3 13 14 3 5 14 12 | 4 3 | 1 8 2 2

Another look

1. Scan the text and circle the correct alternative to complete the sentences.

a. The text consists of **tips/rules**.

b. The readers probably **don't know anything about Instagram/already use Instagram**.

2. Check the elements of this text genre.

a. ☐ use of verbs in the present continuous

b. ☐ organization in topics

c. ☐ use of the imperative

d. ☐ complex sentences

3. Read the text. Why do you think the title is *Instaquette*?

____

www.pcmag.com/article2/0,2817,2412482,00.asp

SHUTTERSTOCK

INSTAQUETTE: THE DOS AND DON'TS OF INSTAGRAM

by Meredith Popolo
November 27, 2012

These unofficial guidelines governing Instagram etiquette will help you play nice with your current followers and win over new ones. While there are no steadfast rules about using Instagram, there are some dos and don'ts that will make you a more effective Instagrammer.

1. DO MATCH YOUR TWITTER AND INSTAGRAM USERNAMES
2. DON'T ASK PEOPLE TO FOLLOW YOU
3. DO BE SOCIAL
4. DON'T LIKE EVERY PHOTO
5. DO TAKE INTERESTING PHOTOS
6. DON'T FLOOD THE FEED
7. DO APPLY FILTERS LIKE MAKEUP
8. DO USE HASHTAGS TASTEFULLY
9. DON'T TAKE HORIZONTAL PHOTOS
10. DO WRITE CAPTIONS OR TAG LOCATIONS THAT EXPLAIN THE PHOTO
11. DON'T USE SCREEN CAPTURE

BIS

Adapted from: <www.pcmag.com/article2/0,2817,2412482,00.asp>. Accessed on: Apr. 4, 2016.

4. Instaquette is the combination of which two words?

____

____

5. Find the expressions in the text that mean

a. people who look at your page regularly: ______________________

b. post too many pictures: ______________________

c. words that explain a picture: ______________________

d. mark electronically: ______________________

6. Write the number of the tip the following explanations correspond to.

a. ☐ Instagram squares up your photos, so make sure you snap shots vertically.

b. ☐ Instagram is, after all, a *social* network and relationships are a two-way street.

c. ☐ Posting one photo a day is a good rule. Posting six photos of your favorite band at a concert in two minutes is not.

d. ☐ Like on Twitter, using hashtags can increase the visibility of your post.

e. ☐ Those who follow you on Instagram will probably want to follow you on Twitter, too.

7. Add one more tip to the list. You can write about security, for example.

____

____

____

1. Are you an Instagram user? If you are, do you agree with the tips presented? Can they be useful in other social media, too? Which ones?

____

____

2. Why shouldn't you flood the feed?

____

____

Reading the world

1. Look at the image and check the correct alternatives.

a. The man in the green shirt has

☐ a mechanism on top of his head.

☐ a machine on his face.

b. He is

☐ the doctor.

☐ the patient.

2. Scan the text and find

a. the name of the patient: ____________________

b. where he is from: ____________________

c. his age: ____________________

d. the name of the technology he is using: ____________________

BIS

QUADRIPLEGIC MOVES HAND WITH BRAIN MICROCHIP

A new device reroutes messages from the brains of patients affected by serious spinal and head injuries to help them move.

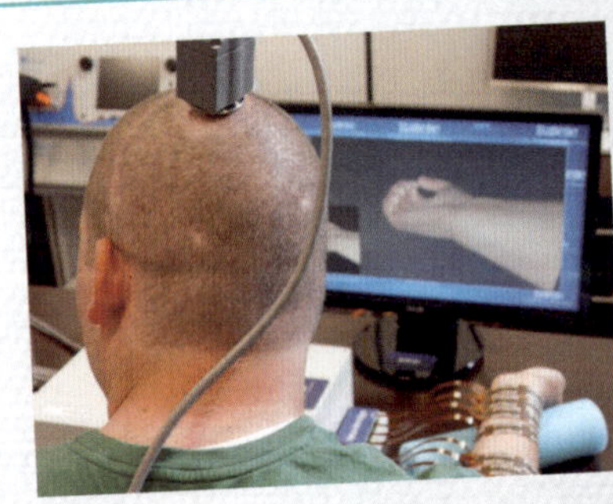

THE WASHINGTON POST/GETTY IMAGES

A paralysed man has been able to move his fingers and hand with his own thoughts thanks to a pioneering operation that implanted a microchip in his brain.

Ian Burkhart, a 23-year-old quadriplegic from Ohio, is the first patient to use Neurobridge, which reconnects the brain directly to muscles.

Scientists at The Ohio State University Wexner Medical Center took almost 10 years to develop the system.

Ian said of the achievement: "Today was great. I mean to be able to open and close my hand and do those complex movements that I haven't been able to do in four years was great. It's definitely great for me to be as young as I am when I was injured because the advancements in science and technology are growing rapidly and they're only going to continue to increase."

Mr. Burkhart was paralysed four years ago during a diving accident that left him unable to move from the chest down.

The Neurobridge technology combines algorithms that learn and decode the user's brain activity and a muscle stimulation sleeve that translates neural impulses from the brain and transmits new signals to the paralysed arm.

In this case, Ian's brain signals bypass his injured spinal cord and move his hand, hence the name Neurobridge.

Adapted from: <http://news.sky.com/story/1288819/quadriplegic-moves-hand-with-brain-microchip>. Accessed on: Apr. 14, 2016.

3. The main topic of the passage is

a. ☐ how a patient is benefiting from a new technology.

b. ☐ the development of a new microchip.

4. Read the text again and write **T** (true), **F** (false) or **NM** (not mentioned).

a. ☐ Ian can now move his hand and fingers with his brain.

b. ☐ Neurobridge reconnects brain directly to muscles.

c. ☐ Ian thinks that it was a great progress for him.

d. ☐ Ian is married and has a small kid.

e. ☐ The technology understands the messages from the muscles.

f. ☐ The next step is to help Ian walk.

5. Answer the following questions.

a. How many patients use this technology? ______________________________

b. How many years were necessary for scientists to develop this technology? ______________

c. Where is Ian wearing the stimulation sleeve? ______________________________

6. Find the words in the text to complete the crossword puzzle.

Across

2. They are tissues that contract to create movement. In this case, they are stimulated by a metal sleeve.

5. The kind of accident that Ian suffered.

6. A person who is not able to move his or her legs and arms.

Down

1. The kind of movement that Ian can do now.

3. His ____ cord was injured in the accident.

4. The most important organ, which is located in a person's head.

UNIT 8

Say no to cyberbullying!

Review the journey

1. Complete the table with the base form or the simple past of the verbs.

Base form	Simple past
call	______
stop	______
kiss	______

Base form	Simple past
______	arrived
______	invited
miss	______

2. Look at the images. What did they do last Sunday?

a.

SHUTTERSTOCK

Katie and Sarah

______

b.

PURESTOCK/DIOMEDIA

Brian

______

c.

MASKOT RF/DIOMEDIA

Ted

______

d.

SHUTTERSTOCK

Donna

______

3. Put the conversation in the correct order.

☐ **Emily:** A farm? Really?

☐ **Emily:** Farm work is hard! How was it?

☐ **Emily:** Hi, Sophie! How was your weekend?

☐ **Sophie:** It was amazing! I even milked a cow!

☐ **Sophie:** It was great! We were on a farm.

☐ **Sophie:** Yes! I helped my aunt with the farm work.

4. Complete the biography with the past tense of the verbs in parentheses.

www.biography.com/people/keanu-reeves-9454211

FILMMAGIC/GETTY IMAGES

KEANU REEVES

Film Actor, Director (1964-)

BIOGRAPHY

BACKGROUND AND EARLY CAREER

Keanu Charles Reeves __________ (be) born on September 2, 1964, in Beirut, Lebanon. Reeves's mom __________ (work) in entertainment as a performer and later a costume designer. He __________ (move) with his mother and sister to New York and then Toronto.

THE MATRIX

Reeves __________ (star) in a sci-fi film that would become a genre game changer–*The Matrix*. Known for its innovative fight sequences, avant-garde special effects and gorgeous fashion, *The Matrix* __________ (be) an international hit. Two sequels __________ (be) filmed together and released in 2003.

OFF THE SET

Reported to be one of the most generous actors in Hollywood, Reeves __________ (help) care for his sister during her lengthy battle with leukemia, and has supported such organizations as Stand Up To Cancer and PETA.

BIS

Adapted from: <www.biography.com/people/keanu-reeves-9454211>. Accessed on: Apr. 14, 2016.

5. Correct these statements about the text.

a. Keanu Reeves was born in Toronto.

____

b. His mother was a teacher.

____

c. There were two *The Matrix* movies.

____

Another look

1. Scan the text and underline the correct option to complete each sentence.

a. The text is **a fact sheet/a poster**.

b. The intended readers of this text are **Internet users/school children**.

2. Read the text. What is its main objective?

a. ☐ To give information about internet safety.

b. ☐ To describe the positive and negative sides of the Internet.

Extracted from: <www.educatorstechnology.com/2012/12/great-internet-safety-posters-teachers.html>. Accessed on: Apr. 14, 2016.

3. Answer the following questions.

a. What's the name of the organization that published the poster?

____

b. Where is this organization from?

____

c. What kinds of opportunities are there online?

____

4. An acrostic is a writing where the first letter of a word is used to make other words. Rewrite the acrostic from the poster.

I ___ ___ ___ ___ ___ ___ ___

N ___ ___   ___ ___ ___ ___ ___ ___ ___ ___ ___ ___ ___ ___ ___

S ___ ___ ___

A ___ ___ ___ ___ ___

F ___ ___ ___ ___

E ___ ___ ___ ___ ___ ___ ___ ___ ___

5. Create an acrostic about a school situation.

1. Do you usually follow the tips presented in the poster? Why?

____

____

2. What online courses and studies are there available? Which ones would you like to attend to?

____

____

Reading the world

1. Scan the text and find

a. the number of children and youth being bullied in the world: ______________________

b. the age when bullies usually get a criminal record: ______________________

2. Read the text and complete the sentence: The main objective of the text is to

a. ☐ alert people of the consequences of bullying.

b. ☐ give solutions to stop bullying.

BIS

www.kidspot.com.au/school/secondary/peer-pressure/facts-and-figures-

Facts and figures about bullying

GETTY IMAGES

With all schools talking about bullying and the media regularly reporting on latest research, it could seem like we're in a bullying epidemic. But, it's not all bad – the incidence of bullying, particularly the traditional face-to-face style, according to expert Dr. Toni Noble, is not increasing.

"Cyber-bullying, on the other hand may be increasing with recent research suggesting that 1 in 10 kids have been cyber-bullied."

Here is why bullying, and policies and strategies to combat it, are such a high priority for communities and governments.

- One student in every four in Australian schools is affected by bullying.
- An estimated 200 million children and youth around the world are being bullied.
- Kids who are bullied are three times more likely to show depressive symptoms.
- Girls who were victims of bullying in their early primary school years were more likely to remain victims as they got older.
- Girls were much more likely than boys to be victims of both cyber and traditional bullying, says a recent Murdoch Children's Research Institute study.
- Children as young as three can become victims of bullying, says Canadian research.
- Young people who bully have a one in four chance of having a criminal record by the age of 30.

Adapted from: <www.kidspot.com.au/school/secondary/peer-pressure/facts-and-figures-about-bullying>. Accessed on: Apr. 14, 2016.

3. Read the text again and write **T** (true), **F** (false) or **NM** (not mentioned).

a. ☐ 10% of kids are cyber bullies.

b. ☐ 25% of students in Australian schools suffer bullying.

c. ☐ Usually, girls bully girls and boys bully boys.

d. ☐ Girls and boys are bullied equally.

4. Match the beginning and the end of the sentences.

a. When a girl was a victim in primary school,

b. 25% of young bullies

c. Face-to-face bullying occurence

☐ may become criminals in adult life.

☐ is not going up.

☐ there was a big chance for her to be a victim when she was older.

5. Answer the following questions.

a. According to the text, is there a face-to-face bullying epidemic?

____

b. How young can the youngest victims of bullying be?

____

6. Imagine you are going to participate in a demonstration against bullying. Write your messages on the posters below.

a.

b.

c.

Connecting ideas

UNIT 1

- **www.ancient.eu/Eros/**
  Definition of Eros, god of love
- **www.bbc.com/culture/story/20130916-mystery-of-a-missing-masterpiece**
  The mystery of the ancient glass masterpiece
- **www.museus.gov.br/wp-content/uploads/2011/05/gmb_norte.pdf**
  Guide of Brazilian museums

UNIT 2

- **www.roughguides.com/gallery/traditional-dress/#/3**
  In pictures: traditional dress around the world
- **www.fashionmuseum.co.uk/**
  The Fashion Museum Bath official website

UNIT 3

- **www.theatlantic.com/photo/2015/06/unusual-homes-around-the-world/395432/**
  Unusual homes around the world
- **http://typeslist.com/different-types-of-housing/**
  List of house types
- **www.youtube.com/watch?v=YWvemw0nj7k**
  Documentary about Nick Olson and Lilah Horwitz, who made a glass house in the mountains of West Virginia, USA

UNIT 4

- **www.todayifoundout.com/index.php/2013/04/the-origin-of-the-7-day-week-and-the-names-of-the-days-of-the-week/**
  Origin of day names
- **www.youtube.com/watch?v=qEw2YFCJmdg**
  Holi, India's Color Festival
- **www.youtube.com/watch?v=Fr1TX5g-IJA**
  Harbin Ice Festival 2015

UNIT 5

- **www.youtube.com/watch?v=_MC3XuMvsDI**
  Inside Out official trailer
- **www.youtube.com/watch?v=wmGVY4T88dc**
  English Vinglish official trailer
- **www.youtube.com/watch?v=xPvPUk96vb0**
  Bollywood dance (*Slumdog Millionaire*)

UNIT 6

- **www.youtube.com/watch?v=JE_Fzt6uT2g**
  Matilda – The Musical trailer
- **www.youtube.com/watch?v=QA_FSCZQCNM**
  Top 10 London Musicals
- **www.nationalgallery.org.uk/**
  National Gallery official website
- **www.royalacademy.org.uk/**
  Royal Academy of Arts official website

UNIT 7

- **www.youtube.com/watch?v=Ol1CeVaX4O8**
  Inside Google – National Geographic
- **http://fortune.com/2014/10/10/how-kevin-systrom-got-started/**
  How Kevin Systrom got started
- **http://mundoestranho.abril.com.br/materia/quais-tecnologias-sao-desenvolvidas-para-ajudar-pessoas-com-deficiencia**
  Article about technologies developed to help disabled people
- **www.youtube.com/watch?v=riLExaDddlg**
  3D Printing Medicine

UNIT 8

- **www.youtube.com/watch?v=bfT2qqrqzgo**
  End Cyberbullying 2015
- **www.chegadebullying.com.br/**
  Chega de bullying campaign